PLATO'S *MENO*

D1604185

Given its brevity, Plato's *Meno* covers an astonishingly wide array of topics: politics, education, virtue, definition, philosophical method, mathematics, the nature and acquisition of knowledge, and immortality. Its treatment of these, though profound, is tantalizingly short, leaving the reader with many unresolved questions. This book confronts the dialogue's many enigmas and attempts to solve them in a way that is both lucid and sympathetic to Plato's philosophy. Reading the dialogue as a whole, it explains how different arguments are related to one another, and how the interplay between characters is connected to the philosophical content of the work. In a new departure, this book's exploration focuses primarily on the content and coherence of the dialogue in its own right, and not merely in the context of other dialogues, making it required reading for all students of Plato, be they from the world of classics or philosophy.

DOMINIC SCOTT is Senior Lecturer in Philosophy at the University of Cambridge and a Fellow of Clare College. His previous publications include *Recollection and Experience: Plato's Theory of Learning and its Successors* (Cambridge, 1995).

CAMBRIDGE STUDIES IN THE DIALOGUES OF PLATO

Series editor: Mary Margaret McCabe

Plato's dialogues are rich mixtures of subtle argument, sublime theorising and superb literature. It is tempting to read them piecemeal – by analysing the arguments, by espousing or rejecting the theories or by praising Plato's literary expertise. It is equally tempting to search for Platonic views across dialogues, selecting passages from throughout the Platonic corpus. But Plato offers us the dialogues to read whole and one by one. This series provides original studies in individual dialogues of Plato. Each study will aim to throw light on such questions as why its chosen dialogue is composed in the complex way that it is, and what makes this unified whole more than the sum of its parts. In so doing, each volume will both give a full account of its dialogue and offer a view of Plato's philosophising from that perspective.

Titles published in the series:

Plato's Cratylus
David Sedley

Plato's Lysis
Christopher Rowe and Terence Penner

Plato's Meno
Dominic Scott

Forthcoming titles in the series:

Plato's Euthydemus
Mary Margaret McCabe

Plato's Timaeus
Dorothea Frede

Plato's Symposium
Robert Wardy

PLATO'S *MENO*

DOMINIC SCOTT

University of Cambridge

CAMBRIDGE
UNIVERSITY PRESS

CAMBRIDGE UNIVERSITY PRESS
Cambridge, New York, Melbourne, Madrid, Cape Town, Singapore, São Paulo, Delhi

Cambridge University Press
The Edinburgh Building, Cambridge CB2 8RU, UK

Published in the United States of America by Cambridge University Press, New York

www.cambridge.org
Information on this title: www.cambridge.org/9780521104685

First published 2006
This digitally printed version 2009

A catalogue record for this publication is available from the British Library

ISBN 978-0-521-64033-6 hardback
ISBN 978-0-521-10468-5 paperback

For Aylin

Contents

Acknowledgements   *page* ix

Introduction   1

PART I

1 The opening: 70a–71d   11

2 The first definition: 71e–73c   23

3 A lesson in definition: 73c–77d   31

4 The third definition: 77b–79e   46

5 Meno as an interlocutor   60

PART II

6 The stingray: 79e–80d   69

7 'Meno's paradox': 80d–81a   75

8 The emergence of recollection: 81a–e   92

9 The argument for recollection: 82b–85d   98

10 The conclusion: 86b6–c2   121

PART III

11 The method of hypothesis: 86c–87c   129

12 Virtue is teachable: 87c–89c   145

13 Virtue is not teachable: 89e–96d   161

14 Virtue as true belief: 96d–100b   176

15 Irony in the *Meno*: the evidence of the *Gorgias*   194

16 Meno's progress   209

    Conclusion   214

Appendices   219
References   227
Index of ancient passages   232
General index   235

Acknowledgements

Most of this book was written while I was a British Academy Research Reader in 2001–3. Needless to say, I am enormously grateful to the Academy for this opportunity. I would also like to thank the Center for Hellenic Studies and its Directors, Debbie Boedekker and Kurt Raaflaub, for a very productive and enjoyable fellowship there in 1998–9. As ever, I owe a great debt of gratitude to the Cambridge Faculty of Philosophy and to Clare College for their continued support.

I have benefited from trying out the central ideas of this book at various seminars and conferences. My debts to individuals who commented at such occasions are too numerous to recall, but I would especially like to thank Hugh Benson, Tad Brennan, Lesley Brown, Victor Caston, Terry Irwin, Thomas Johansen, Geoffrey Lloyd, Mark McPherran, David Sedley, Frisbee Sheffield, Roslyn Weiss and Raphael Woolf. I am particularly grateful to Jimmy Altham, Myles Burnyeat, Gail Fine and Rosanna Keefe for reading earlier drafts of the manuscript all the way through.

I have also been very fortunate that Gail Fine gave me detailed feedback on the manuscript. Her comments, invariably incisive, have saved me from a number of errors.

From beginning to end, M. M. McCabe has acted as gadfly, midwife and occasionally stingray (though only in the most beneficial sense). The series of which this book forms a part is very much her inspiration. I only hope I have done her credit.

As with all my research, I also owe a lasting debt to Myles Burnyeat, who has been a continuing source of inspiration.

For some years, the *Meno* has been a set text on the undergraduate philosophy syllabus at Cambridge, and I owe a special debt to my students. Their obvious enthusiasm for the dialogue has been a constant delight and their feedback yet another source of inspiration. My only regret is that I may have to remove it from the syllabus to prevent future generations hounding me with lists of my errors, now that they have been committed to print.

Finally, I would like to thank the Cambridge University Press, and particularly Linda Woodward, for their help in the final stages of production.

This book has been some years in the making. Doubtless it would benefit by gestating for many more. But the moment of publication can no longer be delayed. My text of the dialogue is now on the verge of disintegration and is threatening to do so at the very page where Socrates remarks on the need to examine the same topic over and over again (85c10–11). No one should ignore such an omen.

Introduction

Meno, a young aristocrat from Thessaly, asks how virtue is acquired. In reply, Socrates professes himself unable to answer: since he does not even know what virtue is, how can he know how it is acquired? Meno agrees to tackle the nature of virtue first and offers Socrates a definition, or rather a list of different kinds of virtue. After some argument, he accepts that this is inadequate, and offers another definition – virtue as the power to rule – which is also rejected. In order to help the inquiry along, Socrates gives a short lesson in definition, after which Meno offers his third and final definition of virtue: the desire for fine things and ability to acquire them. When this is refuted, he despairs of ever making any progress in their inquiry: how, he demands, can you look for something of whose nature you are entirely ignorant? Even if you stumble upon the answer, how will you know that this is the thing you did not know before?

In the face of this challenge, Socrates changes tack (81a). Adopting a religious tone, he asserts that the soul is immortal and has had many previous lives; what we call learning is in fact the recollection of knowledge that the soul had before. At Meno's request, he offers to provide some support for these claims, and summons one of Meno's slave boys to join them. Drawing some figures in the sand, he sets the boy a geometrical puzzle: take a square with sides of two feet and an area of four square feet. What would be the length of the sides of the square whose area is double the original? In response to Socrates' questioning, the boy first gives two wrong answers. But eventually, after continued questioning, he gives the correct one. Socrates argues that, as he has only questioned the boy and never taught him, the answers must have been in him all along. In fact, they must have been in him before birth. Finally, Socrates mounts an argument to show that the truth was in him for all time and that his soul is immortal.

I

They now return to the topic of virtue. Socrates still wants it defined, but Meno persists in asking how it is acquired (86c). Socrates yields to his demand and, to move the inquiry ahead, introduces a new method adapted from geometry, the method of hypothesis. *If* virtue is a form of knowledge, he argues, it can be taught. The task now is to show that virtue *is* a form of knowledge, which Socrates immediately proceeds to do: virtue is the knowledge that enables us to make correct use of our available resources, be they money, power, or qualities of character, such as endurance or self-discipline. So, at this point (89c), Meno's original question seems to have been answered: since virtue is knowledge it must be teachable. But then Socrates raises a doubt: if virtue were teachable, surely they would be able to point to actual teachers and learners of it. Introducing a new character, Anytus (later to be a key figure in Socrates' trial and execution), he tries to find instances of people who have successfully taught virtue to someone else. The sophists are brusquely dismissed as charlatans, and instead they turn to consider four of the most eminent politicians in recent Athenian history. None of them, it turns out, succeeded in transmitting their virtue even to those dearest to them, their own sons, which they would surely have done if they had been able to teach it. Since even these men were unable to teach their virtue, Socrates now suspects that it may not after all be teachable (94e).

Anytus, clearly annoyed, accuses Socrates of maligning the great men of Athens and withdraws from the dialogue, leaving Meno to resume the role of interlocutor. After confirming the conclusion just reached with Anytus, they find themselves in a quandary. At one point earlier on, they thought they had established that virtue must be teachable because it is a form of knowledge. Now they have reached the conclusion that it is not teachable. At 96e, Socrates proposes a way out. They were wrong to think that virtue is only knowledge. It is not just by knowledge that one can act rightly and make correct use of one's resources, but also by having something less – true belief. After explicating the difference between knowledge and true belief, Socrates goes on to draw a parallel with poets and soothsayers who are divinely inspired to say much that is both useful and true, but without any understanding. Similarly, he suggests, the great politicians guided their city not by knowledge, but by true belief. He concludes that virtue comes by divine dispensation, although he adds that they still need to investigate the nature of virtue before establishing with any clarity how it is acquired.

THE QUALITY OF THE ARGUMENTS

The *Meno* is a remarkable work – a philosophical gem, as J. S. Mill called it.[1] Perhaps its greatest claim to fame is the theory of recollection and its purported means of demonstration, the interview with the slave boy. But the dialogue is also remarkable for the sheer breadth of topics covered in so short a space: virtue, definition, philosophical method, mathematical method, education, the origins of knowledge, the immortality of the soul, Athenian politics, and the distinction between knowledge and true belief. In this way, the *Meno* epitomises the synoptic character of so much of Plato's work: here was a philosopher who could rarely broach one topic without stumbling upon a multitude of others.

But this feature of the dialogue also raises acute challenges for the interpreter. For one thing, what is the work about? Over the years, this question has met with quite different responses. Some see it as a dialogue about virtue; others have claimed that the ethical themes of the work are chosen just by way of example: the real topic is inquiry, discovery or knowledge.[2] A different response altogether would be to say that there is no one topic that the *Meno* is 'about'; its interests are irreducibly plural. Even so, we might want to find a complex unity – some rationale for why all these different themes are included within one work. There is such a unity, I shall claim, but that is something which we can only establish after working through all the different arguments one by one.

As we do so, we shall confront what is surely the main interpretative challenge of the work. Because it covers so much in so short a space, its arguments often appear very sketchy. For example, the amount of space that Socrates devotes to proving recollection from the evidence of the slave boy's performance (85b–d) is remarkably brief relative to the enormity of the conclusion; the argument for immortality flashes past just as quickly; and it takes little more than a page (87d–89a) to establish the thesis that virtue is knowledge. (Contrast the much lengthier treatment of the *Protagoras*, 349e–360e.) So with relatively little information at our disposal, it is often very difficult to determine on any one occasion exactly what the argument is. Worse, a sketchy argument can easily be represented as a bad one. Critics of a particular passage will claim that there are gaps not so much in Socrates'

---

[1] Mill 1979: 422.

[2] Thompson (1901: 63) takes the subject matter to be ethical. Crombie (1963: II, 534–5) thinks that philosophical method is the main theme of the dialogue. For Bedu-Addo (1984: 14), it is knowledge and its acquisition. Both agree in saying that the ethical content is chosen by way of example. Weiss (2001: 3) opts for moral inquiry, so straddling the divide.

presentation, but in the argument itself: he just does not have the premises he needs to draw his conclusion. In places, Socrates seems to admit as much. At the end of the recollection passage, he sounds extremely tentative about the conclusions he has drawn (86b6–7), and later on has to correct a mistake in his own argument that virtue is knowledge (96d5–e5). At the end, he stresses the need to resume the inquiry into the nature of virtue before they have any confidence in the conclusions they have drawn about its acquisition.

Furthermore, it is sometimes difficult to pin down exactly what Socrates is trying to conclude in a particular argument, never mind what the argument actually is. There has been disagreement about what Socrates means by saying that everyone desires good things (77b–78b), or that virtue is knowledge (87d–89a). Similar problems apply also to his methodological pronouncements: for instance, determining the exact nature of the hypothetical method has been a thorn in the flesh of many commentators over the years.

The main task of this book is to resolve the indeterminacies surrounding both the arguments and the conclusions that they are meant to support. Where the quality of the arguments is at issue, I shall discuss possible objections and then consider different ways of addressing them. Usually, this involves searching for premises that might be implicit and that would improve the quality of the argument; or, failing that, at least bringing out its interest and importance, whatever the flaws that remain.

There is another strategy. Faced with the prospect of having to redeem what looks like a bad argument, some commentators pronounce it as bad, but add that Socrates was perfectly aware of the fact. Interpreters who take this route claim that he ingeniously tricks Meno into accepting a bad argument, or deliberately confuses him with muddled exposition. In this spirit, individual commentators have targeted the slave boy demonstration, the references to geometry and mathematical method, as well as the entire final section of the dialogue from the appearance of Anytus to the end. If one were to adopt the views of all these interpreters at once, one would end up writing off much of the dialogue as self-consciously bad argument.[3]

Although such an approach might be appropriate for the occasional passage, it risks making the dialogue more of a fake than a gem, at least in philosophical terms. Furthermore, we should note from the outset that Socrates expects participants in a dialogue to speak the truth (75c–d). It is

[3] Weiss (2001: 94–107) takes this kind of approach to the slave boy demonstration, Lloyd (1992) to much of the mathematical material and Wilkes (1979) to the whole of 89–100b.

difficult to see how this is compatible with the use of deliberately misleading arguments on his part. At any rate, I have done my best to avoid this type of interpretation.[4] Almost all the cases I have encountered where commentators adopt it can be better dealt with by a more patient approach to the argument or passage in question. I hope the result is that the dialogue justifies its description as a philosophical gem – even if a little rough cut for some tastes.

CHARACTER AND DIALOGUE

The *Meno* is very much a dialogue – a drama that unfolds between its various interlocutors. Though the same could be said of most of Plato's works, here characterisation and individual psychology are particularly striking. Throughout, Meno's own personality and his reaction to philosophical cross-examination are vividly portrayed. At a number of points Socrates makes explicit reference to his character, even calling him bullying, spoilt and arrogant. How seriously these comments are meant can be discussed in due course, but they ensure that the assessment of Meno as a person, and not just the quality of his answers, is kept well to the fore. The same can be said of Anytus, perhaps even more so.

But if characterisation is such a feature of this work, how are we to relate it to the philosophical content? With this question one needs to steer between two extremes. Some readers may be tempted to treat the dramatic element as mere packaging, or literary *joie de vivre* intended to draw us into the dialogue, which they then go on to ransack for philosophical arguments. But it is possible to go to the opposite extreme, and to be so caught up by Plato's powers of characterisation that one ends up reading a passage merely as an episode in an unfolding psychological drama, without asking what philosophical pay-off is involved.[5]

As far as the *Meno* is concerned, one thing that brings content and characterisation together is moral education. The dialogue, I shall argue, does not just have this topic as one of its central themes; it is also an exercise in moral education. Meno's character is carefully exhibited in the first half of the dialogue, not to leave us with a static portrait of a somewhat unsavoury character, but to introduce us to the educational challenge that Socrates has to face. After reviewing the faults that Meno is shown to possess in the first

---

[4] One exception is Socrates' description of the geometrical method (86e–87b); another is the argument with Anytus. However, in neither of these cases shall I claim that Socrates deliberately misleads his interlocutor.

[5] On the hazards of this approach see Gulley 1969: 162–3 and Burnyeat 2003: 23.

part of dialogue (pp. 60–65), I shall argue that he starts to improve, thus demonstrating the results of Socratic education at work (pp. 209–13).

Over and above the importance of its philosophical content or the brilliance of its characterisation, the *Meno* has another claim to fame: it has long had a fascination for those concerned with Plato's intellectual biography. 'Developmentalists', as they are sometimes called, usually divide his works into three groups. In the early dialogues, he aimed to capture the nature and character of Socrates' thought. While he did not reproduce *verbatim* transcripts of actual Socratic encounters, he at least caught the spirit of his mentor. But eventually Plato grew dissatisfied, especially with the negative character of Socratic philosophy with its emphasis on refutation, and started to develop positive views of his own. Also, he widened his philosophical horizons beyond Socrates' exclusively ethical interests to embrace metaphysics, epistemology and psychology. In the final phase of his thought, Plato adopts a critical approach to some of the views expounded in the middle period, and sometimes even reverts to the apparently negative style of the early Socratic dialogues.

Developmentalists often see the *Meno* as 'the' transitional dialogue.[6] Although it starts in the manner of an early Socratic dialogue, it soon changes and, especially with the theory of recollection, shows Plato in his more positive mode, although without the confidence of some of the middle period works. This episode also shows the broadening of interest associated with Plato's departure from Socratic philosophy. The recollection passage is not the only point of interest to developmentalists. They also point to the distinction between knowledge and true belief (something of which Socrates says he has knowledge), and the interest in mathematics as a helpful parallel for philosophical method.

Developmentalism has been a distinctly mixed blessing for the *Meno*. In the first part of the dialogue, Socrates criticises Meno for breaking virtue into small pieces. The same can be said, alas, of so much recent work on the dialogue itself. Its claim to fame as 'the' transitional dialogue has often made commentators less interested in it in its own right than in how sections of it relate to other works. For instance, Socrates' examination of Meno in the first part is often used by scholars looking back to the earlier dialogues, while the positive epistemological developments that follow are

---

[6] For references, see pp. 202–8.

often viewed as anticipations of later works. So although references to the work are plentiful, they often come as part of broader discussions of Plato's thought and its development.[7]

Nevertheless, 'developmentalism' should not be treated as a dirty word, despite the damage it has done to scholarship on the *Meno*. So long as we are prepared to do justice to the integrity of the dialogue, it can be very illuminating to see the methodological and epistemological achievements of the *Meno* in the context of Plato's broader development. Indeed developmentalists need not confine their interest to these fields alone. In the course of this book, I shall argue that the dialogue's moral psychology and political theory can also be seen as pointing towards other dialogues.

One specific claim that I shall make in this context is that, at various points in the dialogue, Plato puts Socrates on what I shall call 'philosophical trial'. The most dramatic example comes when Socrates introduces the theory of recollection in response to Meno's challenge to the possibility of inquiry and discovery (80d). This passage testifies to Plato's concern about whether it is possible to attain knowledge, and hence whether we have any duty to inquire. The historical Socrates certainly believed that we have a duty to inquire, however arduous that may be. Through Meno, however, Plato deliberately challenges this position, and does so by questioning whether discovery is actually possible: if not, why do we have any duty to inquire? Plato shows the importance of the challenge by putting into Socrates' mouth an unsocratic solution of extraordinary philosophical boldness. Other scholars have suggested such an approach to this passage, but I shall also argue that this is just one example of Plato putting Socrates on trial in the *Meno*. There are three others, which concern the historical Socrates' views on definition, the value of the elenchus and philosophical method. To this extent, at least, I am highly sympathetic to those who see the *Meno* as a work in which Plato wrestles his Socratic inheritance.[8]

---

[7] Such tendencies are epitomised by Vlastos 1991.

[8] Throughout this book, I use 'Socrates' to refer to the character of the dialogue. When making a claim about the historical Socrates, I shall flag the point explicitly.

PART ONE

CHAPTER I

The opening: 70a–71d

Most of Plato's works start with an introductory scene, often of considerable length, giving details about the characters involved in the dialogue, as well as its physical and historical setting. The *Meno*, however, appears to have no introductory scene at all. As one commentator has put it: 'The dialogue opens with an abruptness hardly to be paralleled elsewhere in the genuine work of Plato by the propounding of a theme directly for discussion.'[1] The same commentator immediately goes on to criticise the dialogue for failing to live up to Plato's usual standards of literary composition. It must, he concludes, be a very early work.

Yet, although Meno propounds a theme directly for discussion, Socrates' reply takes a circuitous route, as if trying to slow the conversation down. He talks of how the Thessalians, previously renowned for horsemanship and wealth, have now acquired a reputation for wisdom. By contrast, his own people, the Athenians, are in exactly the opposite state: their wisdom has emigrated to Thessaly, leaving them ignorant about the very nature of virtue, let alone whether it is teachable. This then cues a principle that will be central to the dialogue: one cannot know how virtue may be acquired without knowing what it is (71b3–8). Only now is Socrates ready to start the philosophical discussion. But *en route* to this point, he has peppered his speech with proper names and allusions that send modern readers scurrying to the commentaries. There is no reason to think that this passage is the work of an immature Plato. Rather, it bears all the hallmarks of an author well practised in writing extended and highly allusive introductions, but who has decided on this occasion to use a much more compressed approach.

In fact, it does share something in common with many other opening passages from Plato's works, which very often use the introduction to anticipate some of the themes that will figure in the dialogue to come. The

---

[1] Taylor 1926: 130.

very abruptness in the way that the *Meno* begins anticipates two important features of the work, both connected with the character of Meno himself.[2]

First, the way he springs his question on Socrates highlights something that will become increasingly important as the dialogue proceeds. At a number of places he reveals himself as someone with a peremptory, almost tyrannical streak in his character (75b1, 76a8–c3 and 86d3–8) – someone with an interest in controlling others; at one point he even defines virtue as power pure and simple (73c9–d1).[3] This defect in his personality will be central to the interplay between the two characters and to Socrates' attempts to improve him.

The second theme anticipated by the opening lines concerns Meno's attitude to teaching and learning, which is one of knowledge on demand. By posing a simple and direct question, he expects to receive an answer that will quickly make him an authority on the topic, able to teach others in turn.

This feature may not strike a reader who approaches Meno's question for the first time. But it is amply shown in retrospect. We can see it already bubbling to the surface in Socrates' reply. Referring to Meno's own people, the Thessalians, he claims that they have recently been imbued with wisdom and acquired the habit of answering confidently whatever question one might care to ask (70a5–71a7). The credit for this goes to the sophist Gorgias. Later on in the dialogue, Meno echoes this same point, saying that in the past he has proudly dispensed what he took to be excellent speeches on virtue on numerous occasions (80b2–3); and the way in which he became an 'authority' on virtue has been gradually revealed in the intervening pages: he simply committed Gorgias' views on the subject to memory (71c10, 73c6–8 and 76a10–b1).

To fill out this picture of teaching and learning, we should turn to a piece of evidence that Aristotle gives us about Gorgias. Like other sophists, he travelled from city to city offering his services for money. He did not claim to teach virtue but specialised in teaching rhetoric (cf. 95c1–4), and his own oratorical skills were both innovative and widely admired. But at the end

---

[2] See Klein 1965: 38 and 189, Seeskin 1987: 123 and Scolnicov 1988: 51. For the general thesis that the opening of a Platonic dialogue often anticipates some of its central themes, see Burnyeat 1997.

[3] One can also compare Meno's opening question with his initial reaction to the theory of recollection (81e5). In wording that recalls 70a1, he asks Socrates: 'can you teach me how [learning is recollection]?' Socrates immediately complains that, according to the theory he has just set out, nothing can be taught, causing Meno to reply that he was only speaking 'out of habit' (82a5). There may well be a *double entendre* here: Meno has not only fallen back into a semantic habit, but also into one of expecting an answer to be given on demand. See Klein 1965: 98.

of his work, *Sophistical Refutations*, Aristotle complains that Gorgias never taught his students the principles of his craft, rhetoric – that is, he did not show them how to construct an effective speech from scratch; he merely gave them a collection of speeches or set answers, presumably on topics on which they were likely to be questioned. Aristotle compares him to a cobbler who, instead of teaching his apprentices the fundamentals of the craft, merely gives them several different pairs of shoes to try out on their clients in the hope that one of them will fit.[4] This point resonates throughout the dialogue, especially during the early part: just by memorising what Gorgias told him, Meno thinks that he has learnt to speak well about virtue – not only in the rhetorical sense, but also in the sense that he has actually gained knowledge of what it is.[5]

The assumption that underlies Meno's abruptness in asking his question betrays an approach to education that will be opposed throughout the work: equipped with a collection of speeches, the teacher acts as informant; the learner in turn memorises whatever the teacher has to say. Education is a straightforward process of transmission. The other side of that contrast is the Socratic approach to education, where learning takes the form of a dialogue in which the 'teacher' asks questions, and the learner responds. This is the reverse of Gorgias' model, where the learner asks one short question, and the teacher replies with a speech.[6] The basis of Socrates' approach to education lies in the theory of recollection: learning is a matter of drawing on one's own internal resources rather than receiving information from outside. This approach also turns a learner into an inquirer and casts the 'teacher' into the role of catalyst and questioner; it also helps to explain why the interaction between teacher and learner takes the form of an ordered sequence of questions, facilitating a step-by-step process of recollection.

We shall return to these rival approaches to education in due course.[7] My concern here is merely to show that the contrast between them is foreshadowed in the very opening of the work – in the abruptness of Meno's question and in the sly innuendo that follows in Socrates' immediate reply.

---

[4] *Sophistical Refutations* 34, 183b36–184a8.
[5] This is not to say that he thinks he has acquired virtue from Gorgias (cf. 95c1–4), only knowledge of its nature.
[6] It is true that Socrates replies to Meno's question with a speech. But his concern is not to answer the question – on the contrary, he avoids it. His underlying point is to make clear to Meno all the work that needs to be done before the question can be addressed directly, as well as to criticise, albeit subtly, Meno's presuppositions in posing the question as he did.
[7] See below pp. 143–4.

MENO'S QUESTION

Can you tell me, Socrates, is virtue (*arete*) teachable? Or can it not be acquired by teaching but by practice? Or can it be acquired neither by practice or learning, but comes to mankind by nature or in some other way? (70a1–4)

For want of a better term, I shall follow many other translators and use 'virtue' for the Greek *arete*. This was a term with a bewildering range of connotations, and it is no surprise that Socrates moves so quickly to have it defined. But what Meno has in mind when he uses the term is very much a political concept: the quality or set of qualities that makes for a successful leader (71e3, 73c9–d1 and 91a3–4).[8] Socrates also treats virtue as the quality by which a politician benefits his city, especially as the work goes on (cf. e.g. 89b6–7 and 98c8–9).

Notoriously, however, the word had much wider connotations than successful leadership, and could be used of an enormous variety of different things, animate or inanimate, human or non-human. From Homer onwards, we find it used of such diverse things as horses, soil and cotton.[9] Now the *Meno* only uses virtue of human subjects, but even here there are other connotations at work than the narrow political sense just mentioned. In his first definition, Meno allows that children and slaves may have virtue no less than their parents and masters, demonstrating that virtue must have a broader sense than that of successful leadership. Another connotation of virtue is that of a genus of which such qualities as justice, courage, temperance and wisdom are species.[10] This way of thinking can be found in non-philosophical texts and throughout the Platonic corpus. It is particularly prominent in the first ten pages of the *Meno*.[11]

Since much of this book will be concerned with virtue in one way or another, I shall not dwell on the issue in any more detail at this stage, except to say that Socrates' priority will be to sort through different conceptions of virtue and discover its underlying nature. In Meno he has the perfect interlocutor for the task: someone who manages to hold a large number of diverse and conflicting intuitions on the nature of virtue and so almost personifies the confusions inherent in popular thought.

---

[8] Protagoras has a similar account of virtue at *Prot.* 318e5–319a2. See also Xenophon, *Memorabilia* 4.2.11.

[9] See Guthrie 1971: 252.   [10] This list is supplied by Meno at 74a4–5.

[11] See esp. *Meno* 79a3–5 with 74a1–6; also *Laches* 190c9, and *Prot.* 329c6. For non-philosophical references, see Dover 1974: 68–9.

The question of how virtue is acquired had already been the subject of intense debate for at least half a century, a fact partly explained by the political changes through which Athens was going in that period. The transition from aristocratic rule to democracy in the course of the fifth century produced increased social mobility, allowing those from non-aristocratic backgrounds to attain high political office. In this context, a question naturally arose about the respective roles of nature and nurture in developing the qualities necessary for political success. Partly to meet this need, the sophists appeared on the scene, promising to equip young men ambitious for power with the necessary skills to achieve it. In a democracy this meant, among other things, oratory: the power to persuade both in the law courts and in the political assemblies. This was one skill most sophists professed to teach. But typically, they had a wider range of wares on offer: Protagoras, who unashamedly claimed to teach virtue, was famed for showing his pupils how to argue either side of a case,[12] and Hippias broadened the range to include various kinds of mathematical studies.[13] Add to all this that the sophists expected fees for their teaching, and one can see that any ambitious young man would have had an obvious interest in the question of whether virtue can be taught.[14]

The *Meno* is only one of the dialogues in which Plato takes up the long-standing debate about the acquisition of virtue. It is also central to the *Alcibiades I, Euthydemus, Laches* and *Protagoras*, and there are substantial thematic overlaps between these dialogues and the *Meno*.[15] Because of this, I shall be making occasional reference to some of these works, not in the interests of piecing together a unified account of Plato's thought, but to help illuminate the appearance of these themes in the *Meno*. I shall also be comparing passages in the *Meno* to the *Republic*, a dialogue in which Plato's interest in the acquisition of virtue takes centre stage, since the success of the ideal state sketched there depends above all on the education of its leaders. Here his treatment of the subject is much more extensive than in the other dialogues mentioned although, as we shall see, the *Meno* contains some of the seeds of the ideas that feature in the *Republic*.

If we now turn to the details of Meno's question there are two puzzles to confront. The alternatives he mentions were well established: participants

---

[12] See Aristotle, *Rhetoric* II 24, 1402a24–6 (DK 80 B6).   [13] Cf. *Prot.* 318d9–e4.

[14] On the general background to this debate see Guthrie 1971: 250–60 and Kerferd 1981: 131–8.

[15] Among these are: a general interest in assessing the sophists' claims to teach virtue; the use of the argument that virtue cannot be teachable because no virtuous person has ever succeeded in teaching his own sons; the need to define virtue before asking about its acquisition; the dangers of 'eristic' argument, i.e. debating purely for the sake of winning a victory; and Socrates' own thesis that virtue is knowledge.

in the long-standing pedagogical debate tended to focus upon the different contributions of nature, teaching and practice in accounting for the development of virtue. (The reference to 'some other manner' may be Plato's way of preparing us for the alternative canvassed at the end of the dialogue, divine dispensation.) The first puzzle is that Meno presents these alternatives as mutually exclusive. Admittedly, there may have been precedents for this: decades before, Pindar had espoused nature as the sole origin of virtue,[16] and there is one fragment of Democritus that might be used to suggest that, for most people, practice is the sole route.[17] On the whole, however, it was far more common to claim that more than one factor was involved, often all three, even if individual thinkers gave particular weight to one or other of them.[18] Perhaps we should not be surprised if Meno assumes that virtue comes by a single route: he may simply not have thought the matter through. What is more surprising is that at no point in the dialogue does Socrates challenge the assumption. We shall return to this problem on page 160 below when we come to examine his views on the acquisition of virtue.

Another mystery arising from Meno's question concerns the second alternative, practice. This might refer to repeated 'exercise' in political affairs, by analogy with gymnastic training.[19] What is puzzling is that it is never mentioned again in the dialogue either to be developed or dismissed. Both teaching and nature, on the other hand, are discussed quite explicitly.

At this point, we should note that one of the most important manuscripts for the *Meno* omits the reference to practice in the opening question. This raises the possibility that Plato himself did not have Meno mention practice and that what is printed in most editions is an interpolation from a

---

[16] *Olympian Ode* 9.100 and *Nemean Ode* 3.40–2.

[17] See DK 68 B242: 'more people become good by practice than from nature'. The same thought is attributed to Critias (DK 88 B9). Elsewhere Democritus makes it clear that teaching and nature are also important factors (cf. B33, 56 and 182). So I suspect B242 should really be taken to mean that practice is a more important factor in the acquisition of virtue than nature (cf. Epicharmus DK 23 B33). One text where practice is given all the running is *Phaedo* 82a11–b3: here Socrates talks of 'popular virtue' (though not true virtue) as being acquired solely by practice. See also *Rep.* VII 518d9–e2 and X 619c7–d1.

[18] Aside from the sources already mentioned, see Protagoras DK 80 B3 and 10; Euripides, *Suppliants* 911–17 and *Hecuba* 599–602; Thucydides, 1.121; Anonymus Iamblichi, DK 89 1; *Dissoi Logoi* DK 90.6, 10–11; Xenophon, *Mem.* 3.9.14 and 4.1.4. In almost all these cases, two or more of the triad are thought to be necessary for the acquisition of virtue. For discussions of the issue that refer to some of these passages see Shorey 1909, O'Brien 1967: 144–6 n. 27 and Dover 1974: 88–95. When sifting through the texts cited by these commentators one should be careful to distinguish whether a source is discussing the acquisition of virtue, or becoming a good orator or poet. Shorey frequently blurs these distinctions.

[19] For this conception of practice see Isocrates, *Antidosis* 187–8.

later editor. According to the manuscript in question, F,[20] Meno's opening question reads:

Can you tell me, Socrates, is virtue teachable? Or can it not be acquired by teaching or learning, but comes to mankind by nature or in some other way?

Modern editors and translators are united against F's reading and in favour of keeping the reference to practice in the text. There are three reasons usually given for this. First, as we have seen, practice was a well-established member of the 'pedagogical triad', and we might expect it to be mentioned. Second, commentators sometimes point ahead to a passage from Aristotle's *Nicomachean Ethics*, I 9, 1099b9–11 where he mentions practice alongside nature, teaching and divine dispensation as factors responsible for human development. The reference to divine dispensation as an alternative to teaching and nature seems to recall the ending of the *Meno*, making it all the more tempting to assume that Aristotle is quoting directly from the dialogue. Thirdly, one might try to explain away the original problem about the lack of any further references to practice by saying that the argument by which teaching and learning are eventually discounted (93a5–94e2) could easily be adapted to eliminate practice. For Socrates will argue that, if virtue were teachable, such men as Themistocles and Pericles, the very paradigms of virtue, would have taught it to their own sons – something they manifestly failed to do. Similarly, one might argue, if virtue could come by practice, the great and the good would have trained their sons, just as they had them trained in such things as horsemanship.[21]

None of these points, however, is conclusive. First, although practice was a well-established member of the triad, there is no overriding need for it to be mentioned explicitly. It could as well be accommodated under the final alternative ('some other way'), especially if, as may be the case, it was the junior partner in the triad: the main antithesis seemed to have been nature and teaching.[22] As to the second objection, it is pure speculation to say

---

[20] The manuscript F is thought to derive from a popular edition of Plato's works, compiled by a philosophically unsophisticated editor. So it may have the advantage over other manuscripts that its editor would be less inclined to make philosophical 'improvements' to the text where a more educated editor might consider himself to have detected a previous scribal error or oversight. On the standing of this manuscript see Bluck 1961: 135–40. Unfortunately, the Oxford Classical Text, Burnet 1903, fails to mention F's reading of 70a2.

[21] See Bluck 1961: 202–3.

[22] Another solution could be that, for Meno, teaching might encompass more than just intellectual instruction, and so already include practice, i.e. training. (For this wider sense, see O'Brien 1967: 146, n. 27 and Bluck 1961: 202 with *Prot.* 323c5–324c5, where teaching is broad enough to include non-intellectual elements of education such as punishment.) If so, teaching could then be eliminated by the argument of 93a–94e in exactly the way proposed in the previous paragraph. I doubt that

that Aristotle must have been citing the *Meno*, as if he had no other sources
to draw upon. Besides, we should be wary of assimilating *Meno* 70a1–4
to *N.E.* 1 9, 1099b9–11: while Aristotle may be using similar terminology
to the *Meno*, he is addressing a different (if related) question – about the
acquisition of happiness, rather than virtue.[23]

As far as the third point is concerned, it may be that the 'father argument'
of 93a–94e can work equally well against training and practice as it does
against teaching and learning. But this is not sufficient to dispel the original
mystery. There are two points prior to the argument of 93a–94e where we
should expect to find explicit references to practice. The first is at 86c7–d2,
where Meno is trying to get Socrates to return to the opening question of
the dialogue:

> Nevertheless, I'd most like to consider and hear you answer the question that I
> asked at the outset: whether one should attempt to acquire virtue as something
> teachable, or as coming to mankind by nature or in some other way.

Meno is as keen as ever to have his original question answered and, in an
attempt to bend Socrates to his will, proceeds to spell the question out all
over again. Yet, although he mentions teaching, nature and 'some other
way', he makes no reference to practice. Unless we accept F's reading of
the opening question, this is extremely mysterious: Socrates has not yet
deployed the father argument, so there is no reason at this stage why Meno
should have lost interest in practice.

Another place where we might expect a reference to practice is 89b, just
after Socrates has argued that virtue is knowledge, and hence that it is teachable (on the grounds that all and only knowledge is teachable). What is interesting is that he still feels the need to eliminate one of the alternatives Meno
had suggested at the start: that virtue comes by nature (89a6). Why does he
not do the same for practice, if he is in a mood to eliminate the alternatives
to teaching that Meno had explicitly mentioned in his original question?

On the strength of these considerations, I think that the balance of the
argument shifts in favour of F's reading, despite the consensus of scholars
on the other side.[24]

---

this solution can be applied to the *Meno*, because the notion of teaching it develops is narrowly
intellectual: see 87c2–3. Besides, anyone who defends the inclusion of 'practice' in Meno's opening
question thereby has to admit that Meno himself opposes teaching and practice.

[23] Commentators also point to *N.E.* x 9, 1179b20–1, which is concerned with the acquisition of virtue
and mentions the pedagogical triad, but again there is no reason why Aristotle should be referring
to the *Meno* as such, given the number of other sources that refer to the same triad. (Also, there is
not an exact verbal similarity with *Meno* 70a1–4, as Aristotle uses ἔθος not ἄσκησις.)

[24] It is interesting that the pseudo-Platonic dialogue, *On Virtue*, which tracks parts of the *Meno* very
closely, opens with the question: 'Is virtue teachable? If not, do people become virtuous by nature

SOCRATES' RESPONSE

The disavowal of knowledge

Put briefly, Socrates' reply is that he does not know how virtue can be acquired because he does not know what it is (71b3). In making the point, he uses the following analogy: if someone did not know at all who Meno is, how could they know if he is beautiful, rich or well born? Presumably he is thinking of a scenario in which someone who has never heard of Meno is asked whether he is rich etc. Although the person can infer, just by being asked the question, that Meno is a human being, they are otherwise in a complete blank about him. Overtly, therefore, Socrates is in a similar blank about virtue (apart from thinking that it is some quality attributable to human beings).

Plato frequently attributes disavowals of knowledge to Socrates, and the question arises as to whether we should take such disavowals at face value. In the course of the *Meno* he appears to espouse a number of claims about virtue – for example that it is a unitary property, and that justice, temperance and piety are necessary conditions of virtue; at 87d–89a he propounds the argument that virtue is a form of knowledge, which is based on the premise that virtue is beneficial (87e3). Obviously, Socrates cannot be in the same situation as someone who has never heard of Meno. But if we are not to take the analogy at face value, what is his real position? I take it that he does not know what virtue is in the sense of having a fully fledged philosophical understanding of it. Later on in the dialogue, he makes a distinction between knowledge and true belief, where knowledge requires that one has reasoned out the explanation (98a1–8). It is in this sense that he fails to know what virtue is.

But this leaves us with the question of how to characterise the grasp of virtue that he does have. Some scholars, confronted with Socrates' disavowals in other dialogues, have claimed that he had two senses of knowledge in play. Vlastos, for instance, argues that what Socrates disavows is 'certain' knowledge on ethical matters; yet, since he believes many ethical propositions that have so far withstood cross-examination, he can claim to know them in a weaker sense.[25] Other commentators also attribute to Socrates a secondary, weaker sense of knowledge that he claims for

---

or in some other way?' As the author almost certainly had the text of Plato's *Meno* before him, F's reading of the opening becomes all the more plausible. For a discussion of the relation between the *Meno* and *On Virtue*, see Reuter 2001: 85–90.

[25] Vlastos 1994: ch. 2 esp. 55–8. Vlastos calls this weaker sense 'elenctic' knowledge.

himself.[26] But whatever one may say about other dialogues, this strategy will not do for the *Meno*, which insists so firmly on the unity of definition (cf. 74d3–e2) and duly proceeds to recognise only one type of knowledge – explanatory understanding (98a3–4); anything less is relegated to the status of true belief.

Perhaps then we ought to say that what Socrates does have, if not knowledge, is (at best) a number of true beliefs.[27] This is certainly the more promising approach, but the notion of true belief here needs to be made more determinate. About half way through the work, Socrates attributes true belief to the slave boy, who has only just started to follow a pattern of ordered reasoning for himself (85c6–7), and at the end to the great politicians of Athens, who seem to have achieved many great things, but without having reflected on what they were doing or saying. If we are to characterise Socrates' grasp of virtue in terms of true belief, we surely do not wish to put him in either of these two categories. Rather, he must have a web of beliefs, whose interconnections he has explored extensively in his frequent ethical inquiries. The process of reaching back to underlying explanations is thus well advanced, even if it has not culminated in full understanding.

The priority of definition

Another central theme in Socrates' response is often discussed under the title 'the priority of definition'. He insists that knowing whether virtue is teachable depends on knowing what it is, and bases this claim upon the more general principle that you cannot know what something is like without knowing what it is. Although we shall examine this principle in some detail as the commentary goes on, we need to make some introductory remarks here.

He introduces the principle by asking, 'If I don't know what something is, how would I know what it's like?' (71b3–4). This appeals implicitly to a metaphysical distinction between features that are essential to an object ('what *x* is in itself') and those that are non-essential ('what *x* is like').[28] But

---

[26] See Woodruff 1987 and Brickhouse and Smith 1994: 31. Like Vlastos, these commentators use the distinction between different kinds of knowledge to explain what they take to be a mixture of avowals and disavowals of knowledge in such works as the *Apology, Crito, Protagoras, Gorgias* and *Republic* I.

[27] For this approach see Irwin 1977: 40–1; cf. also Burnyeat 1977: 384–6.

[28] Unfortunately, he says very little about this distinction, e.g. how to assign features to one class or the other. There are other passages in the early dialogues where a similar distinction is invoked, although they do not give us any substantial information to supplement what we find in the *Meno*. At *Euthyphro* 11a6–b1, Socrates complains that, in defining piety as what is loved by the gods, Euthyphro has not given him the essence (οὐσία) of piety, but a 'concomitant feature'. (See *Meno* 72b1 for the use of the word οὐσία to denote the 'what it is' or essence of something.) Other applications of this distinction appear in the *Laches* 189e3–190c2, *Prot.* 312c1–4 and 360e6–361d6 and *Gorgias* 463c3–5.

why does he think that knowing the essence is necessary for knowing the non-essential attributes? I have already anticipated his claim that knowledge requires explanatory reasoning (98a3–4). If this is already implicitly at work at 71b, we only have to add one further assumption to derive the priority of definition: the essence is what explains the non-essential attributes.

On this interpretation, Socrates in the *Meno* is already committed to significant, but as yet undeveloped, metaphysical and epistemological assumptions that were to reach their clearest expression with Aristotle, especially in his *Posterior Analytics*. Aristotle himself endorses this interpretation, claiming that Socrates used definitions as the starting points of demonstrative reasoning.[29] For Aristotle, the distinction was between the essence of something and what he called 'necessary accidents':[30] features that do not belong to the essence itself but are dependent on it for their explanation. For instance, a triangle essentially has three sides; but that it has angles equal to 180° is not part of the essence, but follows from the essence. One only has knowledge – demonstrative understanding – of a necessary accident when one has derived it from the essence. This is an 'apodeictic' conception of knowledge, according to which the definition acts as a principle from which we can deduce other properties.

But if the true rationale for the priority of definition lies in Socrates' implicit metaphysics and epistemology – his 'proto-Aristotelianism' – what are we to make of the support he overtly gives, the analogy of knowing who Meno is (71b4–8)? The analogy is easy enough to criticise. Does Socrates really mean to claim that individual people have essences that can be defined and then used to explain attributes of their character? And what does he mean by 'knowing' here? To determine whether Meno is rich or well born, all I need is some identifying feature by which to differentiate him from other people. But what Socrates goes on to demand by way of knowing what virtue is goes much deeper than this.

The underlying problem with the analogy is the way it uses an individual (Meno) to illustrate something about a property such as virtue. Certainly the analogy should not be pressed too hard, and is best treated as a pedagogical device to give Meno an intuitive hold on the idea of one question ('what is x?') having priority over another ('what is x like?'). If Socrates exploits a verbal similarity in the analogy and glosses over what to a seasoned thinker are important differences, it is not thereby bad pedagogy. By the end of the dialogue, however, once the analysis of knowledge has been given, we

---

[29] See *Met.* XIII 4, 1078b23–5. (Aristotle was notoriously fond of seeing his predecessors as groping towards ideas that he articulated more clearly.) For this interpretation of *Meno* 71b among modern commentators, see Vlastos 1994: 85 and esp. Prior 1998.
[30] For the expression see *Posterior Analytics* I 6, 75a18–19.

should see this analogy for what it is and not attach too much philosophical importance to it.

There are two more introductory points to make about the priority of definition. First, the fact that Socrates appeals to it gives us a valuable insight into the way in which he understands Meno's opening question. Although I have consistently translated it as the question of whether virtue can be taught (etc.), the terms used are susceptible of different interpretations: the verbal adjective διδακτόν can mean either 'can be taught' or 'is taught'; the same applies to μαθητόν, meaning either 'can be learnt' or 'is learnt' (and ἀσκητόν – 'can be acquired by practice' or 'is acquired by practice'). So the very opening question of the dialogue could be whether virtue can be taught, or whether it is in fact taught. Moreover, there is a further distinction between two types of possibility. The statement, 'virtue cannot be taught' could mean that there is no possibility of teaching *as things stand*, e.g. because there happens to be no one at present qualified to teach it. But it could also mean that virtue cannot *in principle* be taught: whatever the circumstances in one place or another, it is simply not in the nature of virtue to be teachable.

Because Socrates focuses the discussion directly on the nature of virtue, we can see that he resolves the ambiguity of the opening question in favour of this last meaning: if he wanted to address either the factual question of whether virtue is taught, or whether it can be as things stand, he could immediately have embarked on a historical survey of Athens.[31] For his purposes, however, such a survey runs the risk of overlooking possibilities simply because they have not been realised in our experience.

Finally, the priority of definition at issue in this passage needs to be distinguished from a different principle, viz. in order to know whether a particular thing is F, you must know what F-ness is. This is a principle whose attribution to Socrates has been the subject of a long-running dispute.[32] The principle at stake at the beginning of the *Meno*, however, is not the priority of definition over instances, but over non-essential attributes. Whether Socrates in the *Meno* also espouses the former principle must at this stage be left as an open question, though it will assume considerable importance when we come to examine the problems that prompt Socrates to introduce the theory of recollection at 81a.

---

[31] He does indeed embark on this sort of inquiry after 90b4 but, as Brunschwig (1991: 595) has argued, this does not show that he has replaced the original question with one about how virtue is in fact acquired. I shall return to this issue on pp. 161–2 and 177–8 below.

[32] See Geach 1966, Santas 1972, Burnyeat 1977, Nehamas 1987: 277–93, Beversluis 1987, Benson 1990, Vlastos 1994: 67–86 and Prior 1998.

CHAPTER 2

The first definition: 71e–73c

SOCRATES *VERSUS* GORGIAS

Meno is surprised at Socrates' claim not to know what virtue is, and no less surprised that he has never met anyone else who does:

MEN. What? Didn't you meet Gorgias when he was here?
SOC. I did.
MEN. Then didn't he seem to you to know?
SOC. I don't have a very good memory, Meno. So I can't say now how he seemed to me then. But perhaps he did know, and you know what he said. So remind me what he said. But if you'd rather, speak on your own behalf: I imagine you think the same as he does.
MEN. I do.
SOC. So let's leave him aside, as he's not here anyway. But you, Meno, by the gods, what do you say virtue is? Speak and don't begrudge me an answer. Maybe it'll transpire that I was telling a most fortunate falsehood, if you and Gorgias turn out to know, while there was I saying I'd never met anyone who did.

(71c5–d8)

Socrates has now set the stage for Meno to give a definition of virtue and, in doing so, continues to draw out one of the central themes of his initial speech: Meno is positioned as someone who will be recalling views enunciated by Gorgias. This exchange also continues the proleptic technique of the previous lines: the references to memory (71c8 and c10) playfully anticipate the most famous theme of the dialogue. Also, to the re-reader there is a double meaning in Socrates' suggestion that he may yet revise his claim never to have encountered anyone who knows the nature of virtue: in one sense everyone whom he has met has been ignorant, in the sense of being unable to give an explicit account of themselves; in another it will turn out that they do have the knowledge, however deeply it may be buried within them.

Gorgias' position

In his first attempt to answer what virtue is, Meno gives a list, describing a man's virtue and a woman's, then adding that there are virtues for children, both male and female, and for older men, both free and slave (71e1–72a5). As we have just seen, Meno has been set up as someone who is merely going to quote Gorgias' views. This will be important for understanding his role as an interlocutor, but for the moment I shall concentrate on Gorgias' position and on its philosophical context.

According to this position, virtue is made to depend on a number of variables – age, gender, social status and occupation. Because these factors vary widely from one human being to another, one cannot expect virtue to be a single determinate feature applicable to all human beings. Compare, for instance, the account of a man's virtue with that of a woman:

> This is the virtue of a man: to be competent at managing the affairs of the city, and in doing so to treat his friends well and his enemies badly, and to ensure that he does not suffer any such harm himself. If you want the virtue of a woman, that's not difficult to describe: it is to manage the household well, looking after its affairs and being obedient to her husband. (71e2–7)

Nothing that occurs in the formula applied to men, which is concerned with activities in the public sphere, is found in the female type, which is exclusively internal to the household.

There is additional evidence that Gorgias pursued this type of relativising approach to virtue from Aristotle's *Politics* I 13:

> For it misleading to give a general definition of virtue, as some do, who say that virtue is being in good condition as regards the soul or acting uprightly or the like; those who enumerate the virtues of different persons separately, as Gorgias does, are much more correct than those who define virtue in that way.[1]

We also have direct evidence from one of Gorgias' own works that he applied a similar approach to 'adornment' (κόσμος) – a term, he claims, that differs as it applies to cities, bodies, souls, actions and speech.[2]

---

[1] 1260a25–8 trans. Rackham 1959.

[2] 'Adornment for a city is the manliness of its citizens, for a body beauty, for a soul wisdom, for an action virtue, for speech truth' (*Encomium on Helen* §1). See Guthrie 1971: 254. It is unclear exactly how this claim is supposed to relate to the first definition of virtue in the *Meno*. Although there is no outright contradiction (the *Helen* does not require that virtue be univocal), the position quoted in the *Meno* makes virtue a property of people rather than of actions, unlike the *Helen*.

It is safe to assume that Gorgias was taking up a philosophical posture and self-consciously refusing to apply to some evaluative terms what I shall call the 'unitarian assumption'. This is the view that Socrates is concerned to defend in the first part of the *Meno*, and it is stated most explicitly as the argument proceeds, especially at 74d5–75a8: whenever we apply the same term F to many different things, and say that they are all F's, each one no less than the others, there is one unitary property, F-ness, that they have in common. Notice, incidentally, that Socrates is not inferring the existence of one unitary form merely because we apply the same word to a number of different things. Using a single word for many items is only the first element in his account of why we should posit a form. The commitment required is stronger: we must also make the claim that the items are all equally cases of F-ness, no one more or less than the others. This commitment goes beyond mere language use.

This, in outline, is the substance of the dispute that will take up the first few pages of the dialogue. Given the lack of evidence about Gorgias, it is difficult to establish his position in much more detail. But there is one further question that needs to be raised – whether he is to be interpreted as advocating a quite general scepticism of there being unitary definitions, as found in Wittgenstein (*Philosophical Investigations* §66):

Consider for example the proceedings we call 'games'. I mean board-games, card-games, ball-games, Olympic games, and so on. What is common to them all? – Don't say: 'There must be something common, or they would not be called "games"' – but *look and see* whether there is anything common to all. – For if you look at them you will not see something that is common to *all*, but similarities, relationships, and a whole series of them at that.

Here Wittgenstein seems to be mounting a quite general attack on the unitarian assumption. But we should be very wary of interpreting Gorgias' point so broadly. The rationale behind his position as reported in the *Meno* appears to be that virtue is relative to a number of factors, which in turn vary across different types of people. But this reason would not generate an argument for a more widespread scepticism about the unitarian assumption; the only other evidence for Gorgias' attitude to the assumption concerns what seems to be an evaluative term, 'adornment'. Thus even if he had an interest in the diversity of evaluative properties, this still falls well short of Wittgenstein's global challenge to the assumption. In other words, Gorgias might have been happy to accept the unitarian assumption in most cases, but thought evaluative terms constituted an important class of exceptions.

Socrates' response

In reply, Socrates complains that he has been given a 'swarm' of virtues, when what he wants is the one thing they all have in common. There are then three stages in his attempt to persuade Meno to accept the unitarian assumption. The first two constitute an argument from analogy. Taking up the allusion to bees, he first insists that all bees have one essence in common, despite their several differences from one another. Natural kinds are perhaps the least problematic case for the assumption, and Meno makes no attempt to hold the conversation up. But when told that there must also be a single property common to all virtues, he says that he does not quite understand what is being said (72d2–3). So Socrates embarks on another stage of the argument from analogy, appealing to a trio of parallels: men and women can be healthy, large or strong. There is not one health for a man, another for a woman, but one form common to all cases. The same applies to largeness and strength.

Socrates has chosen these examples carefully.[3] The manifestations of these properties vary widely: what one expects of a healthy man (e.g. how much he would eat or sleep) is quite different from a child; a strong man can normally lift heavier things than a strong woman; the height of a large child would make a man small. Yet this need not stop us claiming that there is the same underlying property in all cases. For example, despite the outward variety, health might still consist in the same internal balance of bodily elements in all cases. This of course would be a very convenient parallel for Socrates to apply to virtue.

Although Meno has no problem accepting the assumption for these three cases, when asked to find the single property for all virtues, he stalls the conversation again, objecting that virtue cannot be treated in the same way. This prompts Socrates to abandon the appeal to analogy altogether, and put forward a fresh argument for applying the unitarian assumption to virtue (73a6–c5):

1 The virtue of a man consists in managing the city well, that of a woman the household.
2 One cannot manage a city or a household well if one does so intemperately and unjustly.
3 If one manages justly and temperately, one manages with justice and temperance.
4 To be good, men and women need the same things, justice and temperance.

[3] See Irwin 1977: 134.

5 To be good, children and old men also need to be just and temperate.
6 Once they have these two qualities, they become good.
7 All human beings are good in the same way.
8 All human beings are good by having the same virtue.

In describing the virtue of women, Meno said that they must manage the household well (71e6–7). Socrates now takes him to have meant this requirement to apply to everyone: whatever it is that they do, they must do it well. He then argues that 'well' has a single determinate sense, analysing it for everyone in terms of justice and temperance.

There is an obvious problem with the validity of the argument. Steps 1 through 5 establish that justice and temperance are necessary conditions for virtue, wherever it occurs. Step 6 makes the two qualities sufficient for virtue in children and old people. But unless they are sufficient for everyone, 7 does not follow. It might be that justice and temperance form a common core but, in those other than children and the elderly, other qualities are also needed to suffice for virtue.[4] Despite this, however, the argument has some force against Gorgias. Socrates could still insist that the different types of virtue are branches that share a common trunk. Without taking us all the way to the unitarian assumption, he has moved us a significant distance away from Gorgias' original position. What he has done is to remind us – those of us who have the requisite intuitions – that there are certain requirements that apply to all human beings as such.

Even this, however, may be too generous to Socrates. Granted that temperance and justice are common to all cases of virtue, Socrates is still not justified in assuming that these qualities are in their turn unitary: why could men and children not be temperate and just in different ways? Thus, even the more cautious 'common trunk' thesis would have to be modified in some way.

SOCRATES ON TRIAL (I)

Throughout this passage, Socrates appears firmly wedded to the unitarian assumption. But I now wish to raise a question about Plato's stance on the issue. In the Introduction, I said that in the course of this book I would be discussing four passages in which Plato puts Socrates on 'philosophical trial'. This is the first of them. The pattern I shall claim to find repeated in the *Meno* includes at least three elements: first, the Socrates of the dialogue espouses a position that we can safely ascribe to the historical Socrates.

---

[4] See Robinson 1953: 57.

Second, this position is subjected to a serious philosophical challenge in the dialogue. Third, although the challenge comes from Meno, it is far from clear whether he understands its true significance.

There is no difficulty in ascribing the unitarian assumption to the historical Socrates. We find it clearly enunciated in the *Laches* and the *Euthyphro*, and there is also external evidence from Aristotle's *Politics*. Just before stating that Gorgias denied the assumption, he has Socrates affirm it:

> Hence it is manifest that all the persons mentioned have a moral virtue of their own, and that the temperance of a man and that of a woman are not the same, nor their courage and justice, as Socrates thought, but the one is the courage of command, and the other that of subordination, and the case is similar with the other virtues.[5]

What I wish to argue, however, is that Socrates' position is actually being challenged as well as stated in the *Meno*. To some readers, perhaps, all that is going on is that Socrates is trying to explain one of his favourite principles to an unusually obtuse interlocutor. But contrast this passage with its parallels in the *Euthyphro* and the *Laches*, where the same assumption is espoused but with much more dispatch. At *Euthyphro* 5c8–d5 Socrates asks for the quality that all pious actions have in common. When Euthyphro responds with an example, it takes very little to get him on track:

> So do you remember that I did not ask you to tell me one or two of the many pious actions, but that form itself by which all pious actions are pious? You said that all impious actions are impious and all pious actions are pious by one form – or don't you remember? (6d9–e1)

At this point Euthyphro defines piety as 'what the gods approve'. Although ultimately rejected by Socrates, this answer at least satisfies the unitarian assumption.

Laches takes a little longer to grasp the point. Having defined courage as standing fast in battle, he is confronted with other cases and asked to adhere to the unitarian assumption. When he professes not to understand

---

[5] *Politics* I 13, 1260a20–4 trans. Rackham 1959. Saunders (1995: 100) thinks Aristotle here refers directly to the *Meno*, in which case we could not use this text straightforwardly as evidence for what the historical Socrates thought. But Aristotle is clearly talking here of the historical Socrates, because at 1260a22 he refers simply to Σωκράτης, not ὁ Σωκράτης, let alone ὁ Σωκράτης ἐν τῷ Μένωνι, either of which we would expect if he was talking about the Socrates of the dialogue. On this see Newman 1887: II 219 and Vlastos 1991: 97 n. 67. Furthermore, the claim Aristotle attacks is that the specific virtues have a single definition. While this can be used as evidence that Socrates believed the unitarian assumption, it is slightly different from the context of the *Meno*, where it is virtue as a whole that is said to be apply in the same way to men and women alike. None of this, of course, is to deny that Aristotle had read the *Meno*, and knew that Plato's Socrates affirms the unitarian assumption; my point is that his remarks in *Pol.* I 13 are aimed directly at the historical figure.

(191e12), Socrates offers him a sample definition of speed. Thereafter he satisfies the assumption by saying that courage is endurance (although, like Euthyphro, this is eventually refuted on other grounds).

By contrast, the *Meno* makes heavy weather of the assumption. As we have seen, Socrates starts by presenting a rather brisk analogy: all bees must have something in common. Meno accepts this, just as Laches accepted the analogy of quickness, but – unlike Laches – has difficulty in applying the same point to virtue:

I *think* I understand, but I don't yet grasp the question as I'd like to. (72d2–3)

So Socrates has to give him some more parallels – largeness, strength and health. Already we can see this discussion of the unitarian assumption proceeding at a slower pace than in either the *Laches* or the *Euthyphro*. But then comes the most striking feature for our comparison. Meno accepts the assumption for these three properties, but stalls yet again when asked to apply it to virtue:

Somehow I think that this is no longer similar to these other cases. (73a4–5)

This forces Socrates to abandon the appeal to analogy and put forward a completely different argument for applying the unitarian assumption to virtue (73a6–c5). What is interesting about this argument – whatever its shortcomings – is the fact it has to be used at all.[6] Merely stating the assumption (as in the *Euthyphro*) or appealing to parallels (as in the *Laches*) is not enough.

Why does Plato construct the conversation in this way? Let me suggest an analogy for reading this part of the dialogue – and perhaps Platonic dialogues more generally. Imagine a student who has had an article recommended to him by his teacher. The author of the paper is someone whom the teacher greatly admires. On being given a photocopy, the student discovers it annotated by a previous student, and becomes annoyed: any annotation, even if just an underlining or a question mark, is difficult to ignore. As he starts to read, his eye is almost inevitably drawn to the markings and his reading becomes subtly influenced. But imagine further that the teacher who recommended the article, though she had pretended that the annotations were the work of a previous student, had actually written them in herself, using them to guide her student's own reading and make him think more carefully about passages he might otherwise have

---

[6] White 1976: 39–40 rightly emphasises this point.

accepted uncritically. This is one model for understanding Platonic dialogues. We are the readers, Socrates the author from whose views we are to
learn, and Plato the teacher who annotates Socrates' views with comments
from another party, the interlocutor.

To return to the *Meno*: we could imagine this section of the dialogue
moving much faster than it does. After giving his list of virtues, Meno could
have been brought by the use of a single example to accept the unitarian
assumption. If Plato had written the dialogue this way – more in line with
the *Euthyphro* and the *Laches* – he might just have been trying to explain
the distinction between one form and its many instances or species. But
the relatively protracted argument suggests that he has a more complex
purpose in mind. After the bee analogy, we hear Meno saying he does not
yet understand, just as the annotator might underline the script and place
a question mark in the margin; and after three more analogies he decides
to stall, just as one might write a more aggressive comment in the margin.
In constructing the dialogue this way, Plato is using Meno to interrupt
Socrates precisely because he needs interruption: what Socrates took to be
an assumption needs instead to be grounded in argument.

But what are we to make of Meno's role in challenging the assumption?
We should be careful not to accord him too much credit. At 72d2–3, just
after Socrates claims that there is one virtue that applies to all cases as
in the example of bees, he very revealingly confesses not to understand.
Gorgias' position came with a philosophical background and, if Meno had
understood it, he would have grasped the point of the bee analogy perfectly
well, but rejected it. This is indeed what he starts to do when Socrates expects
him to apply the analogies of largeness, strength and health to virtue (73a1–
3): now he objects – though with some hesitation (73a4–5) – that the case of
virtue seems to him to be different. But the fact that he makes this response
relatively late and somewhat weakly shows that he is only just beginning to
grasp the real point behind the view he quoted. Doubtless he has a sense
that Socrates' position is open to serious challenge, but his understanding
of the issues is only partial. To a large extent, he is holding Socrates up out
of obtuseness, and so the reader learns something through him, though not
from him. In this respect, the dialogue operates at two levels. At one, we
find Socrates attempting to win over a somewhat wayward interlocutor; at
the other, Plato communicates a serious philosophical concern to a more
sophisticated audience. It is particularly distinctive of the *Meno* that it
operates at two levels, and we shall find the same feature at work in the
three remaining episodes of Socrates on trial.

CHAPTER 3

A lesson in definition: 73c–77b

THE SECOND DEFINITION

Meno's second definition of virtue comes at 73c9–d1: 'what else, but the power to rule over people, if you are looking for one definition to cover all cases?' The discussion of this definition is very brief. Although Meno claims it satisfies the unitarian assumption, Socrates immediately points out that it does not apply to children or slaves. He then asks whether they should not add the power to rule with justice. Meno agrees, on the grounds that justice is virtue. 'Virtue or *a* virtue?' Socrates asks. Meno does not appear to understand; but after being given a parallel, quickly agrees that there are other virtues: for example, courage, temperance, magnificence (*megaloprepeia*), wisdom and many more besides. Now, however, they are back where they started, with a swarm of virtues and still no common characteristic. When Meno professes himself unable to find this characteristic, Socrates feels compelled to explain at some length what it means to ask for a definition.

In this brief passage, Socrates entirely demolishes Meno's second definition. In the process of doing so, he points towards an account of virtue as a genus with a wide range of species. This will come to the fore in the discussion of the third definition. Another striking feature is the way Meno appears to have forgotten the lessons of the previous discussion so quickly. We shall consider the implications of this when we discuss his character as an interlocutor on pages 60–5 below. But for the moment, I shall pass as rapidly as Socrates does to the next phase of the dialogue, a lesson in definition.

If Meno needs such a lesson, what exactly is his problem? On the basis of his performance so far, there are three possibilities: (a) he does not understand the definitional question, i.e. what it is to seek the one form that many things have in common; (b) he does not understand the difference between virtue itself and *a* virtue; (c) he cannot grasp what the one virtue

31

over the many virtues is, i.e. he cannot find the definition of virtue. Problems
(a) and (b) are very closely related. Someone who does not understand the
difference between virtue and *a* virtue is likely to be baffled by the demand
for a unitary definition: such a demand requires a clear distinction between
the one and the many, the very distinction obscure to someone who has
problem (b).

In the course of the discussion of the first two definitions, Meno has struggled on all of these points. At 72d2–3, he confessed to an (a)-type problem
in saying that he did not understand the request to find the common characteristic underlying different virtues, as he could with the example of bees.
As we have just seen, he then shows a (b)-type problem in the course of the
discussion of the second definition when he fails to understand the question
whether justice is virtue or a virtue (73e1–2). After Socrates introduces a parallel – *schema* (usually translated as 'shape'),[1] which he distinguishes from
one of its species, e.g. curved – Meno quickly lists some of the species of
virtue, suggesting that he now grasps the overall logical distinction between
genus and species. But when asked to find the common form of virtue, he
professes himself unable (74a11–b1). Clearly he is stumbling over problem
(c), and the fact that Socrates says 'reasonably so', shows that the problem
is a serious one. (Contrast the reference to the surprise felt on discovering
someone with an (a)-type problem at 75a3–4.)

A DIALOGUE WITHIN THE DIALOGUE (74b4–75a8)

To have brought Meno to the (c)-type problem at 74a11–b1 is at least a
step forward: understanding what that problem is requires that one has
moved beyond (a) and (b). So it may seem surprising that the first stage
of the lesson in definition, 74b4–75a8, is given over purely to clarifying (a)
and (b). What this shows, of course, is that Socrates still distrusts Meno's
grasp of the basic logical distinction required to understand the definitional
question.[2]

At some length, he proceeds to re-run their previous discussion of virtue
in a parallel dialogue about two parallel forms, *schema* and colour. Socrates
imagines that Meno is asked what *schema* is and replies 'being curved' (cf.
73d9–10); in response to the question whether being curved is *schema* or
a *schema*, he would then reply that it is a *schema*, because there are other

---

[1] As I think that 'shape' is a mistranslation of *schema*, I shall retain the Greek word for the time being
until I come to discuss the issue in detail below. The correct translation, I shall argue, is 'surface'.

[2] To anticipate a later point in the work (98a2), Meno's grasp of the logical distinction is unstable and
might yet take to its heels.

schemata, which he would be prepared to list (cf. 74a1–6). The same scenario is re-enacted, detail for detail, with colour 74c5–d2. Then Socrates spells out, again at some length, what he has been saying ever since the discussion of the first definition (72a8ff.): even though 'curved' and 'straight' may be opposed to one another, they are still embraced by one and the same thing. So that is the question: what is this thing, *schema* (74d3–e9)? The last episode in this parallel comes at 74e11–75a8, where the imaginary Meno has professed not to understand (cf. 72d2–3 and 73e2), leaving his questioner amazed: 'don't you understand that I am seeking what is the same in all these cases?' Eventually, leaving the imagined Meno alone, Socrates turns directly to Meno himself and asks him to define *schema*. Having created a dialogue reconstructing the previous discussion, complete with analogues to Meno's misunderstandings, he takes us up to the point where the (c)-type problem is reached. If he were to follow the procedure through, he would have Meno himself proceed to the positive stage in the parallel and give a definition of *schema*. Such 'practice' is meant to ease the way towards finding a definition of virtue (75a8–9).

There are two striking things about this passage, both concerned with pedagogy. First, in trying to get Meno to understand what giving a definition involves, Socrates makes use of a specific technique that will feature more than once in the work: between 74b4 and 75a8 he creates a dialogue within the main dialogue. This imaginary dialogue features an unnamed questioner with a parallel Meno as the interlocutor and, as we have seen, their conversation closely matches what has just passed between Socrates and Meno in their discussion of virtue. Socrates will go on to use a similar device in the slave boy demonstration, as we can see by comparing the structure of the two passages. At 74a11–b1 Meno is stuck; Socrates constructs a dialogue that re-runs the unsuccessful aspects of their previous conversation and then proposes to add the positive stage at 75a8–9. Similarly, at 79e Meno has reached perplexity (*aporia*), and so Socrates sets up the interview with the slave boy, which explicitly parallels the essentials of the previous attempt to discover the nature of virtue, i.e. the transition from confident answers to *aporia*; finally, he moves on to a positive stage where the boy moves on from *aporia* and gives the correct answer. On pages 169–73 below, I shall argue that the Anytus episode also functions as a dialogue within the main dialogue, and that many of the features he displays in response to Socrates reflect qualities that are already emerging in Meno.

Each of these mini-dialogues is to be seen not as an interruption of the main dialogue, but as an episode for Meno to observe and reflect upon. They all enable him to stand outside himself, to see his own failings from a distance and to further his self-understanding. In the present case, the critical point comes at 75a1–5, where Socrates says that one would be amazed if the imaginary interlocutor could not understand the difference between colour and a colour, or *schema* and a *schema*. This is meant to induce a sense of shame in Meno for his own failure to do the same for virtue: once he puts two and two together, he realises that this absurd figure is none other than himself. He is looking at himself from the outside. On pages 169–73 below we shall see the same effect occurring when Socrates uses the technique later in the dialogue.

The other striking feature of this passage is that Socrates attempts to make progress on a moral topic by putting his interlocutor to work on a parallel but non-moral problem. Of the two examples used, *schema* takes the lime light and, as this is explicitly connected with geometry later on (76a2), the question arises as to whether the choice of such an example is significant. If it is, Socrates is proposing that geometry be used as a preparation for ethics. One then immediately thinks of the way in which he will later use a geometrical problem in the slave boy passage to help steer Meno out of a problem about moral inquiry. Looking beyond the *Meno*, one might also find in this passage an anticipation of a central feature of moral education in *Republic* VII, which advocates a ten-year period of mathematics as preparation for moral philosophy.[3]

However, we should not exaggerate here. Socrates' interest in geometry in 74b–77b is not as strong as this suggests. If he were advertising the benefits of specifically geometrical practice, his interest in colour becomes difficult to explain. Notice that it occurs not only in the first phase of the definition lesson, but also as part of the first definition of *schema* (75b9–11), which also suggests that even his interest in *schema* itself cannot be purely geometrical. So it is far from clear that this passage can be seen as an anticipation of the idea of a specifically mathematical preparation for moral philosophy. In other words, Socrates could have given Meno the relevant practice for defining virtue just by pressing him to define colour. (As for the slave boy passage, Socrates is not actually claiming that, if Meno works on the problem of doubling the square, he will thereby gain insight specifically into the nature of virtue.)

Instead, I would be more cautious and claim merely that the *Meno* constitutes an important step in Plato's emerging theory of education: the historical Socrates may have been fond of using non-moral analogies in discussing the nature of the virtues but, so far as we know, did not go

---

[3] For this comparison see Vlastos 1991: 118–25.

beyond this and advocate the more sustained practice that he does at 75a.[4] This may be a peculiarly Platonic invention and in it lie the beginnings of one crucial element in the educational programme of the *Republic*, even if the specifically mathematical nature of this practice is not yet established.

SAMPLE DEFINITIONS

The first definition of schema *(75a8–d7)*

If Socrates thinks that Meno is willing to give a practice definition of *schema*, he is quickly disappointed: Meno demands that Socrates do it himself. So, after insisting that Meno will define virtue in return, he obliges and defines *schema* as what always accompanies colour. But Meno immediately complains that the definition is 'silly' or 'simple-minded': what would he have to say to an interlocutor who didn't understand what colour is? Socrates replies:

I would tell him the truth. And if my questioner were one of the eristic and contentious types, I would tell him: 'I've given you my answer. If I'm not correct, your job is to take hold of it and refute it.' But if, like you and me on this occasion, the parties were friends and wanted to have a dialogue with each other, they should answer more gently and 'dialectically'. The 'more dialectical' approach, perhaps, is to answer not just by speaking the truth, but also through things that the person questioned[5] first agrees[6] he knows. (75c8–d7)

---

[4] Desjardins (1985: 275) has argued that Socrates' reference to 'practice' (μελέτη) in 75a8 picks up one of the options mentioned in Meno's opening question, that virtue comes by practice (ἀσκητόν). On pp. 16–18 above, I argued in favour of the manuscript reading of 70a1–4 that excludes the reference to practice. In response to Desjardins, I would repeat more or less the same challenge as before: if she were right, why does Socrates make no further reference to practice after 75a8? In the concluding pages of the work, Socrates carefully rehearses what they have agreed, repeating where they stand on the different options available to them: teaching, nature and divine dispensation (98d4–e9 and 99e4–6). In both places he goes out of his way to repeat the options they have rejected, and yet makes no reference at all to practice. This would be quite incongruous if Desjardins were right. In my view, practice features in the work at 75a8 not because it was prompted by Meno's opening question, but because it comes as part of Socrates' own conception of learning.

[5] All the manuscripts have ἐρωτώμενος, meaning 'the person questioned'. This has been emended by Thompson (1901: 239–40) to ἐρωτῶν, 'the questioner', on the grounds that it is the person asking for the definition who must agree that he understands what the respondent says. Thompson's emendation was accepted by Bluck (1961: 246–8) and Sharples (1985: 133–4). But in favour of the manuscript reading is the point that the person who originally asked the question becomes questioned by being asked whether he understands what is being said. So the manuscript reading can be accepted as saying (albeit rather inelegantly) 'to answer through things that, when questioned, the person [who originally asked the question] agrees he knows'.

[6] Some editors, following Gedike 1780: 17, have emended προσομολογῇ in 75d6 to προομολογῇ despite a consensus of manuscripts. The problem with προσομολογῇ is that it ought to mean 'agrees in addition [to another agreement]', which is inappropriate to the context. By contrast, προομολογῇ makes good sense of the procedure Socrates actually follows: before he gives his sample definitions

By mentioning the possibility that the questioner is 'eristic', Socrates is almost certainly having a dig at Meno. The word 'eristic', which comes from the Greek word for strife (ἔρις), denotes a competitive approach to argument, and applies to those who engage in argument as if it were a battle. The implication is that Meno only demanded a definition of colour in order to postpone the moment when he has to give another definition of virtue.[7] Feeling under threat from Socrates, he is increasingly turning the dialogue into a contest and uses this manoeuvre to help him survive. But Socrates will have none of it: just as the conversation looks as if it might turn into a battle, he insists on keeping it as a dialogue.

Socrates' approach, which I shall call the 'dialectical requirement',[8] is that we respond 'through things that the questioner agrees he knows'. What he says in the passage is both interesting in its own right and extremely important in a later section of the dialogue (cf. 79d). As I shall be returning to the requirement below (pp. 56–9), here I shall just flag some of the central points.

Any definition must make reference to certain other items, and these are the 'things' that the other person must agree he knows. In the immediately following passage, Socrates carefully applies the dialectical requirement when defining *schema* as the limit of solid. In the lines leading up to this definition he asks:

Tell me: do you call something a 'limit'? I mean such as a boundary or extremity. I'm treating all these things as the same. Perhaps Prodicus would take issue with us, but *you* call something bounded and limited – this is the sort of thing I mean, nothing abstruse. (75e1–5)

In this case, he checks to see if Meno knows what a boundary is. Although he refers to Meno's use of words, the 'things' through which the definition proceeds are not words, but the entities that the words signify. He is not discussing the mere linguistic familiarity required to understand what the definer is saying.[9]

But when he requires that the interlocutor agree he knows such things, what does he mean by 'know'? On the evidence of the lines just quoted, we might think that the level of knowledge required in the interlocutor is quite informal: Socrates certainly makes no attempt to cross-examine Meno on his knowledge of geometry. If so, the dialectical requirement merely

---

he carefully checks that Meno already understands the elements he is about to use in the definition. I am therefore inclined to follow Gedike's emendation. See further below, p. 85 n. 15. (For a different solution to the problem, see Verdenius 1957: 292, who retains προσομολογῇ and takes it to mean that the interlocutor agrees he knows *as well as the person giving the definition*.)

[7] See Klein 1965: 62.   [8] After Irwin 1977: 136.   [9] See Franklin 2001: 417–19.

demands a sense of familiarity on the part of the questioner, something that is quite different from the sort of rigorous understanding that Socrates normally demands from his interlocutors. However, things will not turn out to be so straightforward, for when the dialectical requirement reappears in the discussion of Meno's third definition (79d–e), Socrates places a more exacting sense of knowledge than he did at 75e1–76a3, and expects a rigorous understanding of the things through which the definition is given. This raises questions over the consistency of the dialectical requirement, which we shall have to address when we come to the third definition.

Another point to flag is Socrates' reference to 'mildness' when introducing the dialectical requirement. He is not just talking about politeness here. This theme will reappear later in the dialogue, firstly when Anytus shows a distinct lack of mildness in his argument with Socrates (cf. 94e3–95a6), and then at the very end when Socrates asks Meno to mediate between them to make Anytus milder and so benefit the Athenians (100b7–c2). This shows just how important the quality was for Plato. The closing passage of the dialogue is doubtless an allusion to the death of Socrates, and in Plato's eyes this tragedy was caused in part by the lack of mildness among the Athenians and their leaders towards philosophy. More generally, mildness is vitally important for successful dialogue, and indeed for the attainment of virtue itself: Socrates will shortly argue that virtue is a form of knowledge, which is attained by patient and co-operative dialogue. So in retrospect, we realise that the dialectical requirement, with its emphasis on mildness, has a moral as well as a methodological dimension.

The second definition of schema *(75e1–76a7)*

Just after stating the dialectical requirement, Socrates offers his second definition of *schema* as 'the boundary of solid' (76a5–7). At this point we have to confront a serious difficulty. So far in this book I have avoided translating the Greek word *schema*, which almost all translators and writers on the dialogue take to mean 'shape' or 'figure'. Although there is no doubt that *schema* can mean this, to take it in this sense at *Meno* 75e1–76a7 causes insoluble problems. In what follows, I shall argue that *schema* in the *Meno* should be translated as 'surface'.

First of all, there is a problem in making Socrates' definition apply both to two- and three-dimensional shapes, as it must if it is to be a unitary definition. To put this in focus, it will help to distinguish two conceptions of shape, which later on became associated with Euclid and Posidonius respectively. Euclid, who does indeed take *schema* as what we would call 'shape', defines it as 'what is contained by a boundary or boundaries'.[10] This is to conceive of *schema* as extension: in the two-dimensional case, an extension bounded by a line or lines, in the three-dimensional, by planes. By contrast, Posidonius defined *schema* as the containing boundary or boundaries of an extension.[11]

The problem with Socrates' definition is that it cannot cover both two- and three-dimensional shapes without equivocating on these two senses. If his definition is to apply to plane shapes, then 'shape' has to be taken in the Euclidean sense. For instance, a square might be called the boundary of a solid because a cube is bounded by six squares.[12] Here one is thinking of shape as a two-dimensional *extension* bounding something three-dimensional, e.g. a cube, like the squares of glass enclosing a space to make a lantern. But now try taking 'boundary of solid' as a definition of three-dimensional shape. The shape of the cube is not its extension (as it was in the two dimensional case), but that which encloses the extension. We have now in effect moved over to the Posidonian conception of shape.

So 'boundary of solid', taken as a general definition of plane and solid shapes, equivocates on two senses of shape. If one wants to avoid this charge of equivocation, and still insist that Socrates is attempting to define shape, one might say that he is thinking only of plane shapes, or only of solid shapes.[13] But then the definition lacks universality, and suffers from exactly the same problem that beset Meno's second definition of virtue. This would be very ironic, since the original point of 74b–77a was to stop Meno from making the same kind of mistake again.

All this reveals another oddity of taking *schema* as shape here. The relation of solid and plane to shape is that of species to genus. Yet when Socrates talks of the species of *schema*, or its 'parts', he does not mention solids and planes, but curved and straight (74d8). This alone should make us suspicious about the standard translation of *schema*.

Perhaps there is nothing we can do to salvage the second definition of *schema*. Geoffrey Lloyd, who assumes that Plato is attempting to define shape or figure in something like Euclid's sense, realises that the attempt fails at several points. He then looks around to find an explanation: was Plato incompetent, or was he deliberately confusing the unwary (and

---

[10] *Elements* I, Def. 14.   [11] Proclus, *Commentary on Euclid's Elements* 143.

[12] Aristotle in fact reports that some had defined plane shape as the boundary of solid at *Topics* VI 4, 141b22. Aristotle's comments here bring out a further problem for defining shape as the boundary of solid: it is not essential to planes as such that they bound solids, for we can conceive of planes in abstraction from solids. (The same problem, however, does not apply to the concept of surface.)

[13] For the latter approach see Thomas 1980: 101.

mathematically uninitiated) Meno?[14] Very revealingly, he adds that boundary of solid works as a definition of surface; and this is in fact exactly how
Euclid defined surface (*epiphaneia*).[15] What is perplexing is that Socrates
should offer it as a definition of *shape*.

But does he? Why are commentators so quick to translate *schema* as
'figure' or 'shape'? Given the muddle that results, we should at least consider
alternative translations. In fact, the word *schema* has a wide variety of
meanings in Plato. One of them is 'surface'.

SCHEMA AS SURFACE

There is no reason to doubt that Plato sometimes uses *schema* to mean shape
or figure in the sense that commentators have assumed in the *Meno*.[16] But
this sense of *schema* is only one of many to be found in his works. The diverse
meanings include a type or species of something,[17] an outline sketch,[18]
deportment, bodily movement or posture, e.g. in dancing,[19] and – most
importantly for our purposes – surface, or surface appearance.

Here is such an occurrence of the word in the *Cratylus*:

The image must not by any means reproduce all the qualities of that which it
imitates, if it is to be an image. See if I am not right. Would there be two things,
Cratylus and an image of Cratylus, if some god should not merely imitate your
colour and *schema*, as painters do, but should make all *the inner parts* like yours,
should produce the same flexibility and warmth, should put into them motion, life
and intellect, such as exist in you, and in short, should place beside you a duplicate
of all your qualities? Would there be in such an event Cratylus and an image of
Cratylus, or two Cratyluses?[20]

In this context the *schema* must be the visible, shaped surface of Cratylus:
visible, because that is what an artist would be thought of as copying;
surface, because it is contrasted with the inner parts. The *schema* is the
boundary of Cratylus' body; it is where the physical Cratylus ends.[21]

---

[14] Lloyd (1992) 176–7. See also Appendix 3 below, pp. 225–6. The suggestion that Socrates deliberately
misleads Meno is inconsistent with 75d5–6, where he says that he will proceed to define σχῆμα in
the dialectical way just described, which includes a commitment to truth.

[15] *Elements* XI, Def. 2.

[16] In *Tim.* 33b1–3, the σχῆμα of a sphere is distinguished from its surface, and at 55c3–4 the cubic
σχῆμα is distinguished from its faces. In both cases, σχῆμα must refer to what is contained by the
surface. See also *Theaet.* 147e6 and 148a4.

[17] *Pol.* 291d6 and *Laws* III 700b1   [18] *Rep.* VIII 548c10, *Laws* V 737d6 and VII 802e5.

[19] *Laws* II 654e3–655b5.   [20] 432b3–c5, trans. Fowler 1926, emphasis added.

[21] I take it that σχῆμα has been used in this sense at 431c6: painters reproduce the appropriate colours
and σχήματα of their subjects. This passage leads in to the point made at 432b–c and is part of the
same discussion.

A similar use of *schema* comes in *Republic* x. Artists, we are told, are concerned with the colours and *schemata* of objects:

As we were just now saying,[22] the painter will fashion, himself knowing nothing of the cobbler's art, what appears to be a cobbler to him and likewise to those who know nothing but judge only by *schemata* and colours.[23]

The problem with artists and those they deceive is that they judge only from the outer surface of an object. The same sense of the word is at work at *Laws* II 669a1 which also talks of the artist representing the colour and *schema* of a human being.

Closely related senses of *schema* can be found in two further passages, though in both the word is used metaphorically. At the beginning of his speech in the *Symposium*, Alcibiades compares Socrates to statues of Silenus figures that could be opened up to reveal statues of gods within. A little later on, he expands on the image:

Socrates is besotted with beautiful boys; he's always hanging around them, driven out of his wits. Again, he's ignorant and knows nothing – to judge from his *schema*. Isn't that just like the *schema* of a Silenus? For he has it wrapped round him, just like the Silenus statue does. But if you opened him up, you can't imagine, my fellow drinkers, how much temperance he has inside. (216d1–7)

The point of using the word *schema* is to capture the notion of an outer surface wrapped around (περιβέβληται) a body – that which presents itself in appearance.[24]

The second passage comes from *Republic* II, where Adeimantus describes how someone comes to adopt a policy of having all the benefits of injustice while appearing to be just:

Such a youth would most likely put to himself the question Pindar asks, 'Is it by justice or by crooked deceit that I the higher tower shall scale and so live my life out in fenced and guarded security?' . . . If I am unjust and have procured myself a reputation for justice, a godlike life is promised. . . . As a front and a *schema* I must draw about myself a shadow-outline of virtue, but trail behind me the fox of the utmost sage Archilochus, shifty and bent on gain.[25]

---

[22] The reference is to 597e10–598c5, where they agreed that artists only imitate the external appearance (φάντασμα) of the subject. See also *Rep.* II 373b5–6.

[23] 600e6–601a2, trans. Shorey 1930.

[24] Bury (1932: 148–9) translates σχῆμα as 'role'. But this misses the point of the Silenus analogy, where there is a strong contrast between the outer shell and what lies within (cf. *Crat.* 432b6–7). Furthermore, τοῦτο in 216d5 refers back to σχῆμα in the previous line, and is to be taken with περιβέβληται. This reinforces the sense of σχῆμα as something that contains a body from the outside.

[25] 365b1–c6, trans. Shorey 1930.

We should also note a use of *schema* in the *Crito*, where Socrates imagines himself having escaped from Athens to Thessaly. He comments that the people there might enjoy hearing how he escaped from prison, using some disguise that enabled him to change his *schema* (53d4–7). Again, the word refers to the surface appearance.

In all these passages, *schema* is used to mark one side of an inner-outer contrast. With respect to the object to which the *schema* belongs, the *schema* is that which contains or encompasses it, its boundary. With respect to the perceiver, the *schema* is the feature of the object that presents itself in appearance.[26] Within this group of passages, some uses of *schema* are non-metaphorical and precise: these are the occurrences in *Crat.* 432b7, *Rep.* x 601a2 and *Laws* ii 669a1. Here *schema* means the surface of a body.[27] This is the sense that I suggest is at work in the *Meno*.

The second definition again

There are two ways to develop the proposal that *schema* in the *Meno* 74b–77a means 'surface'. The first is to claim that the word has very much the same meaning as in the *Cratylus* 432b6, viz. *perceptible* surface. The second is to see it as an abstract geometrical entity, along the lines of the Euclidean notion of *epiphaneia*.

In favour of the former approach is the fact that, so understood, *schema* in the second definition fits well with its appearance in the first and third definitions. As far as the first definition is concerned, it is much more natural to say that perceptible rather than abstract surface always accompanies colour.[28] This chimes in with the fact that in several passages where *schema* occurs in Plato it is paired with colour. It is also worth remembering that there was a precedent for closely associating perceptible surface and colour:

---

[26] Here the word approaches very close to ἐπιφάνεια, which is used by Aristotle and Euclid among others to mean 'surface'. See also Empedocles DK 31 A88. Plato(?) only uses ἐπιφάνεια at *Alc.* i 124c10, where it means 'eminence'.

[27] There are other passages where σχῆμα is found alongside colour, and probably refers to the perceptible surface of an object. At *Gorgias* 474d4 Socrates is discussing the meaning of the word καλόν, and talks of καλὰ σχήματα and colours. See also *Phaedo* 100d1, *Philebus* 51b4 and *Rep.* v 476b4–5.

[28] The first definition of σχῆμα is ambiguous, implying either that wherever there is colour there is σχῆμα, or that wherever there is σχῆμα there is colour. See Sharples 1985: 131–2. I cannot see any way of deciding between these two, but if we take the second reading we have all the more reason to take σχῆμα as perceptible surface. Thomas (1980: 100) thinks it implausible that Socrates should choose to define perceptible σχῆμα in this passage, and so rejects the second reading. But it is only implausible to those who harbour the assumption (unwarranted, so far as I can see) that in the *Meno* 'Plato's new enthusiasm [sc. for geometry] bubbles out all over the text', as Vlastos (1991: 118) puts it. See above, pp. 34–5.

according to Aristotle, the Pythagoreans went as far as to identify colour with surface.[29]

Taking *schema* as perceptible surface also fits well with the third sample definition that Socrates gives to satisfy Meno. Here he defines colour as 'an effluence from surfaces commensurate with sight and perceivable' (76d4–5). The effluence surely flows from the physical surfaces of objects.[30] If *schema* meant surface in an abstract sense, the definition would be much more problematic.

There is, however one advantage in taking *schema* to mean surface in the abstract geometrical sense. When he introduces the terms to be used in the second definition, Socrates asks:

Do you call something a 'plane', and again something else a 'solid', for example such things as feature in geometry? (76a1–2)

From the reference to geometry we might assume that Plato is abandoning the empirical context of the first definition and moving into the abstract realm of mathematics.[31] If so we should expect *schema* to mean more or less the same as abstract Euclidean *epiphaneia*.

Nevertheless we should be cautious about adopting this view, especially bearing in mind the context of the passage. In the earlier discussion of virtue, Socrates insisted that they were dealing with something that had a single nature. It would be at least inelegant if, in giving these three definitions, he started with an empirical conception of *schema* in the first, changed it to an abstract one, and then reverted to the original sense of *schema* when he used it in his definition of colour at 76d4–5. As for the reference to geometry at 76a1–2, perhaps this need not imply an identity between the way in which the terms are being used here and the way they appear in abstract geometry. Socrates may be alluding to geometry merely to give Meno some purchase on what the terms 'plane' and 'solid' signify. So although the abstract reading of *schema* is possible, I am still inclined towards the empirical sense. Either way, so long as we take Socrates to be defining surface, the worst of the problems with this definition are behind us.[32]

[29] *Sense and Sensibilia*, 439a33–4.
[30] This is especially clear in the theories that derived from Empedocles: the pre-Socratic atomists and, later on, Epicurus, who says explicitly that the streams of images flow from the surface of objects (D.L. x 48).
[31] Klein 1965: 65; cf. Vlastos 1991: 121.
[32] Since writing this, I have found two allies in my cause. The suggestion that σχῆμα be translated as 'surface' was made by Friedländer (1964: 279), though without any supporting argument. Klein (1965) translates σχῆμα as 'shaped surface', or 'closed surface of a visible thing'. Unfortunately, he only applies this sense to the first definition (pp. 56–60). Seduced by the apparent reference to

The definition of colour (76a8–77a5)

Now that Socrates has defined surface and fulfilled his side of the bargain (cf. 75b4–6), he expects to be given another definition of virtue. Instead, at 76a8 Meno abruptly asks: 'and what do you say colour is?' After some protesting, Socrates accedes to this demand and gives a definition of colour:

soc. Do you want me to answer in the style of Gorgias, so that you can follow me most easily?
MEN. I do, of course.
soc. So do you talk of 'effluences' of things, as Empedocles does?
MEN. Certainly.
soc. And 'channels' into and through which the effluences pass?
MEN. Absolutely.
soc. And some of the effluences fit with some of the channels, while others are smaller or larger than them?
MEN. That's so.
soc. And do you call something 'sight'?
MEN. I do.
soc. From this, then, 'grasp my meaning', as Pindar put it. Colour is an effluence from[33] surfaces, commensurate with sight, and so[34] perceptible.

(76c4–d5)

Socrates appears to be following the dialectical requirement meticulously, just as he did with his second definition of surface: he introduces every item in the definition by checking that Meno is familiar with it.[35]

Socrates is not surprised when Meno remarks that this is the best of the three definitions: it is what he is used to. Socrates himself prefers the definition of surface, and seems to disparage the definition of colour as *tragike*, a word that probably means something like 'high-flown', or 'rhetorical'.[36] Meno has a predilection for the ornamental, as one might expect from a

abstract geometry at 76a2, he claims σχῆμα in the second definition means figure as defined by Euclid, i.e. that which is contained by any boundary or boundaries (p. 65). Bizarrely, however, he immediately goes on to say: '*Schema*, in Socrates' second definition, is a "technical" word signifying a "bonded surface area" akin to *epipedon* and *epiphaneia*.' He then gives a reference to Euclid's definitions of these terms, thereby suggesting that he is himself confusing Euclid's very different definitions of σχῆμα and ἐπιφάνεια. When he comes to discuss the definition of colour, with its reference to σχημάτων in 76d4, he reverts unequivocally to σχῆμα as 'surface'.
[33] The expression ἀπορροὴ σχημάτων could also mean 'an effluence of σχήματα'. See further below, p. 45.
[34] See Verdenius 1957: 292.
[35] Two points about the provenance of the definition: we need not assume that it was taken over by Gorgias from Empedocles. To say that the definition is 'in the manner of Gorgias' (76c4–5) is not to say that he believed it. Nor can we even be confident that Empedocles believed it himself, *pace* Burnet 1908: 287 n. 5, though there is some evidence that he did from Theophrastus, *De Sensu* 7 (DK 31 A86).
[36] See Hoerber 1960: 95 (who also suggests 'stagy') and Bluck 1961: 252–3.

pupil of Gorgias.[37] This has significant implications for how we understand the dialectical requirement of 75d. In its original formulation it states that a definition should proceed through things that the interlocutor agrees he knows. Taken one way, this demands that a good definition be stated in a way that the interlocutor finds familiar. In this sense, the definition of colour fits the requirement very well, being something Meno is used to (76d8). But Socrates is less enthusiastic about it partly because it is over-blown: although Meno *professes* to understand such things as effluences and their passages, were he to be pressed to give an account of them, he would soon find himself in trouble.[38] This suggests that Socrates already has in mind a more exacting application of the dialectical requirement, where the questioner does not just have a sense of familiarity with the components of the definition, but really understands them. We shall return to this distinction when we come to discuss the reappearance of the dialectical requirement at 79d1–4.

When Socrates says he prefers the definition of surface to that of colour (76e4–7), does he mean the first or the second? It is most natural to take him as referring to the second. 'The definition of surface' is most naturally taken as referring to the definition that appeared most recently. The only motivation for looking back to the first definition would be that one has mistranslated *schema* as shape and is embarrassed at the resulting inadequacy of the second definition. Besides, it is difficult to see why the first definition should rank particularly high in Socrates' estimation. At 75b11–c1 he suggests some reservation about it: 'I'd be happy if you could tell me about virtue *even* in this way.' Perhaps the problem is that we have only been given a concomitant feature of surface, not told what it is in itself. This would recall the distinction made at the beginning of the dialogue between what something is and what it is like (71b3–4). Seen in this light, the statement, 'surface is the only thing that always accompanies colour', though true, does not actually count as a definition at all. But at least it is a formula that has the unity and universality lacking from Meno's first two definitions of virtue, and so is appropriate in the context.[39]

---

[37] Contrast Socrates' phrase 'nothing abstruse' (οὐδὲν ποικίλον) at 75e4–5.

[38] There is no suggestion that Socrates considers his definition of colour to be false. This would conflict with the dialectical requirement, which requires an answer to be true (75c8 and d5–6). We should also note that a similar definition of colour appears in the *Timaeus* 67c4–7 and, even if this is not the same as the definition given in the *Meno*, Plato does appear to be strongly influenced by it, as Vlastos (1991: 122 n. 65) suggests.

[39] Compare the *Euthyphro* 11a6–b1, where Socrates rejects the definition of piety as what is always loved by the gods because it does not explicate the essence of piety, only one of its consequences.

The compatibility of the three definitions

If Socrates is adhering to the dialectical requirement, all three definitions must be true and so consistent with one another. Yet there are problems here. First of all, recall the fact that the Empedoclean account of colour is ambiguous: it could mean either (a) colour is an effluence coming *from* surfaces or (b) an effluence consisting *of* surfaces. Each possibility creates a problem of compatibility with the other two definitions. On (a) colour, *qua* effluence, becomes detached from its surface; yet, according to the first definition, surface is what always accompanies colour. On version (b) the surface becomes detached from its solid, which is incompatible with the second definition where the surface, as the limit of the solid, must always be attached to it.[40] Furthermore this version in effect identifies colours and surfaces, while the first definition keeps them distinct.

I would incline towards reading (a) of the Empedoclean definition: it only generates one problem, which can be dealt with as follows. The incompatibility results from taking the term 'accompanies' (ἑπόμενον) in the first definition literally, to mean that a colour must always be conjoined with a surface. However, we might stretch the meaning of 'accompanies', so that the existence of a surface is a necessary condition of colour: if a colour exists, there has to have been a surface. In this attenuated sense, where 'accompanies' implies a necessary condition, surface always accompanies colour.[41]

---

[40] I am grateful to David Sedley for drawing my attention to this problem.

[41] Another way to resolve the problem is to adopt the manuscript T's alternative reading of χρημάτων ('things') for σχημάτων ('surfaces') in 76d4: to say that colour is an effluence of (or from) things creates no inconsistency with the other two definitions. An objection to this is that all the terms of the definition ought to have been presented to Meno beforehand so that he can confirm that he is familiar with what they signify. The term σχῆμα passes this test as it has already been defined, but χρῆμα (unlike ἀπορροάς etc.) has not been mentioned before. In reply, a proponent of this reading can say that, in introducing the term 'effluence', Socrates did refer to effluences of 'things' (ὄντων, 76c7) and it seems acceptable for Socrates to substitute χρημάτων in the actual definition.

CHAPTER 4

The third definition: 77b–79e

Meno offers his third definition of virtue at 77b2–5:

Well then, I think virtue is, as the poet[1] says, 'rejoicing in fine things and being able to have them'. And that's what I say virtue is – desiring fine things and being able to acquire them.

Socrates' first move is to substitute the word 'good' (*agathos)* for 'fine' (*kalos).* Although he does this very swiftly, the move is not as straightforward as it is made to sound. The word *kalos* can mean 'beautiful', and is commonly applied to physical objects. But it can also apply to actions or characters in the sense of 'noble'. (I have used the translation 'fine' in an attempt to cover both senses.) In Plato's works, the concept of the *agathon* is very closely connected with whatever is beneficial or useful – *prima facie* a different sense from that of *kalon*. Nevertheless, *agathon* and *kalon* draw very close together in other dialogues,[2] and it is interesting that here Meno accepts the substitution without any complaint. This allows Socrates to proceed straight to the business of refutation, which he does by examining each of its two components in turn: that virtue involves (1) the desire for good things and (2) the ability to acquire them.

DESIRE AND THE GOOD (77b–78b)

The underlying assumption of this section is that, if something is to act as a mark of the virtuous, it cannot be common to all people, because

---

[1] We do not know the identity of the poet or the context from which the quotation is taken. Thompson (1901: 100) suggests Simonides.

[2] Another place where Socrates identifies the *kalon* and the *agathon* is *Gorgias* 474d1, though, interestingly, his interlocutor Polus rejects the move. (Also, Socrates himself immediately goes on to shift position and give a disjunctive definition of the fine as either good or pleasant.) It may be that in the *Symposium* and the *Republic* the *kalon* and the *agathon* are treated as the same: see Hobbs 2000: 220–7. We should also note that Xenophon's Socrates explicitly identifies the fine and the good at *Mem.* 4.6.9.

not everyone is virtuous. Socrates refutes Meno by arguing that everyone desires good things, and no one desires bad things, which in turn makes the first component of Meno's answer irrelevant to the definition of virtue.

This argument has a special interest in the dialogue, and in Plato's works more generally. We have seen how Meno's first two definitions give rise to discussions of genuine philosophical significance: the first led to a discussion of the unitarian assumption, the second to a more extended discussion of definition. But the third takes us in a new direction altogether: it gives virtue a psychological dimension, lacking from the previous two definitions, which both analysed virtue solely in terms of externals. By defining virtue partly in terms of desire, Meno allows Socrates to lead him into the terrain of moral psychology, and so to touch on issues treated at more length in famous passages of the *Protagoras*, *Gorgias* and *Republic*. The problem, however, is that the argument of *Meno* 77b–78b is tantalisingly brief. Not surprisingly, there has been considerable disagreement among commentators about the conclusion Socrates is trying to establish and the argument that he uses to draw it.

Before we examine the argument in any detail, we need to be clear about one point. Ultimately Socrates wishes to show that people never desire what they think to be bad. But is he really claiming that no one ever desires what is bad for another person, or merely that no one ever desires what is bad for themselves? The first possibility is made tempting by those translations that render the conclusion as 'no one desires evil'.[3] This of course would be strongly counter-intuitive, and yet Socrates offers no argument for it, which one would expect him to do – especially as Meno is someone who thinks one ought to harm one's enemies (71e4). Instead, we should favour the second possibility, for at 77c7–8 Socrates clarifies what he means when he talks of someone desiring something: they desire that it happen to *themselves* (cf. also 77d2–3). From this I take it that the argument as a whole discusses only desires relating to the agent.

A diagram will help illustrate the course of the argument:

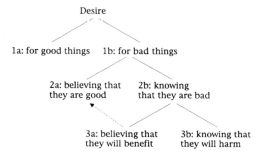

___

[3] See e.g. Lamb 1924 and Guthrie 1956.

Meno thinks that, in addition to those who desire good things, there are those who desire bad things. This gives us the first subdivision into two groups of people, 1a and 1b (77b7–c3). 1b is then divided into those who desire bad things thinking that they are good, 2a, and those who know that the object is bad, 2b (77c3–7). An example of 2a might be someone who desires a drink of water thinking it would be good for him, not knowing that it is in fact petrol. 2b is then subdivided into those who know that the object of desire is bad, but that think it will benefit them, 3a, and those who know that the object is bad and know that it will harm them, 3b (77d1–4). The remainder of the passage breaks into two sections, 77d4–e4 and 77e5–78b2, which deal with 3a and 3b respectively.

The argument against 2a and 3a

Socrates' strategy in the argument is to show that all the classes apart from 1a are empty: we all desire good things, so the first part of Meno's definition is superfluous.[4] But *prima facie*, there is a puzzle about 2a, since they appear not to be mentioned again after their initial appearance at 77c3–5. Yet, for the overall argument to be valid, Socrates must eliminate the possibility of their existence or at least re-describe them as desiring the good.

In fact, there is no cause for concern here. Although he leaves them on one side as soon as he has introduced them, he does so in order to continue the process of subdivision. He then turns his focus on 3a and quickly reduces them to 2a (77d7–e2). Immediately afterwards he argues that both should be described as desiring the good.

The treatment of 2a and 3a proceeds as follows. At 77d3 Meno describes 3a as thinking that the object of their desire will benefit them, even though they know it to be bad. This causes Socrates to object that no one who believes the bad things are beneficial can really know that they are bad, to which Meno immediately agrees (77d4–7).[5] At 77d7–e2 he makes a further move against 3a, assimilating them to 2a:

---

[4] The fact that the argument proceeds by setting out a series of dichotomies may be significant. For it was a style of argument favoured by Gorgias, as the argumentative structure of his treatise, *On What Is Not*, makes clear. (I am grateful to Myles Burnyeat for this point.) If Socrates is deliberately imitating Gorgias in this way, he is repeating a tactic that he used in giving the definition of colour, which was explicitly said to be in Gorgias' style (76c4–5).

[5] Here he assumes that bad things cannot be beneficial. Behind this is probably a general set of assumptions: whatever is bad is harmful, and vice-versa; whatever is good is beneficial, and vice-versa. On this see *Meno* 87e1–2, *Prot.* 333d8–e1, *Gorg.* 474e7–475a3 and 477a1–2 (where 'good' and 'beneficial' are treated interchangeably) and *Rep.* II 379b11. Xenophon, *Mem.* 4.6.8, presents Socrates as making the good and the beneficial co-extensive. On Socrates' assumptions here, see Nakhnikian 1973: 3–4.

So it's clear that these people do not desire bad things – the people who are ignorant of them – but what they thought to be good, though these are actually bad.

Here he assumes that not only do 3a not know that the object of their desire is bad, but they do not even believe it to be bad. Having assimilated them to 2a, he continues:

So the people who are ignorant of them and think them to be good clearly desire good things – or not?

This is the point where he re-describes 3a and 2a jointly as desiring the good. The best way to understand this move is by means of the distinction between intended and actual objects of desire.[6] If someone wants a glass of water and believes that the glass of clear fluid in front of them is water, we are justified in saying that what they desire is a glass of water. If it is in fact petrol, we might say that petrol is the actual object of desire, while water is the intended object. To identify objects of desire by picking out the intended objects rather than the actual ones seems legitimate and more natural than the other way around, and that is what Socrates is doing here: when it comes to deciding whether the people under discussion desire the good or not, we should focus on their intended objects.

The argument against 3b

Having re-described 2a and 3a as both desiring the good, Socrates turns to 3b – those who allegedly know that the object of their desire is bad and that it harms them. These are the stages by which he tries to argue them out of existence:
1 X desires bad things.
2 X knows that the bad things are bad.
3 X knows that the bad things will be harmful to him.
4 X thinks that whatever harms him makes him miserable and wretched.
5 But no one desires to be miserable and wretched. [Lit.: is there anyone who desires to be miserable and wretched?]
6 Therefore X does not desire things that make him miserable and wretched.
7 Therefore, X does not desire bad things.

In this passage, I take Meno to be defending a simple and intuitive point. To take a modern example, imagine someone on a certain kind of medication who knows that if they consume any alcohol the effects of the

---

[6] Santas 1979: 186–9.

drugs will be undone and they will be in great pain. They are totally clear about this and hence know that they will be 'miserable and wretched' if they have a drink. Meno thinks it quite possible for such a person nevertheless to want to drink. As Socrates in the *Protagoras* is well aware (352d4–7), most people would agree. Nevertheless, he is determined to oppose it and argue that, if you really know something is bad for you overall, you cannot desire it.[7]

But what exactly is his argument for this claim? Steps 1 to 4 describe the person with their alleged desire, mapping out the extent of their knowledge: they are completely clear about the consequences of fulfilling the desire. At this point step 5 appears on the scene. As I have indicated, in the text it appears as the question, 'Is there anyone who desires to be miserable and wretched?'. A very natural reading of this is to take it as a rhetorical question asserting the claim that no one desires to be miserable and wretched. If one does so, however, one renders the argument very implausible.[8] Taken this way, step 5 only makes sense if Socrates takes 1 to 4 to commit us to the claim that the person X desires to be miserable. His argument then has the structure of *modus tollens*: if one desires bad things; one desires to be miserable; but no one desires to be miserable, so no one desires bad things. So there must be a suppressed premise in the argument – the principle that, if X desires p, and knows p leads to q, he desires q. This yields the inference that X desires to be miserable, which is then ruled out by the empirical claim stated in step 5.[9] Yet this premise is very easy to dispute. For one thing, it would generate a huge range of desires: I have to desire every known consequence of my actual desires. It is also highly counter-intuitive, almost absurdly so. For instance, if I desire to go to the dentist, I desire all the pain I know that to involve. It might also be said that the principle wrongly assimilates desires to beliefs. It may be true that, if I believe p and believe that p implies q, I believe q. But the same principle does not apply to all mental states.

However, I wish to argue that this is the wrong way to reconstruct Socrates' argument; in particular that he is not committed to the principle just mentioned. Return to step 5, 'Is there anyone who desires to be wretched and miserable?' Imagine being confronted with someone who purports to

---

[7] Here I agree with the interpretation of the conclusion given by Nakhnikian 1973: esp. 5.

[8] I am not referring to the fact that this claim denies the existence of people with self-destructive desires. This is not fatal to Socrates' argument. The exceptions are few and far between; and, given that his concern is to find a criterion that will mark off the virtuous from the non-virtuous, the first half of Meno's definition still allows too many people to count as virtuous, even with the exclusion of self-destructive people.

[9] For this reconstruction see Santas 1979: 315 n. 15.

desire something he knows to be bad for him. If you were Socratically minded, you might try to change his attitude by saying: 'But surely you don't want to be miserable, do you?' Taken literally, the point is that the person does not have a desire to be miserable. But most likely you would be pointing out to them that they have a desire *not to be miserable*, which is quite different. In the same way, I would suggest that at this point in the argument Socrates is claiming that all human beings have a desire to avoid misery, and that this desire is fundamental to whatever else they might desire. The point is not that this desire will always outweigh a conflicting desire for something one knows to make one miserable, but that it will not even allow such a desire to form in the first place. This is the negative corollary of a thesis often associated with Socrates, sometimes called 'psychological eudaimonism': a person desires something if and only if they believe that it contributes to their overall happiness.[10]

So in my view, the argument against 3b is based on psychological eudai-monism, and does not rely on the principle that if X desires *p*, and knows *p* leads to *q*, he desires *q*. I accept that a literal reading of premise 5 – viz. that no one has a desire for misery – suggests that this premise is implicit in the argument, for the reasons given above. But if we read 5 as saying that everyone has a fundamental desire to avoid misery, the argument is much improved.

Even so, however, it is vulnerable to counter-examples. Many readers will feel that, although Meno caves in quickly, he should have stood his ground more firmly: there *are* people who desire what they think is bad for them overall, and Socrates cannot just argue them out of existence by assuming psychological eudaimonism. The objector's stock in trade here is the phenomenon of weakness of the will or acrasia. To most people, it is simply obvious that we sometimes act against our better judgement, and of course such action presupposes that we desire things that conflict with what we know to be best for us. But the counter-intuitiveness of his position does not stop with the denial of acrasia. For if he were right, we would not even be able to desire something that we knew to be bad and still resist that desire – the phenomenon that Aristotle was to call *encrateia*, or 'continence'. Such thoughts lead to the standard criticism of Socrates, that he considers human nature to be rational to a degree that it is not – that he is an 'intellectualist'.

However, dispatching Socrates' argument is not quite so easy as this sounds. To say that the argument is vulnerable to counter-examples is to

---

[10] See Vlastos 1969: 83–4 and Irwin 1977: 300 n. 51.

assume that he has no way of explaining the phenomena on his terms – which he does, in fact. The alleged acratic or encratic, and anyone who has a conflict of desire, may have failed to make up their mind properly. They have not finally decided what is best for them overall, whatever they may say to themselves or others. So they fluctuate between thinking that one or other course is best for them. For instance, someone might decide that giving up smoking is best overall, but when they focus on the pain associated with giving up, they may not after all think that giving up is the best course. They may also start to question the probability of suffering serious consequences as a result of smoking. Perhaps, it will be argued, their thinking is too short-term. That may be, but this can still be construed as a cognitive failing: on the basis of their short-term thinking they form a belief, which leads to a desire to carry on smoking. In arguing against Socrates, therefore, it is not enough just to throw counter-examples in his way; one needs also to show that the explanations he might offer for such phenomena are in some way inadequate.

Here it is instructive to turn to *Republic* book IV, which expressly repudiates the theory of the *Meno*. Arguing that not all desires are for the good, Socrates there claims that, although some desires are for things because they are good, and as such are based on rational judgement, others are just 'brute' or 'raw'.[11] But what is interesting for our purposes is that this move is not made at all lightly. It comes as part of an elaborate psychological theory that involves splitting the soul into different parts, one of which, the rational, forms desires based on its judgements about the good; another, the appetitive, forms desires merely on the basis of perceived pleasures and pains; and a third, the spirited, acts as the source of such emotions as pride, self-assertion, and is a further source of motivation that can come into conflict with either the rational or the appetitive. Now, the position of the *Republic* may well be more plausible than *Meno* 77b–78b. But the point I am making is that when Plato came to repudiate psychological eudaimonism, he did not do so by merely pointing to counter-examples, but by providing an elaborate and (so far as we know) new analysis of conflict. For Plato, arguing against Socrates brought with it a burden of explanation; he rightly saw that it required much more than a quick and easy appeal to intuition.

To return to the text: by 78b, Meno's resistance has collapsed, and he agrees that everyone desires what they think to be good. Socrates now

---

[11] *Rep.* IV 438a1ff., esp. 441c1–2 and 442c5–8. Some commentators have argued that *Meno* 77b–78b is not after all incompatible with *Rep.* IV, and that it does allow for the existence of 'brute' desires. See Croiset and Bodin 1923: 245–6, Irwin 1995: 138–9 and Weiss 2001: 138–9. I argue against their views in Appendix 1 on pp. 219–21 below.

proceeds to examine the second part of his original definition, that virtue involves the ability to acquire goods. But before we proceed, we should pause to draw out an implication of the argument that has just concluded.

Socrates' position is that everyone desires what they think to be good, though of course they do not always desire what is in fact good. This provides a principle for dividing the virtuous from the non-virtuous, namely knowledge. In this way, the argument of 77b–78b can be seen as a step towards a thesis often associated with the historical Socrates, that virtue is knowledge. For if the argument is accepted, all I appear to need to do the right thing, external circumstances permitting, is that I know what course of action will actually benefit me overall. Once I have this knowledge, there is no possibility of my forming any desire to do otherwise than to pursue it, which might seem sufficient for virtue.

However, as we saw above, the argument of 77b–78b has only considered self-regarding desires, and so to secure the thesis that virtue is knowledge Socrates would also have to show that virtue is always beneficial to the agent. This claim, of course, is a matter of dispute, and Socrates has to go to considerable lengths in the *Gorgias* and the *Republic* to argue that the virtue of justice, in particular, is beneficial to the agent and not merely 'someone else's good', as his opponents think. The *Meno*, however, remains silent on this issue: it certainly insists that justice is in some way involved in virtue, but does not really face up to the question of how virtue relates to the good of the agent. For this reason, the argument of 77b–78b only establishes part of what is needed to prove that virtue is knowledge.

Nevertheless, Socrates does explicitly argue for the thesis later on in the dialogue, at 87d–89a, albeit a different version of it and on different grounds from those suggested at 77b–78b.

VIRTUE AS THE ABILITY TO ACQUIRE GOOD THINGS (78b–79e)

Virtue and external goods

Once Meno has agreed to jettison the first part of his definition, he is left with virtue as the ability to acquire good things. Socrates immediately asks whether he thinks health and wealth are goods, to which he agrees, adding gold, silver, honours and power. This seems to exhaust his list of goods (78c8–d1), and so Socrates proceeds to the attack. Step by step, he gets Meno to emend his position, eventually transforming it into the claim that virtue is doing whatever one does with a part of virtue (79b5). Naturally enough, he then proceeds to accuse him of circularity. I shall start by examining stages by which Socrates transforms Meno's definition and then discuss the charge of circularity.

The first stage comes at 78d3–e2. Meno has now defined virtue as the ability to acquire a range of external goods and, as we might expect from his reaction to the second definition, Socrates asks:

soc. Do you add to this acquisition, Meno, 'justly and piously', or does it make no difference to you? Even if someone acquires them unjustly, do you call this virtue all the same?
MEN. Surely not, Socrates.
soc. But vice?
MEN. Of course.
soc. So it seems we need to add to this acquisition justice or temperance or piety or some other part of virtue.

(78d3–e1)

By having Meno agree to the addition of some moral characteristics to his definition, he shows that the acquisition of external goods is not sufficient for virtue. In the next stage, he argues that it is not even necessary:

soc. Not to acquire gold and silver, when that isn't just, either for oneself or someone else – isn't this lack also virtue?
MEN. Apparently.
soc. So the acquisition of such goods would no more be virtue than the lack of them; rather, it seems that whatever comes with justice is virtue and whatever is without all such qualities is vice.

(78e3–79a1)

In the next stage of the transformation, he gets Meno's explicit agreement that justice and the other moral qualities are parts of virtue (a claim slipped in earlier at 78e1), and starts to make the old charge that Meno is breaking virtue into small pieces again. Finally, he summarises Meno's position at 79b4–5: every action done with a part of virtue is virtue, and the transformation is complete.

In this process Socrates makes two important moves: the introduction of the moral qualities (justice, temperance etc.) and the broadening of the type of action involved in the definition. The first move is one we are familiar with from the discussion of the first two definitions. In making the second, Socrates criticises Meno for limiting the arena of virtue too narrowly: it is not just a matter of acquisition; sometimes it might be virtuous to abstain. But it is not even a matter of either acquiring or abstaining: if some types of action are to be mentioned, all should be included. Virtue applies much more broadly than just to questions about acquisition or abstention. This is why Socrates says '*whatever* comes with justice is virtue and *whatever* is without all such qualities is vice' (78e8–79a1). The arena of courage, for instance, does not necessarily concern acquisition, but whether to endure in dangerous situations; temperance is not always about acquisition. Piety may concern acquisition (in the case of temple robbing, for instance), but need not.

All this makes it look as if the argument flows rather smoothly. But if one looks at the text closely, Socrates appears to say conflicting things over the course of the passage. Here again is the first stage of the transformation:

Very good, then: virtue is the acquisition of gold and silver – so says Meno, the hereditary guest-friend of the Great King. Do you add to this acquisition, Meno, 'justly and piously', or does it make no difference to you? Even if someone acquires them unjustly, do you call this virtue all the same? (78d1–6)

But almost immediately he says:

So it seems we need to add to this acquisition justice *or* temperance *or* piety *or* some other part of virtue. (78d7–e1; emphasis added)

In the first text he implies that justice and piety are necessary for the acquisition to be virtuous. In the second, by contrast, the acquisition is virtuous if accompanied by any one of the qualities listed. So neither justice nor piety seems to be necessary, as they were just before at 78d1–6. That text also had virtue involve a package of two qualities, whereas 78d7–e1 now makes any one of the qualities mentioned sufficient to make the acquisition virtuous.

In the next few lines, Socrates' position starts to shift yet again:

soc. Not to acquire gold and silver, when that isn't just, either for oneself or someone else – isn't this lack also virtue?
men. Apparently.
soc. So the acquisition of such goods would no more be virtue than the lack of them; rather, it seems that whatever comes with justice is virtue . . .
(78e3–8)

Here, justice seems to be sufficient to make the acquisition or abstention virtuous and, because it is the only quality mentioned, I assume that it is also necessary.

So it is possible to extract three different positions about the relation of the moral qualities to virtue from this brief passage. However, I think it would be a mistake to make heavy weather of the point. Socrates' overall aim is to manoeuvre Meno into the position of saying that virtue is acting with one or more of the moral qualities mentioned: which one or ones is not important to the argument. Because Meno starts by limiting his definition to acquisition, Socrates focuses (naturally enough) on justice. But he also mentions piety and temperance in the context of acquisition. The reason is that to acquire an external good may sometimes step over a social boundary, which makes it a question of justice, but sometimes, as the example of robbing a temple shows, one of religion, which puts one in mind of piety. On other occasions still, the acquisition may not harm anyone else except oneself, so that the case becomes one of temperance. Depending on the situation, the act of acquiring external goods may require different moral qualities, or a combination of them. Socrates' references to which qualities are involved are merely illustrative of a more general point, and we should not be disturbed if his different illustrations do not quite match each other.

Circularity and the dialectical requirement

Now that Meno has agreed to define virtue in terms of its parts, Socrates chastises him for breaking it into pieces yet again (79a3–b2; cf. 77a5–9). But in his next speech (79b4–e3), he gives this criticism a new dimension:

soc. Do you think that someone knows what a part of virtue is when he doesn't know what virtue itself is?

MEN. I don't think so.

soc. And if you remember, when I answered you just now about surface, we rejected the sort of answer that attempts to proceed through what is still under investigation and not yet agreed.

MEN. And we were right to reject it, Socrates.

soc. So while you are still investigating what virtue as a whole is, don't imagine that you will explain it to anyone by answering in terms of its parts or by saying anything else in the same way . . .

(79c8–e1)

This argument starts by appealing to a version of the priority of definition. At the beginning of the dialogue the principle was applied to the non-essential attributes of virtue (71b3–8). Socrates now declares that we cannot know what any part of virtue is without knowing the whole. Presumably his rationale in saying that virtue is prior to justice is that the genus is epistemologically prior to the species: any attempt to define justice must mention that it is a virtue and so presuppose an understanding of virtue itself. This point established, Socrates reintroduces the dialectical requirement from 75d: a definition should proceed through things that the questioner agrees he knows. Socrates, for the reasons just given, does not know what any part of virtue is, and so rejects Meno's latest attempt.

There is a serious question as to whether the dialectical requirement mentioned at 79d is the same as was introduced at 75d. When discussing its earlier appearance, I looked at the immediately following passage, the second definition of surface, to see what level of knowledge Socrates expected in his interlocutor. Here he seemed to be content with a relatively shallow level; Meno only needed to acknowledge a non-technical familiarity with the items appearing in the definition: limit and solid. Yet when Socrates invokes the requirement at 79d, he has in mind a much deeper level of knowledge: for Meno's definition to be acceptable, Socrates must have a philosophical understanding of the items that figure in it. Of course he is at least as familiar with justice as Meno was with limit or solid; but that is no longer good enough.

However, we should not be led into thinking that there are two distinct dialectical requirements at work. The original formulation of 75d was underdetermined: it merely tells us to proceed through things that the interlocutor agrees he knows. Taken in isolation, this is underdetermined in two ways. First, as should be clear by now, the term 'know' could be taken either as familiarity or as philosophical understanding. Second, the dialectical requirement also makes reference to the interlocutor's agreement (75d6). This remains in play later on, as Socrates does not agree that he understands the definientia.

The reason there appears to be a difference between the two appearances of the dialectical requirement is that the later passage forces us to think more carefully about what sort of agreement is at issue. First of all, notice the way Socrates generalises the dialectical requirement at 79d6–e1:

So while you are still investigating what virtue as a whole is, don't imagine that you will explain it to *anyone* by answering in terms of its parts or by saying anything else in the same way . . . (Emphasis added)

Meno will not reveal the nature of virtue to Socrates by defining it as he has done, or to anyone else – including himself. It is not as if he fulfils the dialectical requirement with respect to himself, but not Socrates. This is because he too, under examination, has agreed that he does not understand any part of virtue. This is then the other respect in which the dialectical requirement was underdetermined when originally introduced: we were not told with what degree of reflection the interlocutor should give their agreement. These two indeterminacies are closely linked. The less one reflects on whether one knows something, the shallower one's conception of knowledge is likely to be.

So it would be wrong to find two separate requirements at work.[12] Rather, in itself the requirement is indeterminate: it is a rule of dialectical engagement, but the sort of rule that can be applied flexibly. How the rule is to be followed on any particular occasion may be decided on various grounds, including pragmatic and pedagogical. Immediately after it is first stated, it is applied with a loose sense of 'know', both in the second definition of surface and in the Empedoclean definition of colour. Here Socrates has no wish to hold things up – far from it, he wants to get Meno back to the nature of virtue. All he wants to do in defining surface is to give Meno a sense of what a unitary definition involves. In defining colour he probably wants to appease Meno and make him more co-operative. In neither case would there be any point in embarking on an elaborate scientific digression about the nature of surface or colour. But where virtue is concerned, Socrates expects neither of them to be satisfied with a definition that fails a strict application of the dialectical requirement. The reason lies in his insistence that they achieve a philosophical understanding of the nature of virtue before they investigate how it is acquired.

In this context, it is interesting to revisit Socrates' response to the definition of colour. On one hand, he presents it as satisfying the dialectical requirement, but only in the sense that Meno feels familiar with the components of the definition. At the same time, Socrates is uneasy with it (76e3–7), and in retrospect we can see that, were he to apply the requirement more austerely, the definition would then prove unsatisfactory. No less interesting is the comment that immediately follows his comparison of the two definitions:

Nevertheless, son of Alexidemus, I'm sure that it isn't a better one – the other one is. And I think you would agree, if you didn't have to leave before the mysteries, as you were saying yesterday, but were to stay and be initiated. (76e6–9)

There are several passages in Plato that make a connection between philosophy and initiation.[13] If Socrates is alluding to a form of philosophical initiation, his point is that Meno would come to see the relative merits of the two definitions were he to look into them more closely. Later on

---

[12] *Pace* Franklin (2001) who thinks that the statement of the requirement of 75d applies to the beginning of an inquiry, while that of 79d to its end. I can see no evidence that the requirement as stated at 75d is applied to the beginning of an inquiry: it is not as if the definitions of surface or colour are used to start a further investigation. Also, Franklin's claim that there are two requirements contradicts Socrates' announcement at 79d1–4 that he is invoking the same principle. This is surely unsatisfactory.

[13] *Gorgias* 497c3–4, *Phaedo* 69c3–d2, *Symposium* 209e5–210a2 and *Theaetetus* 155e3–156a3. *Phaedrus* 249c6–250c6 links initiation explicitly to recollection. The theme is very much at home in the *Meno*, which will go on to see philosophical inquiry as the development of piety. See pp. 225–6 below.

in the dialogue, talking of the slave boy, Socrates says that by the end of the experiment he has only acquired true beliefs about the solution to the problem. But if he were to go over the same problems on many occasions and in different ways he would end up with knowledge (85c9–d1). The idea of revisiting and rethinking the same topic is also, I think, hinted at in 76e. What seemed satisfactory to Meno one day might, after more careful reflection, seem less so in the future, and so he would have opened the way to deeper understanding.

All this brings out the flexibility of the dialectical requirement, because it allows for both parties to return to a definition and re-open the issue of whether the questioner really did understand the terms involved. The definer may think that the interlocutor has now advanced far enough to benefit from revisiting the old definition; or the interlocutor may do so for himself: in the course of the dialogue, or several dialogues, he may become more critical and so dissatisfied with what he accepted in a previous discussion.

Before I leave the third definition, I would like to reject a possible construal of the way Socrates deploys the charge of circularity against Meno at 79b–e. This goes as follows. Asked for a definition of virtue, Meno referred to justice in his answer. Socrates then substitutes 'a part of virtue' for 'justice', thereby bringing virtue into its own definition. But if this is all he is doing, he is in danger of undermining the possibility of any definition. Say, for example, that you define a bachelor as an unmarried man. I then recast this into 'a bachelor is a man with the same marital status as a bachelor', and immediately accuse you of circularity. More generally, in any definition, X is defined in terms of a, b and c. Furthermore, it is true that a, b and c can be specified in terms of some relation they hold to X. So the original definition that one gave of X could be replaced by one in which any of a, b or c is replaced with an expression involving X. Thus any definition can be made to look circular.

But Socrates is not playing this substitution trick. He is not committed to saying that, for any definition, it is legitimate to replace one of the definientia with a synonymous expression involving the definiendum, and then to use the resulting circularity to undermine the original definition. Only in some cases can we do this, namely those in which one of the definientia cannot be understood prior to the definiendum. His point in this particular case is that justice is not something that can be detached from virtue and understood independently of it. This is what marks off this case from the bachelor example: we can understand what a man is independently of what a bachelor is. So to inform someone that a bachelor is an unmarried man does not presuppose that he already has any grasp of what it is to be a bachelor.

CHAPTER 5

Meno as an interlocutor

We have now reached a turning point in the dialogue. Meno's definitions have all been refuted and, in response to the demand to inquire into the nature of virtue, he is about to issue a notorious challenge to the possibility of inquiry and discovery (80d). *En route* to this point, Plato has revealed a number of details about his character, details that will turn out to be fundamental in two ways: first, and more immediately, they will help us understand exactly why Meno issues his challenge at 80d. Second, and more generally, throughout the dialogue Socrates not only discusses education as one of his central themes, but also shows it happening in practice by confronting some of Meno's failings and trying to change them. To appreciate this point, we first need to be aware of what exactly these failings are.

INTELLECTUAL LAZINESS

Right from the beginning, we have seen how Meno appears as someone imbued with the ethos of memorising answers to be recycled at a later date. I mentioned how this was anticipated in the very opening lines and in Socrates' immediate response – his snide comments about the Thessalians and the 'wisdom' they have just acquired from Gorgias. The implied criticism comes still closer to the surface at 71c8–d2 when Socrates asks Meno to recall what Gorgias said about virtue, hastily correcting this into a request for Meno to state his own view (which will of course coincide with Gorgias'). This sets Meno up as someone who will be quoting from a master, a point reinforced at 73c6–8 when Socrates has just refuted the first definition and is asking for a second:

Since it is the same virtue in all cases, try to say and recollect what Gorgias says it is – and you with him.

The idea that Meno has thought for himself is now only appended as a very brief afterthought. Then at 76b1, when Meno has just demanded a definition of colour, Socrates complains that he is bothering an old man with demands and is unwilling to recall 'what Gorgias says virtue is'. Now there is no longer any pretence at all that Meno has thought the matter through for himself.

So it is no surprise that all three definitions Meno goes on to give of virtue seem to be derived from someone else: the first comes directly from Gorgias, the second (as we shall shortly see) was a widely held view with traces of Gorgias' influence, and the third is a quotation from an unnamed poet (77b2–5). Nor is it any surprise that Meno should think the task of defining virtue easy if it is simply a matter of listening to someone else (cf. 71e1–2, 6 and 72a1–2).

In Meno's case, this ethos constitutes a form of intellectual laziness: he has no inclination to engage in active inquiry. Plato's portrayal of this is brutally clear and has been well documented by the commentators. But there is an associated aspect of his intellectual ethos that is less frequently discussed. This is his refusal to think synoptically, which emerges at a number of points in the first part of the dialogue. In his first attempt to answer Socrates' question about the nature of virtue, he borrows Gorgias' practice of merely listing different virtues in place of giving a unitary definition (71e1–72a5). Coming from the lips of Gorgias himself, this answer would have amounted to a self-conscious philosophical position. But on page 30 above, I argued that Meno has only a dim awareness of the context of the view he is quoting. What is so striking is that he has difficulty understanding Socrates' demand for a unitary definition. Gorgias, of course, would have understood it perfectly well, but immediately challenged its application to the case of virtue. But it is only after Socrates has given the bee analogy and then those of largeness, strength and health that Meno is able to graduate from failing to understand the definitional question to objecting (rather hesitantly) that the case of virtue is different (73a4–5). What all this shows is that Meno failed to grasp Gorgias' position in its wider context; for him, it was merely an isolated bit of information.

In the second and third definitions, Meno shows further evidence of a refusal to think synoptically, though in a different way. Following the collapse of the first answer, he defines virtue as the power to rule (73c9). To give him his due, he is at least aware that he must give a single account to cover all cases. To this extent he has learnt something from the previous discussion. But what is striking about this new definition is the way it ignores so much else that has proceeded, in particular two assumptions he has just endorsed: having acknowledged at 71e8–72a1 and 73b5 that children and slaves can be virtuous, he is now proposing something that clearly applies only to freeborn adults; then, in defining virtue as power, he omits any reference to justice, and has to be prompted to include it at 73d7–8. Yet he has only just admitted that it is necessary for virtue (73a6– c5). This shows that he is making no attempt to build an answer on the basis of what he has already agreed. Instead he makes an entirely fresh start, presenting a new conception of virtue quite unconnected to the earlier one.

This second lapse is repeated in the discussion of the next definition, where Meno at one point defines virtue as the acquisition of external goods (78c5–d3), and has to be prompted yet again to make a reference to justice, temperance and piety.

In both places, 73c and 78c, he is in effect recalling a well-known conception of virtue, the 'immoralist' conception, an essential feature of which is the way it dispenses with justice. The conception is articulated by Thrasymachus in *Republic* I, whose ideal is the tyrant – someone who can bring whole cities and races under his power (cf. 348d5–6 with 344a3–c6). In the *Gorgias*, Callicles also insists that the truly virtuous are those with the strength to rule the weak (483c8ff.). Under examination from Socrates, he refines this position to say that the truly and 'naturally' virtuous are those who can manage the city's affairs with sufficient intelligence and ruthlessness so as to exploit its resources for their own ends (491a7–d3).[1]

As we shall see below, there is another reason why Meno twice recalls this conception of virtue, but my present point is that, in giving his second definition, he just grabs at another tailor-made conception of virtue. He makes no attempt to take account of, let alone build upon, the lessons learnt from earlier in the dialogue.

COERCION

At the beginning of this commentary, I suggested that the very abruptness of the dialogue's opening might anticipate two features about Meno: his expectation that knowledge can be easily acquired, and his peremptory attitude to Socrates.[2] Now that we have seen the first feature at work in 70–80, it is time to turn to the second. Although Meno is lazy when it comes to pursuing an inquiry for himself, he is altogether more energetic when it comes to managing the power relations with Socrates, and there

[1] Earlier in the dialogue, Gorgias talks of rhetoric as the greatest good for a man, which also secures him power over others (452d5–8). The fact that he links the good (*agathon*) with power suggests he would have been more than sympathetic to Meno's second definition of virtue. See Bluck 1961: 232 and Canto-Sperber 1991: 223.

[2] See above, pp. 12–13.

is something distinctly aggressive about the way in which he goes about getting what he wants. One point where this comes to the surface is in the lesson on definition. Notice, first of all, the way he responds to Socrates' suggestion that he define surface as 'practice' for defining virtue. He simply refuses, telling Socrates to do it instead (75b1). As this phase of the dialogue proceeds, Meno's peremptoriness increasingly manifests itself as coercion. In reply to Meno's demand for a definition of surface, Socrates attempts to humour him by entering into a bargain: he will define surface if Meno will define virtue. The deal done, Socrates then defines surface as what always accompanies colour. When Meno retorts that the definition is 'silly', Socrates offers his second definition of surface, though not before he has implicitly accused him of being eristic and encouraged him to take a 'milder' approach to the conversation.[3] But then, instead of fulfilling his side of the bargain, Meno demands that Socrates now define colour. The dialogue continues:

SOC. How arrogant you are, Meno! You bother an old man by demanding him to answer, when you yourself are unwilling to recollect and tell me what Gorgias says virtue is.
MEN. I'll answer you, Socrates, when you've told me this.
SOC. Even if one were blindfolded, Meno, one would know just by talking with you that you're beautiful and still have lovers.
MEN. How so?
SOC. Because you simply give commands when you speak, like spoilt beauties: they act like tyrants while they're still in their prime. Perhaps you also realise that I'm susceptible to beauty. So I'll indulge you and give you an answer.
MEN. Yes – indulge me.

(76a8–c3)

Joking aside, there is a sinister undertone here, and the reference to tyranny should be taken seriously.[4] Socrates suggests that Meno's attitude to the conversation is unco-operative to the point of being coercive. To emphasise this point, it is worth briefly looking ahead to a point later on in the dialogue when, immediately after the recollection passage, Socrates proposes that they resume their inquiry into the nature of virtue (86c4–6). When Meno replies that he wants to return to his original question about its acquisition, Socrates protests:

If I had control not just of myself but you as well, Meno, we wouldn't inquire whether or not virtue is teachable before we had first examined what it is. But since you don't even attempt to control yourself (for the sake of your own freedom,

---

[3] See above p. 36.   [4] Compare the end of the *Charmides* (176b5–d5).

presumably), but try to control me – and succeed – I'll give in to you: what else am I to do? So it seems we have to investigate what something is like when we don't yet know what it is. But at least relax your hold over me a little, and agree to investigate whether it is teachable, or whatever, by way of a hypothesis. (86d3–e4)

This comment on Meno's character, together with the earlier references to tyranny should of course be connected to his views on the nature of virtue as revealed in the second and third definitions. In the previous section, I pointed out his tendency to slide back into an immoralist conception of virtue as an illustration of his refusal to think sequentially. But that is not all there is to be said on this point. Clearly the immoralist conception has a persistent attraction for him, and is presumably his own favoured conception among all the different opinions that he has encountered. So it should be no surprise that his behaviour within the dialogue reflects this view: witness his refusal at 76a8 to abide by the bargain that he made with Socrates at 75b4–5.

That said, the strength of his commitment to the immoralist position is not clear. Contrast the single-mindedness with which Callicles or Thrasymachus espouse it. A closer parallel for Meno might be found in another interlocutor from the *Gorgias*, Polus, who starts by expressing an immoralist position, but eventually reveals scruples. In response to the question of whether it is better to do or to suffer injustice, he replies that it is better to do injustice but 'finer' to suffer it (474c5–d2). This shows that he is trying to accommodate two conceptions of value, one dispensing with justice, the other requiring it. Under pressure from Socrates he is unable to maintain both conceptions in play without contradiction, and so is forced to concede defeat. Soon afterwards, Callicles castigates him for his vacillation, as he himself adopts the less muddled position that it is both finer and better to do injustice than to suffer it. But Polus perhaps represents more accurately the condition in which many of Socrates' contemporaries would have found themselves. Meno, I would suggest, is another case of moral vacillation.[5] On one hand, three times and without any hesitation, he agrees to Socrates' inclusion of justice as a condition for virtue. On the other, he shows a propensity to slide back into the immoralist conception.

Even so, we cannot be sure exactly how far Meno differs from the likes of Callicles and Thrasymachus without understanding the exact nature of this vacillation. It could be that Meno's acceptance of the justice requirement

---

[5] See Adkins 1960: 228–30, though I would question his claim that Meno is 'essentially well-meaning' (230).

is sincere, i.e. that he is genuinely attracted to the 'quiet' virtues.[6] The immoralist ideal, however, remains his preferred or default position, as is evidenced by his own habit of breaking his agreements with Socrates. A more critical characterisation is that the immoralist ideal is his real position, were he being honest. He only wants to be seen to accept the value of justice (and temperance), and is prepared to pay lip service to them when challenged. But the way in which he quietly drops any reference to these values when left to give an answer for himself shows his true colours.

In support of this more cynical interpretation, one might appeal to some of the external evidence that we have about Meno. At the time of the dramatic date of the dialogue he is about eighteen. Later he was to become one of the Greek commanders of the mercenary army that went to Persia and whose expedition is narrated in Xenophon's *Anabasis*. According to Xenophon, Meno turned out to be treacherous, greedy and wholly unscrupulous. He was eventually imprisoned and tortured for an entire year before meeting his death.[7] It is interesting to note the reference to Meno's Persian connection ('the hereditary guest of the Great King', 78d2–3) just at the point where his failure to mention justice is being underlined. It might be that Plato intends some wry humour in having his readers come across the by then notorious Meno discussing the nature of virtue with Socrates, and in particular agreeing three times that justice is one of its necessary conditions.

On the other hand, we cannot simply assume that Plato shared Xenophon's assessment of Meno. In my view, his Meno has not yet hardened into the character whom Xenophon so condemns. This will become clearer in the last section of the work, where I shall argue that not only does Socrates attempt to reform the coercive side of Meno's character; he actually has some success, albeit limited.

---

[6] Interestingly, it is Meno himself, not Socrates, who volunteers temperance, another very unCalliclean quality, as a species of virtue at 74a5.
[7] Xenophon, *Anabasis* 2.6.21–9. On the historical Meno see Bluck 1961: 120–6.

PART TWO

CHAPTER 6

The stingray: 79e–80d

MENO'S ATTACK ON THE ELENCHUS

After the third definition has collapsed Socrates asks for yet another, as if things are going to proceed exactly as before. But Meno has finally reached *aporia*:

MEN. Socrates, even before I met you, I heard that you yourself are just perplexed and make others so. Now it seems to me you're enchanting me with witchcraft and potions – in a word, casting me under a spell, until I'm full of perplexity. If it's appropriate to make a joke, you seem to me to be just like the stingray, both in looks and everything else. It also numbs anyone who approaches and touches it, and I think you have done exactly the same to me. I'm genuinely numbed in mind and word, and don't know how to answer you. And yet I've given very many speeches on virtue on thousands of occasions in front of many people – and very well too, so I thought. But now, I'm not even able to say what it is at all. And I think you are well advised not to set sail from here or travel abroad: if you did such things as a foreigner in another city, you'd probably be arrested as a wizard.

(79e7–80b7)

Meno may be making at least three points here. The first and most obvious is that Socrates numbs his victims into intellectual inactivity. If the stingray comparison is to be applied strictly, Socrates stands accused of preparing his victims for some sort of cognitive death, which of course is the last thing he would want to have said of him. Contrast the image he applies to himself in the *Apology*, the gadfly (30e5) – a flattering comparison, meant to capture the way in which he stirred people out of their complacency into reflection. Meno's image stands this on its head.

Second, aside from the fact that he feels himself at a complete impasse, Meno may also feel that he once had something of value to say about virtue (80b3), which has now been destroyed. If so the implication would be that Socratic cross-examination (the 'elenchus') eradicates the good as well as the bad.

Third, Meno might be using the stingray image to make a point about Socrates' motives. If the stingray is a predator,[1] the suggestion may be that he inflicts *aporia* on his interlocutors to harm them, perhaps to further his own interests (e.g. intellectual self-promotion). Again, this conflicts sharply with his self-image. At 75c8–d7, he emphasised the contrast between those who argue 'eristically', i.e. for contentious purposes, and those like himself who argue dialectically. Very importantly, he says that dialectic is appropriate for friends, implying that the motives of those engaged in argument are supportive rather than manipulative. By contrast, eristic is by its nature predatory: this is the clear message of the dialogue devoted to the topic, the *Euthydemus*, where two sophists subject a philosophical novice to a battery of refutations and exploit his embarrassment to show off their own argumentative skills.

The suggestion that Socrates is intellectually manipulative is also implicit in the way Meno compares him to a magician (80a2–3 and b6–7). Given the reference to arrest at the end of the speech (80b4–7), this allusion is clearly meant to have sinister overtones. An interesting parallel for this image can be found in the *Gorgias*, where Callicles uses almost identical imagery in his tirade against conventional standards of justice. These, he claims, are merely used by the weak to protect themselves against the strong. According to his ideal of 'natural' justice, the strong would impose their might over the weak. But as it is

... we shape the best and strongest among us, taking them from infancy, like lions, and enslave them by spells and witchcraft [κατεπᾴδοντές τε καὶ γοητεύοντες – cf. *Meno* 80a2–3], telling them that they must have an equal share and that this is the fine and the just. (483e4–484a2)

The reference to enslavement shows that those who use witchcraft are doing so to exploit the other party for their own ends, which recalls the notion of manipulation, echoing the way Meno characterises Socrates as a predator.[2]

There are two ways in which to react to Meno's speech. One is to be dismissive. Since he has fallen into the habit of relying on ready-made answers provided by another party, he naturally feels vacant when these are

---

[1] Cf. Aristotle, *History of Animals* 620b19–25.

[2] The witchcraft image is also used at *Euthydemus* 288b8. There may be a further parallel between *Gorgias* 483e and *Meno* 80a–b in that Callicles uses the witchcraft imagery to complain that something of real value has been stifled. Yet another accusation implicit in the witchcraft image in the *Meno* may be that, despite all his claims, Socrates is actually resorting to a non-rational means of dealing with his interlocutors. Interestingly enough, Gorgias himself made use of the witchcraft imagery to describe the power of rhetoric to manipulate an audience: see *Helen* §10.

found wanting. Had he ever exploited his own resources and accustomed himself to building on what could be learnt in the course of reaching *aporia*, he would not feel as blank as he does. To recall the analogy that Aristotle used against Gorgias,[3] if he had never learnt how to make shoes for himself but had merely relied upon someone else's supply of ready-made articles, he would have nothing to offer when none of them turned out to fit.

What passes between Meno and Socrates in the immediate aftermath of the stingray speech may encourage us to take this dismissive approach. Socrates responds by appearing to belittle his complaint: he pretends that Meno has an ulterior motive, which is to describe him with an image so that he will have one in return. Then he adds:

And now, as regards what virtue is, I don't know, but perhaps you did know before you came into contact with me, though now you resemble someone who doesn't know.[4] Nevertheless, with your help I'm willing to inquire and search after what it is. (80d1–4)

Notice the terms in which he proposes that they return to the nature of virtue. When he asked Meno for another definition of virtue at 79e5–6, he did so in the same way as he had done earlier in the dialogue, addressing him as someone who, along with Gorgias, has the answer and is ready to give it (71d4–8 and 73c6–8). But after Meno's admission of *aporia*, he makes a different request – that they take part in a joint inquiry. In effect he is challenging Meno to adopt an entirely different approach, to move towards an ethos of inquiry from one of 'acquiry', as it were. Yet, as we shall shortly see, this merely provokes Meno into deploying an argument that denies even the possibility of inquiry, a move that seems to confirm Socrates' worst suspicions: in his view, Meno is using the argument to avoid having to change his underlying ethos.

SOCRATES ON TRIAL (II)

All this helps to support the image of Meno as the disgruntled apprentice caught out by an unusually demanding customer. Yet there is another way of looking at the stingray speech. Whatever his motives, Meno has put

---

[3] *Sophistical Refutations* 34, 183b36–184a8. See above, pp. 12–13.
[4] We should probably see the first sentence as an anticipation of recollection. In one sense, Meno did explicitly know the nature of virtue before he met Socrates; because he still has the knowledge latently, he only resembles someone who does not know. Plato has already made a similar anticipation at 71c7–d8. See above p. 23.

his finger on something genuinely important. Having initially dismissed Meno's complaint at 80c3–6, Socrates does return to offer a more systematic reply in the course of the slave boy demonstration, an episode that acts as a small-scale elenchus reflecting some of the features of the previous encounter with Meno.[5] The boy starts out confident that he knows the answer but, like Meno before him, is soon reduced to *aporia*. The similarities are most explicit at 84a3–c9, just after the boy has admitted to his ignorance. Socrates turns to Meno and questions him about the boy's progress. He stresses that in ridding the boy of his pretension to know and reducing him to *aporia* the stingray has done him no harm (84b6–7). Then, in a particularly close parallel to Meno's earlier speech, Socrates pretends that before encountering the stingray the boy would have prided himself on his ability to speak about geometry (84b11–c1; cf. 80b2–3). The 'stingray' implants the motivation to inquire, and so is of clear benefit.

In this interlude, one can find replies to all three points suggested by the stingray speech. By ridding the interlocutor of intellectual complacency, the elenchus has the very opposite effect of stifling him: Socrates stresses that the boy will be positively eager to inquire (84b10). Secondly, if Meno feels that something of value had been destroyed, Socrates can reply that all his previous definitions were false, and his self-confidence groundless. Finally, if the stingray is beneficial, as Socrates stresses twice (84b3–4 and c8), there can be no substance in the claim that his motives in using the elenchus are malicious.

Nevertheless, even if Socrates can meet the challenge of the stingray speech relatively easily, the way in which Plato presents the whole issue is striking. He gives Meno an extremely articulate speech whose imagery is both ingenious and fecund; he has Socrates go out of his way to reply to it in a later passage, as if still preoccupied by it. In all this, Plato may be signalling some lingering unease to the reader.

In fact, this passage should be seen as another episode of what I have called 'Socrates on trial'. We have already encountered one episode of this phenomenon in the discussion of the first definition (pp. 27–30). There, a challenge was presented to Socrates, and the target of that challenge was the unitarian assumption, a specific claim that we can attribute to the historical Socrates. We also noted that Meno, the author of the challenge, has (at best) only a partial understanding of its significance. The same features can be found in the stingray passage and its aftermath. It should already be evident that a distinctively Socratic position is being challenged – that the elenchus

---

[5] We noted some of these on p. 33 above.

is beneficial and incites the interlocutor to further inquiry. This claim is implicit in the gadfly image of the *Apology*. And if we want evidence that this was a challenge Plato took seriously – not merely a one-off complaint from an unusually petulant interlocutor – we only have to turn to other dialogues where parallel concerns are aired: the *Euthydemus* and, more explicitly, the *Phaedo* and the *Republic*.

The *Euthydemus* is an extensive comparison between Socratic dialectic and the manipulative and predatory use of argument practised by two well-known sophists. In essence the distinction is the same as that expressed at *Meno* 75d – that eristic uses argument purely for competitive purposes, whereas dialectic is milder and more suited to friends who have each other's welfare at heart. But one of Plato's main purposes in presenting the reader with the juxtaposition is to bring out the differences between two modes or uses of argument – supportive and manipulative – that might be easily confused. The fact he feels the need to do so at such length testifies to his concern about the psychological impact of the elenchus on Socrates' interlocutors.[6]

In a famous passage in the *Phaedo*, Socrates warns his interlocutors about the dangers of 'misology' (89c11–90d7). Those who suffer repeated refutation may eventually lose faith in argument and conclude that no argument can ever be reliable, so lapsing into a form of scepticism. They develop a hatred of arguments (analogous to misanthropy), and give up philosophising. This suggests that over time the elenchus could have the opposite effect of the gadfly, even for interlocutors much more determined and sophisticated than Meno. This is not to say that the criticism is unanswerable. In the *Phaedo*, Socrates makes it clear that the misologists have simply over-reacted to the experience of refutation.

Finally, there is *Republic* VII 537d7–539d6, a passage in which we actually find severe restrictions placed on the use of the elenchus. Here, Socrates warns against the dangers of starting dialectic too young. The problem is that young men who engage in question-and-answer sessions about values become easily corrupted: on being refuted many times themselves, they do so to others and end up overturning the 'lawful' precepts with which they were brought up; then, pleasures and appetites rush in to fill the moral vacuum and direct their lives thereafter. In view of this danger, Socrates requires that there be no involvement in question-and-answer sessions about justice and the like until the age of thirty, by which time

---

[6] See also *Charmides* 166c4–6, where Critias complains that Socrates' real interest lies not in the argument (i.e. the truth), but in refutation. Like Meno, his reaction to the elenchus is to feel under personal attack.

the trainee guardians will have completed their mathematical studies and attained more order in their souls (539b1–d6).

What is particularly striking about this passage, in contrast to the *Meno*, *Euthydemus* and *Phaedo*, is that concerns about the elenchus lead to proposals to limit its use. The elenchus is not unqualifiedly beneficial: in principle it can incite one to further inquiry, but only when used with care and in the right conditions, otherwise it may be counter-productive. This amounts to a qualification of the claims made in the *Apology* on behalf of the elenchus.[7]

The moral of all these texts is that, although the elenchus is in principle highly beneficial, it can have disturbingly negative effects. Along with the *Phaedo*, the *Euthydemus* and the *Republic*, the *Meno* is one text where Plato shows a tendency to worry about the use of the elenchus – to act as a meta-gadfly – despite the rosy image he gives us in the *Apology*.

Finally, there remains a question over Meno's motivation in issuing this challenge. At the beginning of this section, I gave some reasons for thinking that he might be driven by resentment to criticise Socrates as he does. Doubtless, this is part of the picture. The ending of his speech, in which he warns Socrates not to travel abroad (80b4–7), has a sinister edge to it, to which we shall be returning below. On the other hand, there is no reason to deny him any credit at all for spotting a problem with the elenchus, just as he had some inkling that the unitarian assumption was open to serious philosophical challenge. Plato's portrait of Meno is not one-sided. Towards the end of this book, I shall argue that he improves as the dialogue goes on, which implies that he always had the potential to do so. If so, it would be natural for some positive characteristics to show through, even before he has started to improve.

---

[7] It is a further question whether the *Republic* is criticising the historical Socrates for using the elenchus with the people he did, e.g. Alcibiades. This is not the same as the question of whether the elenchus can in certain contexts cause harm. Even if that is agreed to be possible, it might still be true that Socrates was right to take the risk, as it were, of using the elenchus on the likes of Alcibiades. For someone who thinks *Republic* VII does criticise the historical Socrates, see Nussbaum 1980: 87–8 with n. 87. Irwin (1995: 277) takes a contrary view, and I would agree with him. *Rep.* VII 537d–539d is concerned with the ideal state, not with Socrates' Athens, where there were artistic and other influences with the potential to corrupt. Even while writing the *Republic*, Plato could have claimed the Athenians needed a counter-balance to such forces and that Socrates was right to use the elenchus to provide it, despite the dangers involved. But in the ideal state there is no point in taking the risk, as the young will not have been exposed to corrupting influences. Nussbaum acknowledges that 537d–539d is primarily about the ideal state, but says that the same ought, more or less, to apply in the non-ideal state on the grounds that the non-ideal should still approximate as far as possible to the ideal. But the relationship between prescriptions for ideal and non-ideal cases is more complex. To take an example: in a non-ideal state philosophers have no duty to rule at all (496c5–497a5 and 520a9–b4); Plato does not say that they ought to rule as much as possible, even if not quite as much as in the ideal state.

CHAPTER 7

'Meno's paradox': 80d–81a

We now come to one of the most well-known passages in the dialogue. In response to the stingray speech, which concerns the psychological effects of the elenchus, Socrates has just proposed that they jointly inquire into what they do not know. Meno's counter-response is to pose an epistemological challenge to the very possibility of inquiry and discovery. This challenge has become known as 'Meno's paradox'. One thing that has made it seem so important is that it prompts Socrates to introduce the theory of recollection and, with it, the examination of the slave boy. The challenge has also attracted a good deal of scholarly interest because of the interpretative issues it poses. First, it has proved very difficult for scholars to agree on what the problem behind the 'paradox' actually is.[1] Second, there is the question of whether Meno uses the challenge merely as a dodge to evade further cross-examination, or whether he is motivated by a serious philosophical concern.[2]

In dealing with the first issue, it is very important to recognise that Plato structures this phase of the dialogue in two stages: first, he has Meno challenge Socrates with a posse of three questions (80d5–8); then Socrates reformulates the challenge into what he calls 'the eristic argument', a dilemma about the impossibility of inquiry (80e1–5). In what follows, I shall call the first 'Meno's challenge' and the second the 'eristic dilemma'. I shall avoid the expression 'Meno's paradox', as it has been used confusingly to apply to one or both these stages.

---

[1] To get a sense of the variety of interpretations available, contrast Phillips (1948: 88), who thinks it 'contains in embryo one of the central contentions of sophistic nominalism as a philosophical position', Calvert (1974) who interprets the problem as Eleatic in origin, Nehamas (1985) who takes it to concern the lack of teachers of virtue, and Vlastos (1994: 78–9) who thinks it based on the priority of definition. For other interpretations see Moline 1969, White 1974, Ryle 1976: 7, Desjardins 1985: 262–9, Fine 1992, McCabe 1994: 53–7 and Weiss 2001 52–63. I have also discussed the paradox in Scott 1991 and 1995: 24–32.
[2] See Nehamas 1985: 1–2.

The second issue – Meno's motivation – is very germane to one of the running themes of this book: Socrates on trial. As we have seen in the previous section and in discussing the unitarian assumption, Plato uses Meno as the occasion for questioning assumptions that were central to the philosophy of the historical Socrates. By challenging the very possibility of inquiry or discovery Meno might render the Socratic life of examination pointless. In response, the Socrates of the *Meno* advances a theory of genuine importance, which resonates in at least two other dialogues, the *Phaedo* and the *Phaedrus*. But even as he considers the challenge, Socrates suggests that Meno is merely being contentious or eristic. Here we have all the elements needed for another episode of Socrates on trial. At the end of this section, when I have analysed the problems raised through Meno's challenge and the eristic dilemma, I shall argue that this is indeed a text-book example of how Plato puts Socrates on philosophical trial.

THE SURFACE PROBLEMS

Meno's challenge

In the wake of the stingray speech, Socrates insists that the two of them should still persevere and inquire into what they do not know. Meno now protests (80d5–8):

(M[1]) And how will you inquire, Socrates, into something when you don't know at all what it is? Which of the things that you don't know will you propose as the object of your inquiry? (M[2]) Or even if you really stumble upon it, how will you know that this is the thing you didn't know before?

This challenge consists of two closely related points, which I have labelled M[1] and M[2]. M[1] is expressed in the first two questions: how can you even start to inquire in the absence of any specification of the object of inquiry? It is important that Meno adds the qualification 'at all' when he talks of the person having no knowledge of the object of inquiry. He is imagining the would-be inquirer to be in a total blank, lacking any specification of the object in question. If Meno were not thinking along these lines, the second rhetorical question in M[1] would make no sense. For this clarifies[3] the first by picturing the absurd situation of attempting to choose one blank out of many for inquiry.

The weakness of M[1] is clear, at least in the context of the dialogue so far. Although the problem would arise if one really were in a cognitive

---

[3] Cf. γάρ d6.

blank, this hardly represents the situation of either Meno or Socrates in the dialogue. Doubtless, Meno is echoing Socrates' claim at the beginning of the dialogue when he said he did not know 'at all' what virtue is (71b3). But when Socrates says this, and when he talks of being in *aporia* at 80c9–d1, he does not mean that he has no ideas about virtue – that is manifestly untrue – but that he has not yet achieved true philosophical understanding.[4] The first ten pages are rich in ideas and beliefs that can constitute a specification of virtue. The section just preceding the stingray passage shows that they are looking for a unitary form, which involves such qualities as justice, piety, temperance and courage. In the immediate aftermath of the elenchus, Meno may *feel* quite numbed, but this is because he is used to relying on other people's answers and has no more in stock. The reality is that, in the process of refuting Meno, Socrates has aroused a number of beliefs about virtue that can yield a specification sufficient to launch a fresh inquiry.

What then of M^2? While M^1 focuses on the beginning of an inquiry, this part of the challenge envisages a problem about ever completing it (even if one could, *per impossibile*, get started). It will be crucial to my reading of this passage that M^2 is susceptible of two quite different readings. One of them is continuous with the problem raised in M^1: if you are in a cognitive blank about some object, you cannot make a discovery about it by means of inquiry. To make this point, Meno asks us to envisage a situation where you are attempting to assert that one thing (that you have just stumbled upon, x) is another thing (that you started out with, y). But this is impossible: you may be able to grasp x, but since you have never had any specification of y, how can you make any sense of the statement 'x is y'? So interpreted, M^2 stems from exactly the same source as M^1 and can be dealt with in the same way, viz. by distinguishing between grasping a subject sufficiently to have a specification of it, and attaining full knowledge: equipped with this distinction, our would-be discoverer can now make sense of the statement 'x is y'.

We shall see below that M^2 is capable of a deeper reading; but I now wish to proceed to Socrates' reformulation of the problem, as this is directly continuous with the way I have read Meno's challenge.

The eristic dilemma

In the face of the challenge Socrates replies:

I know what you want to say, Meno. Do you realise what an eristic argument you're bringing up – that it's impossible for someone to inquire into what he knows or

---

[4] See pp. 19–20 above. Contrast Nehamas' view in 1985: 5–7.

doesn't know: he wouldn't inquire into what he knows, since he already knows it and there's no need for such a person to inquire; nor into what he doesn't know, because he doesn't even know what he's going to inquire into. (80e1–5)

Socrates claims to be re-articulating what Meno has just said. But although the dilemma that he produces is continuous with Meno's challenge, it is slightly different. M^2 is missing, and there is an addition. This latter point becomes clear if we set out the dilemma more schematically:

S^1 If you know the object already you cannot genuinely inquire into it.
S^2 If you do not know it you cannot inquire, because you do not even know what you are inquiring into.
[Implicit premise: S^3 Either you know something or you do not.]
S^4 Therefore you cannot inquire into any object.

S^2 is taken from Meno's challenge, and corresponds very closely to M^1. S^1 is Socrates' own addition and together with S^2 and S^3 is used to generate a conclusion that is broader in scope than Meno's challenge, which had not attacked the possibility of all inquiry, only inquiry into what you do not know.

Despite these differences, Meno makes no comment and approves of the revised version (cf. 81a1–2). One explanation of this is that the eristic dilemma existed externally to the dialogue, and when Meno set out his challenge he was alluding to part of a larger problem, leaving Socrates to recall it in full. This explanation is supported by the fact that Socrates uses the present tense when he starts to set out the dilemma: 'do you realise that what you are bringing up (κατάγεις) . . .'.[5] It would of course be no surprise if someone else were the author of the eristic dilemma – Gorgias, perhaps. The argument proceeds by the use of dichotomy, a technique favoured by Gorgias in his treatise, *On What is Not*, and the Greek makes heavy use of some of his favourite stylistic traits, repetition and assonance.[6] Once again, it may be that Socrates is proceeding in a way that Meno will find familiar (cf. 76c4–5 and above pp. 44 & 58).

---

[5] The verb κατάγεις suggests three metaphors, two of which pick up themes from the dialogue so far. It can apply to fishing and, if so, Socrates is suggesting that, by issuing his challenge, Meno has only half fished an argument out of the water, leaving Socrates to complete the task. As Klein (1965: 91) argues, this fish really is like a stingray, as it would stifle all inquiry. Another possible connotation of κατάγειν (although this may only be a later usage) is that of conjuring something up, like summoning a genie. The genie – perhaps Gorgias – is waiting there in Meno's memory to give assistance when he gets into trouble. This of course repeats a pattern set up in the first part of the dialogue. See Gaiser 1963: 442 and Canto-Sperber 1991: 248. It is quite possible that Socrates intends the verb κατάγεις to point to both the fishing and witchcraft images at once, especially as they have already featured Meno's stingray speech. κατάγειν can also apply to spinning, meaning 'to draw out'.

[6] For other echoes of Gorgias' style see p. 48 n. 4. For the suggestion that Meno is relying on Gorgias in this context, see Hoerber 1960: 101, Ebert (1974) 91, and Canto-Sperber 1991: 247–8, n. 104.

If this is right, we have some explanation of why Socrates allows M^2 to drop out of view: although Meno had raised two different questions in his original challenge, his real interest was in recalling M^1 rather than M^2. Socrates duly tailors his response to Meno's interests. There is, however, more to be said here, because M^2 is susceptible of another interpretation; and Meno's failure to see this is of some significance, as I shall argue below. But first we need to examine Socrates' response to the eristic dilemma.

Is recollection proposed to solve the dilemma?

The obvious way to deal with the dilemma is to point out that it relies on a false dichotomy. For S^1 to be true, we have to assume that the person has complete knowledge of the object so that any inquiry would be a mere charade. S^2 is true only when the lack of knowledge in question is a cognitive blank, as with M^1: if we were in such a state about an object we would indeed be unable to inquire into it. But these two options do not exhaust all the possibilities, as we can have a partial grasp of something. This will allow us to formulate a problem without thereby solving it.

But how does Socrates respond to the dilemma? A straightforward answer is to say that he attempts to solve it with the theory of recollection. According to the dilemma, a necessary condition of inquiring is that one knows the object of inquiry, so that one has an initial specification; but another necessary condition is that one does not know it, so that there is room for an inquiry. These conditions cannot apparently be fulfilled together. *Ergo* inquiry is impossible. Thus one might think that Socrates uses recollection to show how we can know and not know the same thing at the same time: latently we know the object but, because we have forgotten it and appear like those who do not know (cf. 80d3), there is a point to inquiry.

However, there are three strong reasons against supposing that Socrates introduces recollection to disarm the eristic dilemma. The first is philosophical. As we have just seen, the way to solve the argument is to differentiate between full knowledge of a subject and a partial grasp of it. An obvious way of expressing this is to appeal to the *Meno*'s own distinction between knowledge and true belief (97c9–98b5). This would unravel the dilemma, because having a true belief about something will enable us to identify it as an object of inquiry without knowing all about it. If Socrates really is concerned to solve the dilemma, we should expect him to invoke his distinction between knowledge and true belief rather than recollection.

By contrast, recollection is neither necessary nor sufficient to solve the dilemma. It is clearly not necessary. The dilemma purports to show that inquiry is logically impossible, and does so by exploiting an all-or-nothing conception of knowledge. The correct solution to this problem merely consists in showing that it is logically possible to have a grasp of an object (suitable for the initial specification) that falls short of full knowledge. Recollection is an account of where our cognitive states come from, and as such is not necessary to the solution. The partial grasp could come from a number of sources – perception or hearsay, for instance.

Nor is recollection sufficient for solving the problem.[7] According to the interpretation given above, recollection was supposed to solve the dilemma by distinguishing between two types of knowledge, explicit and latent. Now imagine that we espoused recollection, but rejected the distinction between knowledge and true belief or in general any view that allows for partial understanding. We would be forced to say that, if we know something explicitly, we either know everything about it explicitly or nothing about it explicitly. As a result, our theory of recollection will be powerless to solve the dilemma, because if we recollect we have to recollect everything about it at once. But if recollection is to solve the problem of inquiry, we need to be able to recollect some partial knowledge, which will allow us to specify the object of inquiry. On the view under consideration, any act of recollecting about the object will land us with full knowledge, hence making the inquiry superfluous.

The second reason for doubting that recollection is introduced to solve the eristic dilemma comes from considering the dynamics of the relationship between Socrates and Meno. As I claimed when discussing the stingray speech, Meno's behaviour throughout this section needs to be put in the context of his intellectual character. Why does he challenge Socrates on the possibility of inquiry in the first place? An important clue, as we have already seen, lies in Socrates' use of the term 'eristic' to describe the dilemma. Although the term is pejorative, it does not on its own imply that the argument itself is bad; but it does imply that Meno's motives for using the argument are bad. We saw on page 36 above that Socrates implicitly accuses Meno of being eristic at 75c8–d2. As the contrast between eristic and dialectic there suggests, eristic arguments are used to defeat interlocutors rather than aid their understanding. Similarly at 80e2, Socrates (perhaps

---

[7] Cf. Calvert 1974: 151 and Fine 1992: 214.

still smarting from the insinuations behind the stingray speech) accuses Meno of being obstructive and belligerent and of trying to forestall any further requests to exert himself intellectually.

That this is Socrates' view is confirmed a little later on at 81d–e, just after the first appearance of recollection. After talking about how it is possible for us to recollect what we once knew, he adds:

So one shouldn't be persuaded by that eristic argument. It would make us idle and is pleasant for the faint-hearted to hear. But this one [sc. recollection] makes us hard working and eager to inquire. Trusting it to be true, I'm willing to inquire with you into what virtue is. (81d5–e2)

What is significant is that Socrates presents the eristic argument as something that would be welcomed by the weak, as if to say that Meno was not proposing it as a genuine epistemological concern; rather, he was already daunted by the prospect of further, post-*aporia* inquiry. Only then does he look to the eristic argument as a way of blocking Socrates' request to engage in co-operative inquiry. The argument is not presented as something that he has considered impartially and accepted on its logic alone.

This supports the claim that Socrates is not trying to solve the eristic dilemma directly with recollection. Having introduced the theory, he makes no attempt to explain in logical terms how it disarms the dilemma. Rather, he starts to deploy a psychological strategy of carrot and stick: the latter, because in the lines quoted he attempts to arouse a sense of shame in Meno for being weak;[8] the former, because he uses recollection as an incentive to make Meno eager to inquire, and almost panders to his desire for the exotic in the initial exposé of recollection.[9] This includes references to priests, priestesses and divinely inspired poets – all of whom immediately arouse Meno's curiosity, as does the prospect of hearing about a new theory (81a7–9). The use of allusions to ancient myths and a recitation of lyric poetry is part of the same strategy: whetting his appetite for the exotic and thus luring him into making the effort to inquire for himself. We might see Socrates as trying to create a gestalt shift in his interlocutor: what Meno previously saw as wearisome now becomes something irresistibly intriguing.

---

[8] The pejorative comparison between Meno and his slave at 84a3–c9 is part of the same strategy, as is the reference to manliness at 86b8–9. Because Meno has an interest in power and the use of coercion (see above pp. 62–5), Socrates can be assured that allusions to a lack of manliness will have some purchase on him.

[9] See Umphrey 1990: 20 and Weiss 2001: 65. This passage should be set alongside the definition of colour 76c2–d5 and dichotomous structure of the argument of 77b7–d3: in all these places Socrates adapts himself to suit Meno's tastes, a strategy related to the dialectical requirement of 75d. See above p. 48 n. 4.

But to repeat: what Socrates does not do is to disarm the eristic dilemma directly.

There is a third reason for doubting that Socrates uses recollection to solve the eristic dilemma. This comes from a passage that concludes this whole section of the dialogue.

As for the other points, I wouldn't absolutely insist on the argument. But I would fight, both in word and deed, for the following point: that we would be better, more manly and less lazy if we believed that we ought to inquire into what we do not know, than if we believed that *we cannot discover what we do not know* and so have no duty to inquire. (86b6–c2, emphasis added)

Here he seems to return to the challenge that had initially prompted him to introduce recollection. But notice how he describes it. The challenge comes from someone who thinks that we cannot discover what we do not know and hence have no duty to inquire. Although Socrates seems clearly exercised by this challenge, it is quite different from the eristic dilemma. That attempts to argue that it is impossible to inquire. By contrast, 86b–c alludes to the claim that it is impossible to discover; on this view inquiry is pointless rather than impossible. The difference between the two challenges can be captured by an analogy. Zeno argued that it is impossible to move. This is analogous to the conclusion of the eristic dilemma that it is impossible to inquire. By contrast, the claim that it is impossible to discover and hence pointless to inquire is analogous to the claim that it is impossible to find one's way to a particular destination, even though one can make the attempt.

In short, recollection should not be seen as the philosophical solution to the dilemma. First, the theory is not actually relevant to solving it. On grounds of philosophical clarity alone we ought to be wary of casting recollection in this role, especially as Socrates has the necessary materials to deal with the dilemma in his distinction between knowledge and true belief. Second, in his explicit dealings with Meno, Socrates ignores any epistemological problems the dilemma might raise, and instead focuses on Meno's psychology: his motives for deploying the argument and the incentives he needs to restart the inquiry. Third, Socrates' own statement of the challenge that faces him at the end of the passage suggests he is concerned with the possibility of successful inquiry, rather than inquiry *per se*.[10]

---

[10] Some commentators, e.g. Fine (1992: 213) and Day (1994: 26), see Socrates' primary response to Meno to be the slave boy demonstration, rather than recollection; the latter is only introduced to explain how the slave boy could come to the right answer. Even if this were true, we should still resist the idea that Socrates' concern is with the eristic dilemma, for the slave boy demonstration is clearly not geared up to serve as a response to it: there is no suggestion that the boy might be unable

The question of whether Socrates uses recollection to solve the dilemma is not the same as whether he takes the dilemma seriously. It might be that, although recollection is not intended to be its solution, he still thought the problem serious (whatever Meno's motives for introducing it). Although I consider this very unlikely, I shall leave the question open, and instead continue to focus on finding an epistemological problem commensurate with recollection.[11]

THE PROBLEM OF DISCOVERY

The suggestion that Socrates is really concerned with a problem of discovery rather than inquiry should put us in mind of the second half of Meno's challenge, which Socrates omitted in formulating the eristic dilemma:

(M²) Or even if you really stumble upon it, how will you know that this is the thing you didn't know before? (80d7–8)

Above, I interpreted this as following on closely from M¹: if you are in a total blank about the specification of the object of your inquiry (y), you cannot match it up to anything you might propose as an answer (x); for you cannot even make sense of the statement 'x is y'. Put like this, the problem can be dealt with in the same way as M¹, by distinguishing between the partial grasp of an object, sufficient to act as a specification, and full knowledge about it.

But M² is capable of a deeper interpretation. Suppose that you do have an initial specification of the object. This allows you to start the inquiry. When you propose a candidate answer, you test it against the specification to see if the two match each other. (Again, we no longer have a problem about making sense of the statement 'x is y'.) But this means that the assumptions included in the specification play a crucial role in determining the direction and outcome of the inquiry; they constitute its premises. Yet, unless you already know that the specification is correct, how can you know that this proposed answer is the right one, even if it happens to be?

This problem, which I shall call the 'the problem of discovery', can also be stated in terms of true belief and knowledge. Someone might launch a definitional inquiry with true beliefs about the object in question; it is also possible that they might find the right answer. Nevertheless, it might

---

to start an inquiry or understand the problem; rather, the demonstration is about discovering the solution.

[11] Irwin (1977: 139–40) argues that the dilemma is to be taken seriously and that the distinction between knowledge and true belief is intended as its solution.

be said, all they can claim is that this answer matches their *beliefs* about
virtue. But why should this amount to *knowing* that the definition is true
of virtue? This new problem applies to the context of the *Meno* in a way
that the other reading of M² does not. For Socrates and Meno may well
have some true beliefs about virtue from the very outset; they may have
gathered others in the course of discussing the first three definitions. All
of these they can use to decide between future candidate definitions. Even
so, it may be claimed, they will never get knowledge of what virtue is: they
will always be trapped within a circle of belief. Thus, while the distinction
between true belief and knowledge can be used to solve the eristic dilemma,
the same distinction merely helps to bring the problem of discovery into
sharper focus.

It is very likely that the problem owes its ancestry to the philosopher
Xenophanes, whose own words are strikingly similar to those of *Meno*
80d7–8:

No man knows, or ever will know, the truth about the gods and about everything
I speak of; for even if one chanced to say the complete truth, yet oneself know it
not, but seeming rules over all.[12]

The problem might also be seen as an epistemological application of the
Parmenidean claim that 'what is' cannot derive from 'what is not': knowledge can only come from pre-existent knowledge.[13] What is distinctive
about the problem is its underlying assumption that discovery or learning
is a process of realising that one thing matches something that one already
knows.

The foreknowledge principle

My claim is that Socrates takes the problem of discovery seriously. One reason he does so is that he shares the assumption that knowledge must derive
from pre-existent knowledge, the 'foreknowledge principle' as I shall call it.
To find this assumption at its most explicit, we have to jump ahead briefly
to a passage that comes towards the end of the slave boy demonstration.
At the end of the session, the boy has found the solution to the geometrical problem. Socrates insists that he only has true belief, but claims that
he will end up with knowledge if the process of questioning is continued

---

[12] Sextus *M.* VII 49 (DK 21 B34), trans. Kirk, Raven and Schofield 1983: 179, modified.
[13] Parmenides DK 28 B8, ll. 7–8. Aristotle begins the *Posterior Analytics* with the announcement, 'all intellectual teaching and learning derive from pre-existent knowledge' (71a1–2; cf. II 19, 99b28–30). The fact that he opens the work with this claim suggests he takes it to be obvious and widely held.

(85c9–d1). Projecting into the future, he imagines the boy to have achieved this knowledge and argues as follows (85d3–10):

(a) So without anyone having taught him, but only by being asked questions, he will recover for himself the knowledge within him?

(b) And recovering knowledge for oneself that is in oneself – is this not recollection?

(c) So the knowledge, which he has now, he either acquired at some point or else always possessed.

The ensuing argument (85d12–86a10) attempts to decide between these two possibilities. But either way, Socrates has already betrayed allegiance to the foreknowledge principle, as is evident at three points. First, in (a) he assumes that, if the boy attains conscious knowledge of geometry in the future, the knowledge will already have been in him waiting to be recovered – or recollected, as he infers in (b). Second, in (c) he talks of the knowledge the boy 'has now', which shows he has assumed that, if the boy has knowledge waiting to be recovered at some point in the future, that knowledge must pre-exist and be present in him now.[14] Third, in the same sentence, he goes on to assume that the latent knowledge the boy has now must have pre-existed the present time as well: if he has it now, 'he either acquired it at some time or else always had it'. Ultimately, Socrates concludes that any act of learning must be explained by the existence of conscious knowledge in a previous life. My concern at this point is not to assess the merits of this argument but to show that, when it comes to explaining how the boy will come to know about geometry, Socrates takes it for granted that knowledge must derive from pre-existent knowledge.[15]

The priority of definition

Because he shares the foreknowledge principle, we can begin to see why he should take the problem of discovery seriously. Even so, it could be objected, he might still be able to shrug it off. Taken literally, the problem requires that the initial specification consist in knowledge of the very thing being sought. But instead of having to know what virtue is in the sense of knowing the actual definition, one might only need to know that certain

---

[14] On this sentence see further below, pp. 109–12.

[15] For another application of the foreknowledge principle, see 79d1–4. Recalling the dialectical requirement, Socrates stipulates that one cannot explain anything by appeal to what is 'not yet agreed and still under investigation', i.e. there must be no unresolved questions concerning the items that are to figure in the definition. Thus, if one is to define X by reference to a, b and c, one must already have acquired knowledge of a, b and c. See also above p. 35 n. 6.

things count as instances of virtue, allowing one to specify virtue as the property that all these instances share. One might also know some of the attributes of virtue. Such pieces of knowledge might be enough to help check any proposed candidate. None of this appears inconsistent with the foreknowledge principle.

However, the suggestion that one might know something connected with virtue without knowing the definition needs to be set against the possibility that Socrates endorses a broad principle of the priority of definition in the *Meno*: unless we know the definition of virtue, we cannot know anything else about it. If he does indeed endorse this principle, which I shall abbreviate to 'PD', the problem starts to look more threatening to him, for none of the claims included in our specification can count as knowledge.

Does Socrates assume the priority of definition in the *Meno*? We encountered a narrower version of the principle at the beginning of the dialogue: you cannot know what something is like without knowing what it is (71b3–4).[16] As this concerns the priority of definition over (non-essential) attributes, I shall call it 'PDA' for short. I also raised the question of whether the priority of definition extends more broadly. In the context of other dialogues, commentators often debate whether Socrates applies the priority of definition to instances of a form. Such a principle, which I shall call 'PDI', amounts to the claim that, if one fails to know what *F*-ness is, one fails to know if something is an instance of *F*-ness.[17] For example, commentators on the *Euthyphro* have disputed whether Socrates commits himself to the claim that we need to know the definition of piety to know whether or not any action is pious.[18]

Is Socrates in the *Meno* committed to PDI as well as PDA? If he were only committed to PDA, he would allow us to know instances of virtue without the definition; such knowledge could be used to guide us towards the definition. So the reply just given to the problem of discovery would still hold. It has to be admitted that, unlike PDA, there is no explicit statement of PDI in the *Meno*. In fact, Socrates has little to say about instances. What he does discuss is the distinction between virtue itself and its species or 'parts', especially in the examination of the second and third definitions.[19]

Nevertheless, there is good reason for attributing PDI to the *Meno*. Suppose for a moment that we could have knowledge of instances without the

---

[16] See p. 20 above.
[17] For the distinction between PDA and PDI, see Robinson 1953: 50–1, Santas 1979: 118–26, Benson 1990: 19–20 n. 1, and Vlastos 1994: 69 and 78.
[18] See p. 22 above, n. 32.
[19] See 72a6–d1, 73e1–74a10, and 78d7–79c9. This does at least show that he espouses a third species of PD: the priority of knowing the definition over knowing the parts of virtue.

definition. What kind of knowledge would this be? Presumably, it would be some sort of non-apodeictic knowledge. Commentators on other dialogues have indeed ascribed such a type of knowledge to Socrates. But, as we have seen (p. 20 above), this will not do for the *Meno*, which recognises only one type of knowledge: understanding that requires explanatory reasoning (98a3–4). Thus, if someone knows that a particular (e.g. action) is virtuous, they would have to be able to give the explanation for this. The explanation in question, I would argue, has to be the form of virtue. For at 72c7–8, talking of the relation between virtue and specific types of virtue, Socrates says:

> . . . even if they [sc. the specific types of virtue] are many and various, they all have the same single form *because of which* (δι᾽ ὅ) they are virtues . . .
>
> (emphasis added)

Virtue as a genus explains why the specific types are virtues. Although this is explicitly concerned with the relation between the form virtue and its types, rather than particular instances, it is plausible that the explanation for a particular being *F* is also the form that it possesses: it is difficult to see what else could be the explanation. So, to know that a particular is *F*, one would have to have knowledge of the form, expressed in the definition. For this reason, it is plausible to attribute PDI as well as PDA to the *Meno*.

So if Socrates in the *Meno* espouses both the foreknowledge principle and the priority of definition, he seems to have boxed himself into a corner where definitional discovery is concerned. There is, apparently, no pre-existent knowledge to fall back upon – except knowledge of the definition itself. But then one will not be discovering anything, as one already knows the object of inquiry. This, of course, cues the appearance of recollection, a theory that allows us to make sense of the extraordinary claim that we can 'discover' something that we already know, so long as we have forgotten it. Equipped with this solution, he concedes that in a definitional inquiry we have to begin with mere belief – at the conscious level. But latently there already exists within us knowledge that was once explicit. It is in virtue of this knowledge, as it gradually comes to the surface, that we are able ultimately to know that the answer we have hit upon is the right one.

SOCRATES ON TRIAL (III)

At the beginning of this section, I mentioned that there has been considerable disagreement about 'Meno's paradox', both about the problem itself and Meno's attitude in raising it. In retrospect, this is not so surprising: the text does after all send out conflicting signals. Socrates appears to dismiss

Meno's puzzle as eristic, just as he is about to propound a theory that he takes very seriously, both here and in other dialogues.

My strategy for dealing with these conflicting signals has been to read the passage on two levels.[20] When Meno issues his challenge, Socrates does indeed treat him as trying to conjure up a puzzle for contentious purposes, and responds by engaging with him on his own terms. By accusing him of being 'eristic', Socrates is implying that his concern is less with epistemology than with finding a successful debating tactic. So he does not attempt to disarm the eristic dilemma, but rather grapples with the psychological source of the problem, Meno's unwillingness to engage in active inquiry.

All this sounds like grist to the mill of those who downplay this whole section as bad behaviour on Meno's part. But there is another level. In spite of himself, Meno has stumbled upon a problem of real importance in M^2, even though he has only a fleeting grasp of it: this is why he fails to protest when Socrates ignores the reference to discovery in reformulating the original challenge into the eristic dilemma. Highlighting this deeper problem allows us to make sense of Socrates' undoubted seriousness in propounding the theory of recollection.

There is an obvious irony here in the way that Meno stumbles upon the problem of discovery without appreciating its real significance. Just as one might hit upon the answer to an inquiry without knowing it, Meno has stumbled upon a serious epistemological challenge. We could also say that he has hit upon a true belief about the difficulty of discovery, but almost immediately let it slip again like a runaway slave (cf. 97e3–4). He speaks without understanding what he says, like the soothsayers mentioned at the end of the dialogue (99d4–5).

The fact that this passage operates on two levels makes it an obvious candidate to be seen as another episode of Socrates on trial. To an extent this claim is uncontroversial, as other commentators have suggested that in the passage Plato uses the dialogue to raise a serious challenge to assumptions made by the historical Socrates.[21] Yet, as soon as one tries to establish exactly which of his views is being challenged, one quickly runs into serious controversy.

In the first two episodes of Socrates on trial, the Socrates of the dialogue espouses a particular position (respectively, the unity of definition and the

---

[20] In Scott 1991 I argued that Socrates does not take the eristic dilemma seriously, except as being symptomatic of Meno's laziness. In Scott 1995 I argued that there is a deeper epistemological problem in the *Meno*, commensurate with recollection: a problem of discovery, as distinct from one of inquiry. My current position combines the essentials of both views. I am grateful to Weiss 2001: 60–1 and Tad Brennan (in discussion) for helping me to see how to do so.

[21] See e.g. Phillips 1948: 88–90, Bluck 1961: 8 and Vlastos 1994: 78 (cf. also 28–9).

benefits of the elenchus), which is then subjected to challenge. In each case it was relatively easy to show that the historical Socrates also held the same view as his counterpart in the *Meno*. The present case, however, is not as straightforward. For one thing, the Socrates of the dialogue holds a complex position: he thinks that discovery is possible and that we have a duty to inquire; he also espouses two epistemological principles, the priority of definition and the foreknowledge principle that, taken together, conflict with his belief in the possibility of discovery; this in turn can be used to undermine his belief in the duty to inquire.

But what position, if any, did the historical Socrates take on these issues? There is a famous controversy about his stance on the priority of definition, and determining his views on the possibility of discovery is no less easy. Depending on where one stands on these issues, one will give different versions of the thesis that the historical Socrates is on philosophical trial in this section of the *Meno*.

One thing of which we can be sure is that the historical Socrates believed in our duty to inquire. This is clear from his famous assertion, 'the unexamined life is not worth living' (*Apology* 38a5–6). The *Euthyphro* and the *Laches* also stress the need to inquire, even though the sheer difficulty of acquiring knowledge makes the interlocutors inclined to give up. Laches, for instance, finds himself struggling to give a definition of courage: he has tried 'standing fast in battle' and 'endurance', and both have been refuted. At 194a1–c3, sensing that he wishes to give up, Socrates enjoins him to endure and search courageously for the definition, storm-tossed though they are by the argument (194c2; cf. 191d4). They are not to give up the hunt or slacken off (ἀνιέναι: 194b6); to do so would be tantamount to a moral failing. Similarly, at the end of the *Euthyphro*, Socrates is determined to press on and inquire into the nature of piety, even though Euthyphro is flagging:

So we have to examine the nature of piety again, right from the beginning, for I shan't willingly give up (ἀποδειλιάσω) until I learn this. (15c11–12)

The Socrates of the *Meno* makes exactly the same demand on his interlocutor, insisting on the duty to inquire and accusing intellectual stragglers of moral weakness.[22] To this extent, at least, there can be no doubt that the dialogue recalls a distinctively Socratic attitude.

---

[22] 81d5–e1 and 86b8–9. At 79e5, Socrates asks Meno to start all over again 'from the beginning' (ἐξ ἀρχῆς) and give another definition, just as he does with Euthyphro at 11b2 and 15c11. He makes the same kind of demand (using the same phrase) with a weary Protagoras at *Prot.* 333d3 (cf. 349a7). See also *Charmides* 163d7 and 167b1 and *Laches* 198a1.

But the *Meno* also targets the possibility of discovery. Indeed it is because this is under attack that the duty to inquire is challenged. Yet whether the historical Socrates actually believed in such a possibility is a matter of controversy. On one hand, we might think that Socrates would not have spent his life engaged in moral inquiry if he thought knowledge impossible to attain. Also, the passage just quoted from the ending of the *Euthyphro* (15c11–12) could be interpreted as the words of someone who thought knowledge attainable, if only with difficulty.[23] On the other hand, Socrates nowhere says outright that knowledge is attainable, and in the *Apology* makes some remarks that have been taken to imply the contrary. Knowledge of virtue would constitute 'divine wisdom'; all he has, and all anyone has ever had, is mere 'human wisdom' – the awareness that one does not have divine wisdom (cf. 20d6–e3 and 23a5–b4). Some have taken this to mean that one cannot attain to divine wisdom: the point of calling it divine is that it is beyond human reach.[24]

Unfortunately, there seems to be no evidence to clinch the issue. I can find no text to show conclusively that Socrates thought knowledge attainable; and, while he does say in the *Apology* that no one actually has divine wisdom, he does not actually deny that humans might acquire it, or say that it would be impious to make the attempt.

It is also extremely difficult to determine the historical Socrates' position on the two principles that are needed to create the problem of discovery in the *Meno* – the priority of definition and the foreknowledge principle. In the first case, we walk straight into a well-known scholarly minefield.[25] It is no less easy to determine whether he espoused the foreknowledge principle, although the issue has not received any great attention in the literature. (I argue on pp. 141–2 below, however, that he probably did espouse the principle in the specific case of knowing what something is before inquiring how it is acquired.)

It is possible that the historical Socrates believed all the claims that Plato attributes to his counterpart in the dialogue. However, if this can be shown,

---

[23] See also *Laches* 201a2–7 and Benson 2000: 180–5.
[24] See Vlastos 1994: 62–3 and Weiss 2001: e.g. 8–9. The debate over whether Socrates thought knowledge attainable is complicated by the fact that several commentators attribute to him a distinction between different forms of knowledge. Taking this into account, we should express the point at issue by asking whether knowledge in a 'strong' sense, e.g. certain knowledge, is attainable. See above p. 20 n. 26.
[25] The most detailed case for attributing the priority of definition to the historical Socrates can be found in Benson 1990 and 2000: 112–41. I find his arguments very persuasive, though even he admits that there is no single text that compels us to accept his view – 'no such smoking gun is to be found', as he concludes in 2000: 141. For other contributions to this long-standing debate see above p. 22 n. 32.

it would take a monograph in itself to do so. Alternatively, we might say that he thought knowledge attainable, but had not articulated the priority of definition or the foreknowledge assumption. It was Plato who came to adopt them, and so to question Socrates' confidence that discovery is possible. But even this weaker position would require an extensive digression from the main purposes of this book. Instead, I shall rest content with a position of which we can be confident: the historical Socrates believed adamantly in our duty to inquire, and it is at least for this claim that Plato is putting him on philosophical trial in the *Meno*.[26]

---

[26] If this is in fact all that Socrates believed, Plato's criticism in the *Meno* is to a large degree 'external': he takes a claim of the historical Socrates about the duty to inquire and only renders it problematic by adding in further claims, which the historical Socrates never endorsed. See Irwin 1995: 373–4 n. 44.

CHAPTER 8

The emergence of recollection: 81a–e

THE RELIGIOUS BACKGROUND

When Socrates proposes to reveal a doctrine (*logos*) that he has heard from various religious sources, Meno is agog: what is this *logos* and who originated it? The doctrine, Socrates replies, comes from priests, priestesses and divinely inspired poets:

They say that the human soul is immortal, and sometimes it comes to an end – which they call 'dying' – and sometimes it is re-born, but it never perishes. Because of this, one must lead one's life as piously as possible. For those

> *from whom Persephone accepts requital for ancient wrong* [or: *grief*]
> *Their souls she sends back to the sun above in the ninth year.*
> *From these grow noble kings and men swift in strength and greatest in wisdom.*
> *For the rest of time men call them sacred heroes.*   (81b3–c4)

First, we need to make some sense of these extremely allusive lines. Socrates starts by making two claims – that the soul is immortal and is subject to reincarnation – and from these he derives the injunction to live as piously as possible, something that the verses are supposed to explain (cf. γάρ 81b7). The point seems to be that, because of some ancient wrong (perhaps committed against Persephone herself), our penalty is to pass through a series of incarnations. If in the course of them we act piously, Persephone may be satisfied and reward us. This would be done after a fixed period of time spent in the underworld, viz. nine years. At this point our souls would be sent upwards (i.e. from Hades) to the sunlight where our reward would come in two phases: first an earthly but happy existence as a king, an athlete or a sage; thereafter we would attain the status of heroes for the rest of time.

One point of detail about the first quoted line of the poem: what is Persephone accepting requital for? It could be an ancient sin,[1] or some grief suffered long ago: the word *pentheos* is ambiguous between these two

---

[1] For this reading see Thompson 1901: 121.

possibilities. In the first case, Persephone is involved because she is charged with the punishment of crimes in the underworld. In the second, she has some more direct involvement – if, that is, the grief in question is her own. In an effort to explain what this grief might be, many scholars have found an allusion to the myth of the Titans. Persephone, who was the daughter of Zeus, had a child called Zagreus or Dionysus, to whom Zeus intended to bequeath his power. But the Titans lured the child away and devoured him. Athena saved his heart and a new Dionysus was born. In punishment, Zeus struck the Titans with lightning, but mankind came to be born out of their ashes. The Titans' crime is the 'ancient grief' for which Persephone demands requital.[2]

Either way, we are faced with a further question: what is the relevance of all this to recollection? At 81b3–7, Socrates asserts that, because we are immortal and subject to reincarnation, we shall always have the opportunity to redeem ourselves. Now look ahead to a passage at the end of this whole section, just after Socrates has offered a proof of the immortality of the soul:

> If the truth of things is always in our soul, it should be immortal. So you should take heart and endeavour to seek out and recollect what at present you happen not to know (that is, what you do not remember). (86b1–4)

At 81b he inferred from immortality to the duty to live piously; here at 86b, he infers from immortality to the duty to recollect. A natural way of putting these texts together is to say that piety in some way requires or involves recollection. By recollecting, we shall enable ourselves to escape the cycle of incarnation and achieve the rewards mentioned at 81c1–4.

The idea that piety might require recollection could be grounded in the thesis that virtue is knowledge, for which Socrates will shortly be arguing at 87d–89a, just after the recollection episode (cf. also 77b–78b). If this is also in the background within 81a–86b, the link between recollection and piety is obvious: although the two are not identical (piety is a form of knowledge, while recollection is the process by which we recover knowledge), it is clear that recollection is necessary for achieving piety in the fullest sense.[3]

That recollection has an important religious dimension is particularly clear in the *Phaedrus*, which provides a useful parallel to the *Meno*. Here the interdependence of religion, epistemology and ethics is quite explicit. Having argued that the soul is immortal, Socrates goes on to discuss its

[2] On the background to this myth see West 1983: 164–6.
[3] The notion that philosophy has a religious dimension is implicit in the reference to initiation at 76e7–9. See also pp. 58 and 225.

nature in terms of an allegory, likening it to a winged charioteer drawn by two horses (246a–257a). At first the soul is described in a discarnate state, following a procession with the gods to catch a glimpse of the forms. If a soul does not have an adequate view of the forms, it loses its wings, and falls to earth to be imprisoned in a human body. Thereafter it goes through a cycle of incarnations, human and animal, but can only return to its discarnate state by living philosophically and engaging in recollection. (Recollection of the forms enables the wings, its means of release, to re-grow.) In other words, recollection is the process of expiation that ultimately releases us from the cycle of incarnation.

Of course there are many differences between the *Meno* and the *Phaedrus*: quite apart from differences of eschatological detail, the later dialogue assumes the existence of transcendent forms, entities separate from the world of physical particulars, a commitment absent from the *Meno*. Also, the *Phaedrus* identifies contemplation of forms for its own sake with the good life, a life loved by the gods. In the *Meno*, on the other hand, the theory of transcendent forms is lacking, as is any trace of the contemplative ideal of happiness. Nevertheless, these differences should not obscure the point that the *Meno* adumbrates the same sort of approach as we find in the *Phaedrus*, suggesting a similar interconnection of themes. In both works, recollection is intimately connected to pious living, and hence to the idea of earning one's expiation during the course of successive incarnations.

In the light of all this, we can see that Socrates' purposes in introducing the theory of recollection in the *Meno* are multi-layered. In the previous section, I argued that he expects the theory to help solve the serious epistemological problem lurking behind Meno's challenge. At the same time, he hopes that the exotic details associated with the theory will intrigue his wayward interlocutor and lure him back into inquiry. However, this is not to deny the importance of the religious context of the theory: far from it. As Socrates draws Meno into the world of the priestly *logos*, he expects him to take the injunction to piety very seriously indeed.

SOCRATES' APPROPRIATION OF OLDER DOCTRINES: TWO FURTHER PUZZLES

Throughout this passage Socrates is self-consciously appropriating doctrines already in existence: reincarnation was espoused by the Pythagoreans, the Orphics and Empedocles – as well as Pindar, who is most probably the author of the verses quoted at 81b8–c4. Yet the notion that Socrates is appropriating other people's views raises complications. First, it may seem strange that it is now Socrates rather than Meno who is quoting from other people. But Plato is careful to distinguish Socrates' approach to appropriation from his interlocutor's. The sources mentioned at 81a10–b2 come divided into two groups, the first consisting of priests and priestesses who are concerned to 'give an account' of their practices, the second including 'Pindar and many other poets who are divine'. Presumably these two groups are discrete, the implication being that the poets do not give an account of their views, even though they may be true. This point anticipates the distinction between knowledge and true belief made at the end of the dialogue, where knowledge depends on reasoning out the explanation, which is close to the sense of 'giving an account', while those who have true belief at the end of the work are said to be divine, and include poets as well as soothsayers (cf. 81b1–2 with 99c11–d1). At 81a10–b1, Socrates is quite clear that, unlike the poets, the priests do not fall into this class. In the light of the ending of the work, we can infer that the priests rather than the poets are to be taken as Socrates' model.[4]

In fact, this point is already hinted at in the course of 81b–82b. As soon as Socrates alludes to a doctrine that he has heard from older sources, Meno (unsurprisingly) wants to know both what the doctrine is and who originated it. Socrates, on the other hand, insists that Meno must decide for himself whether the doctrine is true (81b2–3). This theme continues after the initial sketch of recollection. When Meno asks Socrates to teach him about recollection, Socrates refuses, and instead proposes to give a demonstration of the theory (81e3–82b2). This turns out to involve an extended question-and-answer session based on the interview with the slave. Throughout, Meno, like his slave, is only to answer what he himself thinks true. Thus, although Socrates begins this whole section in quotation mode, he does so without reneging on the epistemological stance adopted in the rest of the dialogue. The idea of recollection was originally derived from other sources, but it is something that Socrates in the dialogue intends to make very much his own.

This raises the further difficulty of deciding which aspects of the older doctrines he will keep and which he will discard. One passage where this

---

[4] Socrates' reference to giving a *logos* (81a11–b1) for what he is about to tell Meno tells strongly against Weiss' assertion in 2001: 64 n. 37: 'by having Socrates cite priests and priestesses as his source, Plato emphasises the doctrine's extrarational character and indicates thereby the improbability that Socrates endorses it'.

question is particularly pressing is the point where recollection is first described, especially the sentence at 81c5–7:

Since the soul is immortal and has been born many times, and has seen both what is here and in Hades – all things, in fact – there is nothing that it hasn't learnt.

Prima facie, this point seems very straightforward, especially if one reads it in the light of the preceding passage: the soul has had many incarnations and at least one spell in Hades. As a result, it has acquired a great deal of experience, which it is able to recollect in future incarnations. But in saying this, has Socrates yet moved on to his own version of recollection, or is he still reporting the views of others?

Although the first is possible grammatically,[5] on philosophical grounds, we should be inclined to the latter. There are two issues here, both arising from the phrase 'there is nothing that it has not learnt' (81c7).

The first is one of scope. Given what has preceded, the phrase is most likely a reference to the soul's experience of particular events, both when incarnate and when in Hades. Thus things learnt by sense experience will fall under the scope of recollection. This is what Pythagoras seems to have believed, claiming to remember particular experiences from previous lives.[6] Yet it is usually thought that Plato's theory of recollection dispenses with this,[7] and makes the objects of recollection abstract: mathematical theorems, definitions, perhaps general concepts, but not particular events that were once perceived. Certainly, Socrates in the *Meno* makes no use of the idea that one might recollect particular experiences from a previous life. (At *Phaedo* 81c8–82c8, he does allow that individual character traits might persist from one incarnation to another, though this is different from talking about memories of particular experiences.) For all we know, Plato himself did believe in the possibility. The point is merely that he gives it no part to play in the argument of the *Meno*. So if 81c7 is to be read as referring to the soul's memories of particular events, there is no reason to see this as a view actually endorsed in the *Meno* either by Plato or by the character Socrates. At this stage, we are still hearing the views of the priests and priestesses as they are reported to us.

A second problem about 81c5–9 is that Socrates talks of the soul 'having learnt' as a result of its worldly and underwordly experiences. From what he goes on to say, this includes the soul having learnt about virtue (c8). But did it *learn* about virtue in an earthly existence? If so, the epistemological

---

[5] After 81c5 he no longer uses the accusative and infinitive.   [6] Diogenes Laërtius VIII 4–5.
[7] For a representative statement see Bluck 1961: 9–10 and Brown 1991: 606–7.

case for introducing recollection is immediately undermined: if the soul could learn about virtue before, it can do so now.

Here it is very important to look ahead to a passage at the end of the whole section, where, instead of assuming the immortality of the soul, as he does here, he argues for it (85d9–86b2). In doing so, he rejects the view that the soul ever actually acquired its knowledge. True, he starts the argument with this idea as an option, but eventually rejects it in favour of the idea that the soul was always in a state of knowing.

The truth of the matter is that the initial statement of recollection represents a process of transition for Socrates. There are some elements that he will discard, or at least fail to endorse, and others that will be central to his argument. That the soul can recollect about virtue (81c8) is obviously crucial to him, given the wider context. The same can be said for the following sentence:

Since all nature is akin, and the soul has learnt everything, nothing prevents someone from recollecting just one thing (which people call 'learning') and so discovering everything else . . . (81c9–d3)

Although this picks up an older idea,[8] it also introduces a significant epistemological theme, viz. that the recollection of one proposition creates an associative link that leads to the next. This will be picked up when Socrates insists that the boy recollects sequentially (82e12), which will be crucial for understanding what exactly the whole demonstration is trying to prove. Also, the account of knowledge sketched at the end of the dialogue suggests a view of knowledge as a systematic whole, in which the parts cannot be understood in isolation from each other (98a1–4).

Of course, all this is to anticipate; my point is merely to show that, although Socrates has started within the framework of his predecessors, he is already weaving in his own interests at 81c–d.

---

[8] At least, the Pythagoreans believed that all creatures were akin. See DK 14 8a.

CHAPTER 9

The argument for recollection: 82b–85d

OVERVIEW

To give a demonstration of his theory, Socrates questions a slave boy on a geometrical problem. The boy speaks Greek but, as Meno confirms later on, has never been taught geometry. Throughout, Socrates insists that he is merely asking questions and not teaching the boy, i.e. telling him what to think. So when the boy eventually gives the right answer, we are meant to conclude that he did not learn it from any source outside of himself.

Socrates starts the examination by drawing a square with two-foot sides in the sand and, after establishing that its area is four-feet, asks the boy to determine the side of the square whose area is double. The examination then falls into three stages. In the first, the boy confidently gives an answer, which he soon realises to be mistaken; in the second he gives another answer, also wrong, and eventually admits his ignorance; in the third, he moves towards the correct answer.

Although most of the passage is a dialogue between the slave boy and Socrates, Meno is also involved. At crucial points Socrates turns to him to ask about the progress the boy is making. This means that there are two dialogues: one about geometry between Socrates and the slave, and a meta-dialogue between Socrates and Meno about what is happening in the first dialogue. The table below shows the main divisions in the geometrical dialogue and the points at which it is interrupted by the meta-dialogue:

SOCRATES AND BOY	SOCRATES AND MENO
82b–e	
Q. If a square with sides of 2ft has an area of 4 ft² what would be the length of the sides of a square with an area of 8 ft²?	
A. 4 ft.	
	82e–83a: the slave boy thinks he knows the answer but in fact he doesn't.

83a–e
Q. If the area of a square with 4 ft sides
is 16 ft², and the area of a square with
2 ft sides is 4 ft², what length of sides
would a square of 8 ft² area have?
A. 3 ft.
Q. But wouldn't that give an area of
9 ft²?
A. It seems so.

83e–84d: now he is aware of his
ignorance

84d–85c
Solution of problem:
ABCD is a square whose sides are 2 ft
and whose area is 4 ft². Area of BDEF
is double that of ABCD; so its area is
8 ft²; so the diagonal BD is the length
of the 8 ft² area.

85d: the correct answers must have
been in him all along.

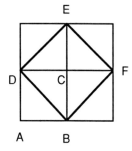

From the way in which the whole episode is introduced at 81e3–82b2, we can
infer that its primary purpose is to support the theory of recollection. We
might therefore expect the meta-dialogue to be concerned exclusively with
showing Meno how far each stage of the slave-boy examination has supported the theory. But the demonstration also plays another role: Socrates is
intent on reforming Meno's intellectual character – or at least changing his
attitude to inquiry and to the benefits of the elenchus. This is very clear in
the first two stages of the meta-dialogue, where Socrates deliberately brings
out the parallels between the slave boy's performance and that of Meno
himself in the first part of the work. In the first aside, Socrates remarks to
Meno that the boy thinks he knows the answer when he does not (82e4–13),

and in the second he goes out of his way to show Meno the benefit that the stingray is doing to the boy (84a3–c9).

This is the second point where Socrates constructs a dialogue within the main dialogue to make Meno reflect on his own failings from the outside. The first was the imaginary conversation about definition at 74b4–75a8 (see pp. 32–4 above); the third will be the argument with Anytus. Seen in this light, the function of the slave-boy demonstration, at least in the first two stages of the meta-dialogue, is to provide a direct reply to Meno's stingray speech.[1]

It is only in the third part of the meta-dialogue that Socrates argues directly for the recollection thesis (85b8ff.). For the time being, I shall concentrate on this argument. Later on, when we come to the Anytus episode, (pp. 169–73), I shall return to Socrates' technique of using a dialogue within the main dialogue and look at all three instances side by side.

Socrates' argument in the third part of the meta-dialogue can be broken down into three phases. First, he aims to show that the answers, which so far constitute true belief rather than knowledge, were the boy's own (85b8–c8). Then he argues that, if the boy is subjected to continued questioning, he will attain knowledge and that in doing so will be extracting latent knowledge already in him (85c9–d10). Finally, he goes on to ask about the origin of this latent knowledge, and eventually concludes that the soul contains 'the truth of all things' within it for all time and so is immortal (85d12–86b2).

THE BOY ANSWERS FOR HIMSELF

Socrates' argument

soc. What do you think, Meno? Is there any belief that he hasn't answered for himself?

men. No – only for himself.

soc. And yet he did not know, as we said a little while ago.

men. That's true.

soc. But these beliefs were in him, weren't they?

men. Yes.

(85b8–c5)

Socrates claims only to be asking questions, without giving away the answers. If the boy nevertheless manages to arrive at the correct answers, they must have come from somewhere. We know they were never taught to him during his lifetime, so they must have been in him all along. This, on

---

[1] See above, pp. 71–2.

the face of it, is Socrates' argument. As such, however, it raises a notorious objection. The vast majority of his questions already contain the correct answer. They take the form, 'such and such is true, is it not?'. Although there are a few occasions where he asks an open question these, one might argue, have little significance: on two of them the slave gives wrong answers (82e2–3 and 83e2), on another he replies 'I don't know' (85a4–5), and on the rest Socrates is merely asking him to perform a very simple multiplication. The objection is simply that Socrates is feeding the boy the answers, the very thing he so emphatically denies.

There is a more subtle interpretation. A vital clue can be found in the first stage of the meta-dialogue where Socrates announces that one should recollect 'in sequence' (82e12–13). This, together with the mathematical context, should put us in mind of the notion of following a proof, which in turn helps to clarify the contrast Socrates draws between merely asking questions and teaching. He uses the term 'teaching' in this passage to denote the transmission of information. In a simple case, we can imagine Gorgias telling Meno p and, as a result, Meno believing p. But take a more complicated case, where Gorgias tells Meno p, q and r, which are in fact three steps in a proof. Gorgias also tells Meno that p implies q, and that q implies r. As Meno believes everything he has been told, Gorgias has now succeeded in transmitting five beliefs to him.

Although Meno now has these five beliefs, he has not followed the proof for himself.[2] He does not believe q because p, nor r because q. Each proposition is grasped atomistically. There is a clear distinction between accepting propositions in this way and 'perceiving the logical relationships' between them.[3] We might say (intuitively) that Meno has not yet 'seen' the truth of each proposition for himself; he has not felt that internal click of understanding that distinguishes someone who has followed the proof from someone who has not. The point can also be put in terms of logical necessity. Someone who follows a proof realises at each stage that only one answer can follow. In contrast to the transmission case, they would be utterly surprised if someone informed them that another proposition followed instead. In this way, they are cognitively independent of the other party.[4] One person who helped to clarify this point was Augustine, who claimed that, far from taking the questioner's words on trust and treating

---

[2] Anscombe 1979: 151–2. See also Nehamas 1985: 28–9.   [3] Cf. Vlastos 1965: 157.

[4] Arguably, this is part of what attracted Plato to the theory of recollection. Here too the notion of inevitability is crucial. On recollecting one thing, one is led by association to the next step (cf. 81c9–d3). In other words, the attraction of recollection is that, via the notion of association, it highlights the movement from one proposition to another that is a hallmark of proof. The disadvantage is that it appears to assimilate subjective or psychological necessity (i.e. association) with the perception of objective necessity (logical entailment).

him as the authority, the learner is himself independently assessing each of the suggestions contained in the questions and reaching his own verdict on them. The authority lies with the learner; he acts as the judge.[5]

What is the role of the questioner in this process? Obviously they prompt us to see for ourselves each step in the proof. The reason it is essential for them to ask their questions in the right order is that they need to place the learner in the right position, as it were, to perceive each successive logical relationship. But they do not, and indeed cannot, instil by transmission the perception itself. By analogy, think of the difference between transmitting by hearsay an empirical belief to someone, and their seeing the event for themselves. In the latter case, they may still need a guide, but only in order to be given the opportunity to see for themselves.

In my view, this is the most plausible account of Socrates' interaction with the slave boy. It explains why, despite so many 'leading' questions, he can still deny that he is teaching the boy, i.e. instilling information in him, and that the boy is making a substantial contribution from his own resources.

Yet the original objection might return in a modified form. According to Vlastos, the slave-boy demonstration provides the data that makes up the ostensible evidence for the theory of recollection.[6] We have just shown that the data can be interpreted in such a way as to favour the theory. Nevertheless, we have not ruled out the other interpretation – that the boy is merely parroting the answers from Socrates. As yet, both interpretations are possible, and the theory is underdetermined by the data. So, while the original objection asserted that the data can only be interpreted in one way, the modified objection tries to manoeuvre us into an agnostic position as between two interpretations: the slave-boy demonstration still cannot be used to support the theory.

Vlastos, however, insists that we can eliminate the 'parrot' interpretation altogether. Socrates tells the boy 'answer just as you think' (83d2) and also plants two booby-traps (82e1–3 and 83d4–e1)

. . . which teach him that he cannot rely on Socrates to make the right suggestions to him: he cannot adopt towards Socrates the attitude an inexperienced mountain-climber can and does adopt towards an experienced guide. If the climber sees or guesses that his guide wants him to take a certain path, he is entitled to use this as good evidence of its being the right path. By misleading him badly a couple of times, Socrates makes the boy realize that he is not entitled to the same assumption.[7]

What Vlastos does here is to press the text for additional data, revealing details of the slave boy's attitude to Socrates; he then uses that data to rule out the parrot interpretation. But, tempting though this strategy is, it risks losing sight of a fundamental point: as far as we know, this experiment never took place. If it had, and if Plato had been writing as faithful a report as he could, it would be worth pursuing Vlastos' strategy. But this passage is just a fiction and should not be treated as if it were an experiment being written up in a scientific paper.

So what can a fictional experiment ever show? Consider the following parallel. In his novel, *Lord of the Flies*, William Golding imagined a group of young teenage boys deserted on an island in the Pacific with no adult supervision. In the end most of them turn into savages. The moral of the story, perhaps, is that human nature is civilised only on the surface, and it takes relatively little to bring out the darker side. Now, if a critic were to say, 'But this never actually happened, so the moral is worthless,' we might be inclined to accuse him of missing the point. But why do we take the moral of this fictional situation seriously? Presumably because it helps us to crystallise views that we already hold on the basis of our own experience, views supported on non-fictional grounds.

Similarly, the real point of the demonstration is illustrative. It draws our attention to the distinction between forming a belief by hearsay and thinking for oneself. We can hardly deny that some people do some of the time follow a proof for themselves (whatever we may say about the slave boy). We are familiar with this from our own learning of geometry when we were at the same stage as the slave boy. Also, Plato's own readers may well have been engaged in discovering new geometrical proofs that no one had ever taught them. Such readers will be vividly aware of what it is like to follow a proof, and the effect of reading the demonstration will be to ask oneself how this is possible. If Plato is right that such insight cannot be instilled by testimony, his argument has at least got off the ground. In other words, the experiment, though only fictional, certainly chimes in with our own cognitive experience. It reminds us of something that we already know.

Recollection, sense perception and a priori knowledge

Before we go on to see how Socrates uses the slave-boy demonstration to support recollection, it is worth pausing for a moment to view his argument in a wider historical context. Readers of the passage often assume that it is concerned with the problem of *a priori* knowledge.[8] Indeed some may even be tempted to hail the passage as the point where the issue of

---

[8] See e.g. Calvert 1974: 148, Moravscik 1978 *passim*, Wilkes 1979: 146–7 and 152, Bostock 1986: 114 and Day 1994: 22. For a cautionary remark on this topic see White 1974: 305 n. 29.

a priori knowledge is introduced into Western philosophy. But in the light of the interpretation just given, we should be cautious. Nowhere in the recollection passage does Socrates allude to sense perception or discuss its shortcomings. For this reason, the tendency to see him as concerned with the problem of *a priori* knowledge is misleading, if only on terminological grounds. For although there is much room for debate as to exactly how to define the notion of *a priori* knowledge, a typical opening move is to characterise it as knowledge whose justification is independent of sense perception.[9] But throughout the passage, Socrates discusses the possibility of knowledge whose justification is independent of testimony, not sense experience. Occasionally philosophers may talk of the *a priori* in terms of testimony, and in this sense, it is right to apply the term to the *Meno*. But this is an unusual sense.

To clarify the point, compare the following argument, which is derived from Leibniz's *New Essays on Human Understanding*. When we assert that $2 + 2 = 4$ we claim this as a necessary truth. It is to be contrasted with a generalisation from experience of the type 'all As are B': even if this proposition is true of all the cases we have met, it is only contingently so. According to Leibniz, experience alone can never justify a necessary truth: were we to rely on experience to show that $2 + 2 = 4$, we would establish only that all the 2s and 2s in our experience made 4.[10] My interpretation of the slave-boy demonstration has obvious affinities with this argument: allowing for some rational reconstruction and application of the principle of charity, Socrates can also be interpreted as edging towards the problem of necessary truths and our knowledge of them. But what he does not do is to characterise the issue in terms of what the senses can or cannot tell us. Rather, his attention is focused solely on whether or not the verbal input contained in his questions can explain the boy's achievement.

Elsewhere, of course, Plato does have Socrates talk of the deficiencies of sense perception, and in no uncertain terms. This is what happens in the recollection argument of the *Phaedo*, which makes almost no reference to testimony, but to perception. Yet what is interesting about this argument is that it does not edge any closer to Leibniz's argument in the *New Essays*. Socrates does not reopen the question of how it is we can grasp necessary truths; and he does not supplement the argument of the *Meno* with an explanation why the senses cannot enable us to do this. Instead he takes a quite different approach. Assuming the existence of transcendent forms,

---

[9] See e.g. Moser 1987: 1: '. . . an instance of knowledge is *a priori* if and only if its justification condition is *a priori* in the sense that it does not depend on evidence from sensory experience'.
[10] Preface and 1 i = Remnant and Bennett 1982: 49–50 and 79.

he contrasts these with objects of perception and asserts that, because of their nature, the forms are accessible only by the mind, even if perception acts as a catalyst (65c11–e5, 74b4–75b8, 79a1–11).

Unlike Leibniz's argument, which is based on logical considerations, this is based on ontology. If one is looking for a historical parallel, one should turn instead to Descartes. He argued that a geometer might prove that one line is double the length of another. But when he draws a diagram to help his students grasp the point, he does not for a moment think that the actual figure he draws has these properties. The lines he draws, however precise, are not even straight, let alone in the exact proportions that he describes. We never actually perceive through the senses the objects of geometrical knowledge, only rough approximations to them. So our knowledge of them cannot derive from the senses; it is *a priori*.[11] The similarity is only very general, but Descartes treats mathematical objects rather as the *Phaedo* treats the forms. But none of this bears much resemblance to the *Meno*, which steers clear of any robust ontological commitments, as well as any statements about the inadequacy of sense perception.

So we should not attribute to the *Meno* arguments about sense perception that are absent from it, nor should we elide the difference between it and the *Phaedo*. And if we are to talk about *a priori* knowledge in Plato, it is safer to start from a more general concept of the *a priori* than is standard, and talk of knowledge whose justification is independent of external sources, whether testimony or perception, and then judge which species of the *a priori* is at issue in any one passage.

THE MOVE TOWARDS RECOLLECTION: 85c9–d10

To return to the argument of the *Meno*: let us assume that, through Socrates' interview with the slave boy, Plato is drawing the reader's attention to the ability to follow a proof – to perceive logical relationships. We still have a long way to go to the recollection thesis. Socrates takes a further step in this direction at 85c9–d10:

SOC. At present, these beliefs have just been stirred up in him like in a dream. But if someone questions him about the same matters on many occasions and in many ways, you can be sure that he will end up with as exact a knowledge of them as anyone.
MEN. So it seems.

---

[11] Descartes, *Reply to Objections* v = Cottingham, Stoothof and Murdoch 1984–91: II, 262; see also Augustine *Confessions* x 12.

soc. So without anyone having taught him, but only by being asked questions, he
    will recover for himself the knowledge within him?
MEN. Yes.
soc. And recovering knowledge for oneself that is in oneself – is this not
    recollection?
MEN. Certainly.
soc. So the knowledge that he has now – he either acquired it at some time or else
    always possessed it, didn't he?

The fact that Socrates includes this phase of the argument at all is striking.
Immediately after establishing that the slave's answers are his own, he could
have inferred that the boy extracted these from himself and that this was
recollection. If the inference to recollection works in the extrapolated case
at 85d3–7, it must work just as well with the actual case before them, that of
true belief. Instead, he delays the inference to recollection until he can also
argue that the boy will have knowledge within him (85d6). The obvious
explanation for this is that Socrates' ultimate aim in this argument is to
establish that we can attain knowledge, and that we can do so only if we
already possess it latently. This is what we should expect: Socrates hopes
that the theory of recollection can help solve the problem of discovery, a
problem caused in part by his commitment to the foreknowledge principle,
which demands that any successful inquiry must start out from pre-existent
knowledge.

There are two principal claims in this passage, which we need to discuss
separately: first, that if the boy continues along the same track he will attain
knowledge; second, that in doing so he will be drawing out knowledge that
has been latent all along.

Socrates' 'egalitarianism'

In the first part of the passage quoted, 85c10–d1, Socrates says that the
boy can attain knowledge of geometry, and claims that he will do so if
he undergoes further questioning. Before we examine his justification for
claiming that the boy could eventually attain knowledge, we should take
note of his reference to continued questioning, as it has significance within
the dialogue as a whole. Socrates makes the point by saying, 'if someone
questions him about the same matters on many occasions and in many
ways . . .'. Some translations render the point as 'if the *same questions* are
put to him on many occasions and in different ways . . .' [emphasis added].[12]
This is possible given the Greek, but makes little sense. Socrates can hardly

---

[12] See Guthrie 1956 and Grube in Cooper 1997; also Bostock 1986: 112.

be saying that, in order to convert your true opinions into knowledge, you need to be asked exactly the same questions, for you would most likely just continue to repeat the same answers.

Rather, the point is that we should revisit the same topic or problem but from different angles, and with increasing depth and complexity. The reference to different contexts is very important: the more varied the contexts in which one places the original problem, the more interconnections one makes within one's set of beliefs. This ties in, of course, with the emphasis on synoptic reasoning that I have stressed at various points in this book. It will also be important when we come to examine Socrates' distinction between knowledge and true belief at 98a.

The idea of revisiting a topic with increasing depth is also one that resonates throughout the work. We saw it, for instance, at 76e, where Socrates suggests that, were Meno to stay longer in Athens and be initiated [sc. into philosophy], he would reconsider his views on which was the best of the sample definitions just given to him.[13] We shall soon see Socrates himself revisiting the argument that virtue is teachable in the final stages of the dialogue. Furthermore, the general notion of revisiting a topic is built into the way the dialogue is written. This is a work designed to be re-read: it is peppered with allusions that take on a deeper level of meaning only when one reads the work for the second or third time. Plato expects his reader to go over the same text several times in different ways (perhaps in the light of his other works), rather than to be content with a single reading. Indeed, many of the claims in the *Meno* are revisited and scrutinised in later works, notably the *Phaedo* and the *Republic*.

What then of Socrates' assertion that, if the boy continues along the same lines, he will end up with as a good a knowledge of geometry as anyone? The claim is as contestable as it is striking. How do we know that the boy would not just plateau at a certain stage? Socrates seems to ignore differences in natural ability. This itself is very interesting if we glance across at other dialogues. One might concede that everyone has buried within them latent knowledge of geometry, virtue and so on, but still think that in some people the knowledge is more deeply buried than in others. This seems to be the position of *Phaedrus* 248c2–e3. The *Republic* makes no mention of recollection but almost certainly espouses an innatist theory of some sort (cf. 518b6–d1). Yet it claims that most people are not suitable for intellectual education and proposes a rigid class system with citizens divided according to their natural ability. So it is not true that everyone can become

---

[13] See above pp. 58–9.

as expert as each other in geometry as long as they do enough dialectic.[14] By contrast, the *Meno* suggests a more egalitarian view of the matter.[15] And the point is not confined to geometry. At 85e1–3 Socrates asserts that the boy will be able to do the same (i.e. become as expert as anyone) in every subject, which includes virtue. This point also has a provocative edge to it, suggesting that the slave boy is no inferior to his master, let alone to Anytus, a well-known Athenian leader.

Latent knowledge

According to the second claim, the boy's projected acquisition of explicit knowledge will be explained by the presence of knowledge that is already latent in him. But how does Socrates move from our ability to follow a proof to the thesis of latent knowledge? On the Augustinian approach suggested above, the boy will act as the judge, listening to the proposals made in the questions so as to make up his own mind whether to accept them. Now, in order for the boy to have this kind of independence, he must already have his own criteria by which to accept or reject any suggestion put to him. It is precisely these internal criteria that are lacking in someone who takes someone's word on trust – hence their cognitive dependence on the other party. In other words, the presence of internal criteria underlies the difference between merely being informed about propositions in a proof and perceiving their logical interrelations. According to Socrates, the existence of these criteria amounts to the possession of latent knowledge.

One can challenge this thesis by offering what to many would seem like a more plausible philosophical alternative. This would be to adopt some form of 'dispositional' innatism. At birth, so this theory goes, we are born with certain cognitive predispositions. To explain the development of mathematical knowledge, for instance, we could say that the mind is innately disposed (under appropriate conditions) to follow certain rules of inference, and assent to specific axioms. There is no suggestion here that we have latent knowledge of these principles. As Descartes suggested, this case can be compared to the phenomenon of congenital diseases. In using the analogy he emphasised that members of certain families who are perfectly healthy as children can have a propensity to contract a particular disease at

---

[14] This is not to say that deep down the souls of the producers and auxiliaries have any less knowledge of the forms, but that in their current incarnation their endowment is more encrusted with bodily accretions than the souls of those who are fitted to rule.

[15] As Popper (1966: 129) rightly remarks.

a later stage in their lives. But there is no sense in which they suffer from the disease before that time.[16]

We should also ask about the extent of the latent knowledge that the boy is said to have. From the way Socrates talks, it sounds as if the boy has latent in him the very answer to the problem of doubling the area of the square. At 85e1–3, Socrates says that not only geometry but also all scientific disciplines are innate, and if the proposition about doubling the area of the square is innate presumably every other proposition of similar specificity within these disciplines will be innate. The number of propositions known latently will be enormous.[17]

A more economical approach would be to limit what is innately known to principles of some sort. In mathematics, these could be thought of as the axioms that Euclid later formulated. Together with certain rules of inference, these might then generate knowledge of the other propositions in the system. And we do not have to look very far ahead for a more economical approach, as Plato himself leans in this direction in the *Phaedo* and *Phaedrus*. Here Socrates argues that knowledge (of definitions) of forms is innate. These definitions act as principles ('explanations' or 'causes', to use the terminology of the *Phaedo* 100b1–102a2). Even though the *Meno* avoids any mention of transcendent forms, the priority of definition implies that definitions of forms constitute principles from which other propositions can be derived. To develop this idea, we would have to go well beyond what is in the text, and this is not my intention here. Rather, I simply wish to bring out a viable alternative to the somewhat generous innatism that we actually find proposed at the end of the slave-boy examination.

Throughout this section, I have taken it as read that Socrates attributes latent knowledge to the boy. This seems natural enough, given that in 85d9 he refers to 'the knowledge that [the boy] has now'. Clearly the boy does not have explicit knowledge, so Socrates can only be referring to latent knowledge.[18] But scholars are not unanimous in this view. It is noticeable that in the rest of the argument, 85e6–86b2, Socrates never refers to

---

[16] *Comments on a certain Broadsheet* = Cottingham, Stoothof and Murdoch 1984–91: I, 303–4. In my view, dispositional innatism first appeared with the Stoics. See Scott 1988 and 1995: ch. 8.

[17] As well as applying recollection to our learning of scientific disciplines (85e2–3), does the theory also apply to cognitive achievements that do not count as expertise in this sense? What about the concepts that all normal human beings develop in the course of their childhood, in other words, early learning? I have argued at length in Scott 1995: chs. 1–2 that recollection only applies to 'higher' learning. I shall not repeat the arguments here, although I discuss a new argument for this interpretation below on pp. 158–9, when commenting on the argument that virtue does not come by nature (89a–b).

[18] For this view see Calvert 1974: 147–8, Sharples 1985: 155 and Weiss 2001: 114 n. 79; cf. Bluck 1961: 313.

knowledge again, but only talks of true beliefs being in the boy, or 'the truth of all things'. So perhaps we were wrong ever to have read a thesis of latent knowledge into the passage. In this spirit, Gail Fine has claimed that Plato does not hold a theory of innate knowledge after all. He believes that once – long ago – the soul had explicit knowledge, but lost it; what it retains is a tendency to favour true over false beliefs, which enables it to inquire successfully. She explains the phrase, 'the knowledge that [the boy] has now', by taking it to be 'forward-looking': transplanting himself into the future, Socrates uses the present tense and talks of what is the case 'now' to refer to the boy as he will be once he has acquired explicit knowledge of geometry.[19]

In my view, there is no getting away from the fact that 85d talks of latent knowledge. Further below, I shall offer an explanation as to why he ceases to talk of latent knowledge in the rest of the passage (85e7–86b4), and shall argue that this does not mean he ever retracts his commitment to latent knowledge in 85d. But for the time being, I shall attempt to show that, whatever happens later on in the argument, Socrates does espouse a theory of latent knowledge at 85d. To do this, I shall first set out why the argument of 85c–e as a whole is best understood by means of the distinction between explicit and latent knowledge, then raise specific objections to Fine's interpretation.

At 85c2–7 Socrates stressed that the slave boy does not have explicit knowledge of geometry; at 85c9–d1, he claimed that he will acquire this explicit knowledge if he undergoes further questioning. Then he re-describes what this moment of achievement will involve: recovering the knowledge from himself (85d4). If one were to take this to suggest that there must already be in him knowledge to be recovered, one would be quite right. For, according to the next sentence, 'recovering *knowledge that is in him* is recollection' (85d6–7). There can be no doubt as to what Socrates is saying here: first, that when the boy acquires explicit knowledge he will be recollecting; second, that recollection consists in the recovery of knowledge that is already in him. So at this future point, at least, there exists latent knowledge in the boy. Fine's suggestion that knowledge arises merely from the operation of tendencies to favour true over false beliefs cannot be right. Explicit knowledge emerges from knowledge already latent.

We now come to 85d9, with its reference to 'the knowledge that the boy has now'. On my view, having asserted that there is latent knowledge waiting to be aroused in the boy in the future, Socrates further assumes that it is latent in him now as well. This makes good sense of the fact that

---

[19] Fine 1992: 213 with n.40 and 2003: 5. See also Vlastos 1965: 153 n.14.

he inserts the word 'now', as well as using the present tense: he is signalling the fact that a further move is being made in the argument. The initial assertion (that there *will* be latent knowledge in the boy) may be highly questionable but, once granted, the further assumption is quite natural: if the knowledge is latent in him then, why not now as well? His next move, again quite naturally, is to ask about the origin of this knowledge; he then canvasses the two most likely options: either the boy's latent knowledge was acquired at some previous point, or it was always in his soul. In what follows he discounts the first and settles on the second.

Let us now turn to Fine's view, according to which 85d9 only refers to the explicit knowledge that the boy will have in the future. What then are we to make of the rest of this sentence, where Socrates immediately assumes that the boy either acquired this knowledge at some point previously or else always had it? Socrates would have to be saying that either the boy has had *explicit* knowledge for all time, or he acquired it. But there are three severe difficulties for this view. First, it is unclear why Socrates should think it so natural to propose these as the options open to them. On Fine's interpretation, the boy will have acquired his knowledge merely by exploiting his tendencies to favour true over false beliefs in the process of inquiry. The assertion that either he acquired the same explicit knowledge at some earlier point or always had it comes out of nowhere. By contrast, if Socrates has already assumed that the boy has latent knowledge now as well as in the future, it makes sense to ask just how long this knowledge has been in his soul.

There is also a problem for Fine with Socrates' second option in 85d10: that the boy has always had the knowledge that he has now. If Fine identifies this knowledge with the *explicit* knowledge the boy will have, Socrates would have to be considering the possibility that the boy has always been in a state of having such *explicit* knowledge of geometry (and all disciplines: 85e2–3). Yet this is clearly absurd: they have already stressed that he does not have knowledge even at the end of the demonstration (85c6–7). That he did not have explicit knowledge at the beginning is obvious. Why then does Socrates now even consider it as a possibility that the boy is in a perpetual state of explicit knowledge?

The third problem is that Socrates presents only two alternatives to explain the origin of 'the knowledge that the boy has now'. According to Fine, he believes that neither of them actually obtain. His own view is that the knowledge has not always been in the boy; nor did he acquire it at some point. The boy has always been in a state of 'having learnt', i.e. the soul, equipped with its explicit knowledge, had no beginning; later it forgot it and, on Fine's view, retained only innate dispositions. This constitutes a third option, which would have to be in Socrates' mind at 85d9. So why does he not mention it as a possibility, and talk as if there are only two options, neither of which he actually espouses?

In short, Fine's attempt to resist the obvious reading of 85d9 – obvious because of the emphatic use of both the present tense and the word 'now' – is difficult in the surrounding context. As I have said, it is indeed a puzzle that, after this point, Socrates ceases to talk of knowledge being in the boy, and speaks instead of true belief or simply 'truth'. I shall address this puzzle below (pp. 118–20).

THE ARGUMENT FOR IMMORTALITY

The remainder of the argument appears to be given over to deciding between the two options set out at 85d10: either the boy acquired his latent knowledge at a particular point, or he always had it. Having dismissed the possibility that the boy acquired it during this life (85d13–e6), Socrates looks to the previous history of his soul. His conclusion is that there was no moment of learning: the boy has always been in a perpetual state of 'having learnt' and the truth was in his soul for all time. In this way, the argument as a whole segues into an argument for immortality.

This argument is one of the more neglected passages in the dialogue. There may be two reasons for this. One is that it seems a mere digression from the main interests of the dialogue. Socrates' principal aim is to persuade Meno to resume the inquiry. Belief in recollection – that knowledge is already in us, waiting to be recovered – ought to have been sufficient for this, and so it is not clear what immortality adds.[20] However, I have already given reasons for thinking that this is no mere digression from Plato's deeper interests. Recollection brings with it a very wide context, fusing religious, moral and epistemological themes. Immortality is very much a part of this grander vision, as the *Phaedrus* also demonstrates.[21]

Another reason why commentators have steered clear of the immortality argument in the *Meno* may be that it appears as bad as it is brief. Immortality is a theme to which Plato returns again and again, and this may be one of the first attempts at a proof. But for some readers, the interest of the passage stops there: if we want a decent argument, we must look to other texts.[22] It has to be admitted that Socrates' argument is seriously flawed. Indeed it may well be that Plato is signalling some unease with Socrates'

---

[20] See Thompson 1901: 142–3.   [21] See above, pp. 93–4.

[22] Robinson (1995: 18) writes of *Meno* 86ab: 'No formal proof is offered; the step is simply taken. One can hardly doubt that friendly criticism of such strange-looking assertions led Plato to more serious

argument through Meno's reaction to its conclusion: 'I think you're right, Socrates – though how, I'm not sure' (86b5). At any rate, in what follows, I shall attempt to pin down the faults in the argument, as well as to suggest how it might have been improved.

Here are the stages of the argument as they appear in 85d9–86ab4. Socrates has just assumed that the boy has knowledge already within him.

1 The boy either always had the knowledge he now possesses or he acquired it at some time.

2 He was not taught geometry during this life.

3 Therefore he (a) possessed (εἶχε) and (b) had known [or: had learned, ἐμεμαθήκει] the answers in some earlier period when he was not a human being.

4 Therefore they exist in him both while he is and is not a human being.

5 At every time he either is, or is not, a human being.

6 Therefore his soul is forever in a state of having known [or: having learnt, μεμαθηκυῖα].

7 If the truth about reality is always in our soul, the soul must be immortal.

Having offered two options in 1 that he takes to be exhaustive, Socrates considers the possibility that the boy acquired the knowledge, and focuses on the sub-possibility that he did so during this life. To make this sub-possibility easy to reject, he claims that the slave knows the whole of geometry, not just the answer to the particular problem just considered. If challenged, he could reply that the geometrical problem was chosen at random, and that any other problem would have sufficed. But at 85e2–3 Socrates further claims that the boy already has knowledge of all disciplines (*mathemata*). The reason for making the point in the present context is that Socrates can ask Meno whether the boy has been taught *all* of this during this lifetime – an easy enough question to answer.

In 3 Socrates assumes that, if the boy did not acquire the answers during this life, he must have had them in an earlier existence, which he takes to be a non-human life, presumably a discarnate state. Next he concludes that the answers are in his soul both when he is a human being and when he is not.

---

attempts at proof in the *Phaedo*.' See also Gulley 1962: 21–2. In the *Apology*, Socrates appears agnostic on the question of an afterlife (40c4–41c7). Plato, it seems, soon came off the fence, as the *Meno* shows. The *Phaedo* argues for the thesis much more systematically and at much greater length. There are also proofs to be found in *Republic* x (608d3–611b10) and *Phaedrus* (245c5–246a2). Plato is not always consistent in his approach to the subject. The *Symposium* is often thought to claim that the human soul is not immortal in the strict sense (cf. 208a7–b4), and the *Timaeus* 41c3–d3 appears to hold that the human soul is created, in contrast to the *Meno* where the soul has no beginning. See also *Phaedrus* 245d1–3. The *Phaedo* is also committed to indefinite pre-existence, as is clear from the cyclical argument: the cyclical process goes on for all time (72a12–b1).

These times, incarnate and discarnate, or human and non-human, exhaust all the possibilities for the kind of existence he can enjoy. Therefore the truth is in him for all time, i.e. forever. If so, his soul must be immortal (86a8–b2).

The move to pre-existence

One objection is that in step 3 Socrates overlooks the possibility that the boy's latent knowledge may never have been explicit; he was simply born with it.[23] This is the challenge Leibniz issues to the Platonists at different points.[24]

It may be that the *Meno* moves to pre-existence as quickly as it does simply because some version of recollection was already in circulation – the Pythagorean, for instance. If so, the accusation is that Socrates lacks any distinctively philosophical motivation for espousing pre-existence. By contrast, the *Phaedo* furnishes an argument that attempts to fill this gap, by explaining why certain cognitive achievements in this life imply the existence of knowledge before birth (73c1–76d6).[25]

Nevertheless a Platonist should not be too cowed by Leibniz's challenge. Simply to assert that we are born with latent knowledge (or, for that matter, predispositions to know) fails to address the question of where the innate endowment comes from. Without an answer to this question, innatism is considerably weakened as an epistemological theory. It may be possible to demonstrate that the mind has innate resources waiting to be activated by external stimuli, but we have no reason as yet to think that any beliefs arising from this endowment will be true, let alone why they should count as knowledge.

Innatists in the seventeenth century tended to meet this challenge by claiming that the innate endowment is the work of a benign and veracious deity. But in doing so, they show that their disagreement with Plato is really one about theology and about rival theories of the soul. Certainly, they cannot claim any obvious advantage in terms of philosophical economy, if that was ever a part of their case. Furthermore, Socrates in the *Meno* would probably be very wary of this theological approach. On my interpretation he seeks to establish the existence of innate knowledge, not merely

---

[23] For this criticism see Stock 1904: 22.

[24] Leibniz recognises his relationship to Platonic recollection at *New Essays* Preface, 1 i and 1 iii = Remnant and Bennett 1982: 52, 78–9 and 106. See also *Discourse on Metaphysics* 26 = Parkinson 1973: 36. For a discussion of the relation between Platonic recollection and Leibniz's innatism, see Brown 1991.

[25] The crux of the argument for prenatal knowledge comes at 74e9–75c5. I have discussed this in Scott 1995: 61–3.

true belief. But given his views about the inability of testimony to justify knowledge, he would not be content with a theory that relied ultimately on divine providence. At the end of the dialogue, he does in fact refer to divine providence, when he concludes that the virtuous men of Athens derived their true beliefs from divine dispensation. But they did not have knowledge, as divine dispensation is a form of hearsay, albeit supernatural hearsay. So Socrates' inference to the pre-existence of the soul certainly needs more argument than we find in the *Meno*. But seen from an epistemological perspective, his insistence on tracing the history of our endowment is well motivated. And the fact that he did not avail himself of the solution of so many of his successors is at least philosophically intelligible.[26]

Indefinite pre-existence?

A different objection concerns Socrates' claim that the soul contains knowledge for as long as it exists. Even if the boy did have explicit knowledge in a previous life, he could still have acquired it in the course of that life, having not had it before;[27] and even if he did have it for the whole of that life, there would have been yet another earlier life in which he could have acquired the knowledge *de novo*. Perhaps it is to block this move that Socrates introduces step 5: at every time the boy exists, he either is or is not a human being. If so, his reasoning is as follows. The boy has the knowledge in a human life, and also had it in a prior non-human life.[28] So he has had it both when a human and not a human. But, according to step 5, these exhaust the possibilities for the type of existence he can have, so in every period of his existence he has had the knowledge. Hence he has had it for all of his existence.

From the way in which the argument actually proceeds, particularly from the presence of step 5, this does seem to be what Socrates has in mind. As such, the argument is clearly fallacious. However, the defect could have been remedied as follows. I have interpreted the theory of recollection as the thesis that one *cannot* be taught to follow a proof or to perceive logical relationships. The text focuses our attention on the sense of recognition we

---

[26] Modern theories, of course, can appeal to evolution to explain why we have cognitive dispositions favouring true beliefs over false. On the different varieties of innatism see Barnes 1972, Savile 1972, Hacking 1975: ch. 6, Jolley 1984: ch. 9, Scott 1988 and 1995: 91–5, 188–90 and 213–16, and Cowie 1999, esp. ch. 1.

[27] As Anscombe (1979: 150) puts it, we could imagine his soul coming into existence a short while before incarnation, learning the truths and then entering into human form.

[28] Note that Socrates also assumes that this prior existence was non-human (86a3–4). Presumably, there must be intervals of bodiless existence between incarnations, as in the cyclical argument of the *Phaedo*. But no argument is given as to why human incarnations could not stand back-to-back.

have when we grasp the logical interconnections between propositions in a proof, and the suggestion is that this recognition should be taken quite literally as 're-cognition'. This requires the existence of latent knowledge in the soul, which in turn points to a prior state of awareness. This, incidentally, is why Socrates claims that *all* learning (of *mathemata*) is recollection. He is not just saying that on some occasions, the ability to follow a proof is explained in this way, but that it need not always be: it is not as if one could follow a proof either by recollection or by learning from a teacher.

In discussing recollection in his *New Essays on Human Understanding*, Leibniz points out that the theory entails an infinite regress:[29]

The Platonists thought that all our knowledge is recollection, and thus that the truths which the soul brought with it when the man was born – the ones called innate – must be the remains of an earlier explicit knowledge. But there is no foundation for this opinion; and it is obvious that if there was an earlier state, however far back, it too must have involved some innate knowledge, just as our present state does: such knowledge must then either have come from a still earlier state or else have been innate or at least created with [the soul]; or else we must go to infinity and make souls eternal . . .

Leibniz is quite right: if *all* learning is recollection, the soul must have pre-existed indefinitely. The regress involved in this argument will be vicious to anyone who believes that the soul is created; but in the context of the *Meno*, of course, it would have been virtuous.

All this is useful for answering the objection. At 85d3–9 the slave boy's projected success in attaining explicit knowledge of geometry is taken to imply that he already has geometrical knowledge in his human life (time *t*). In stage 3 of the immortality argument Socrates draws two inferences from this: (a) that the boy had the knowledge prenatally, i.e. at t^{-1} (εἶχε), and (b) that, at some point still further back (t^{-2}), he had it or had learnt it (ἐμεμαθήκει).[30] Because of the recollection thesis, (a) implies (b). For there can be only two explanations for why at t^{-1} the soul has the knowledge: either it was always there, or it was acquired at some previous time. In the latter case, the thesis that *all* learning is recollection will again be applied, yielding a still earlier state of knowing or learning at t^{-3} and so on.[31]

I am not saying that this is the explicit line of argument that Socrates uses. If he really meant to deploy it, he need not have bothered with most

[29] *New Essays on Human Understanding* i i, trans Remnant and Bennett 1982: 79.
[30] That two different times are involved here, t^{-1} and t^{-2}, is clearly marked by the use of two different tenses in the verbs εἶχε and ἐμεμαθήκει, imperfect and pluperfect respectively.
[31] The verb ἐμεμαθήκει could mean either 'he had known' or 'he had learned' (cf. *Euthydemus* 277e3–278a5). On either sense the regress is established.

of what we actually find in the text, i.e. stages 1 to 7. But it could be used as 'rational reconstruction': the argument now shows both that the soul contains knowledge for as long as it exists and that it has pre-existed indefinitely.

Socrates' conclusion that the soul must always be in a state of knowledge or 'having learnt' should also be seen in the light of the foreknowledge principle discussed on pp. 84–5 above. There, I argued that recollection is introduced to solve the problem of discovery, a problem based upon the Eleatic principle that knowledge must derive from pre-existent knowledge. It is partly because Socrates agrees with the principle that he takes the problem as seriously as he does. As evidence, I looked ahead to the current passage, 85c–d, where he cheerfully assumes that there can be no attainment of knowledge without pre-existent knowledge.

In retrospect, we can see the ingenuity of his argument. Concerned to solve the problem of discovery, he proposes the theory of recollection. To demonstrate the truth of the theory, he stages the slave-boy demonstration, aiming to show that the boy works out the answers for himself. But even if he can do this, he still needs to show there must have been *knowledge* in the soul all along, otherwise he will not have answered the problem of discovery, based as it is on the foreknowledge principle. Throughout 85c–d, we find him assuming the foreknowledge principle to prove that the soul has always been in a state of knowledge. He thus matches his solution to the problem, using the same principle that was assumed in the original challenge in order to derive recollection and the indefinite pre-existence of the soul from the evidence of the slave-boy demonstration. Note that there is no circularity in this argument, because the foreknowledge principle is not something that the problem of discovery challenges him to prove; on the contrary, it is just assumed. Dialectically speaking, Socrates is entitled to make the same assumption when drawing his inferences from the slave-boy demonstration.

The move to post-existence

However, none of this proves anything about the future of the soul, and here a third objection comes into play. Even if it has been shown that the knowledge is in the slave boy for all the time that he exists, indeed for all past time, this does not show that it is in him for all time, period.[32] Hence it has not been shown that the soul is immortal. Socrates in the *Meno* has

---

[32] See Gulley 1962: 21 and Sharples 1985: 156.

not succeeded in proving the future survival of the soul, which is important in the context of expiation and redemption. That said, this objection is not actually lethal to his overall concerns: even if he cannot establish that the soul will continue to exist after this life, he can still insist that we need to recollect our prior knowledge in order to acquire virtue in this life.

Interestingly enough, there is a parallel mistake in the final argument of the *Phaedo*, where Socrates argues that, for all the time that it exists, the soul does not 'admit' death. From this he attempts to prove that the soul is deathless for all time, period (105e2–107a1). At least in this work, however, Plato shows himself to be aware of the problem and attempting to solve it.[33]

LATENT KNOWLEDGE OR BELIEF?

If the immortality argument is unsound, at least its faults do not seem to affect the rest of the recollection passage. Unfortunately, there is a further difficulty with the argument – one that does have consequences for how we understand the theory of recollection.

When Socrates embarks on the argument at 85d9, he sets out two alternatives: either the boy had his knowledge for all time, or he acquired it. As he goes on to argue against the second option and in favour of the first, we would expect him to conclude that the knowledge is in the boy's soul for all time. But halfway through the argument, he appears to switch tack and talk of *true beliefs* being in the boy's soul for all time (86a7). Eventually, he concludes with a third, less determinate claim: that the truth is in the soul for all time (86b1–2). This third claim is compatible with both the second and the first. But that still leaves us wondering whether he means to say that our souls have knowledge in them for all time or merely true belief.

If Socrates does eventually espouse the latter option, there are serious problems. First, we have seen that he undoubtedly does assert that the boy has latent knowledge at 85d3–10. Second, I have argued that, in attempting to solve the problem of discovery, Socrates wishes to remain faithful to the foreknowledge principle in some form, and uses the thesis of latent knowledge to this end. Third, it would be very strange if he were to claim that the soul possesses true beliefs (rather than knowledge) on all subjects for all eternity: for at 97e2–98a8 he will insist that true belief is by its nature unstable.

---

[33] See also *Phaedo* 77c1–d5, where Socrates acknowledges that recollection only establishes the prior existence of the soul, and attempts to establish its post-existence by means of a separate argument, the cyclical argument.

To understand what is happening in the immortality argument, we need to recall Socrates' strategy in the lines immediately preceding it, 85b8–d7. First, he argued that the slave boy's answers, which were only true opinions, came from within (85b8–c8). Then – more boldly – he projected into the future, claiming that the boy could attain knowledge; this, he proceeded to argue, is only possible if he now has this knowledge latently (85c9–d7). There are thus two conclusions that Socrates is drawing. In the earlier stretch of argument (85b8–c8), he merely claims that the boy had true opinions within him, which were then made explicit in the course of the interview. But at 85c9–d7 he draws a bolder conclusion based on the projected scenario: that all along the boy has latent knowledge. When he then starts on the immortality argument, he takes off from this bolder conclusion, and so couches the two possibilities in terms of knowledge: either the boy has had the knowledge forever, or he acquired it (85d9–10). However, at 85e7 they refocus their minds on what the boy has just achieved and so step back to the more modest conclusion – that there must have been true beliefs in him. What this means is that Socrates is now attempting to establish the immortality thesis on the basis of the modest conclusion of the boy's actual rather than projected achievement. Thus, the immortality argument does not continue as it started: it began by assuming the bolder conclusion, but then switches midway, proceeding on the basis of the more modest one.

In other words, the whole of the immortality argument could be run in two different ways. Version [A], as I shall call it, starts out from the case of someone who has been proven to have knowledge both latently and explicitly, i.e. the slave boy as projected in 85c10–d7; version [B] from someone who has as yet only been shown to have true belief (latently and explicitly), i.e. the boy as he actually is.

Version [A]:

1 X now has knowledge.
2 Either he acquired it, or he always had it.
3 He didn't acquire it during this life, so he must have had it in a previous life, when he wasn't a human being.
4 So he has had the knowledge both when he was a human being and when he was not.
5 For all time, he has had the knowledge.
6 Therefore his soul is immortal.

Version [B]:

1 X now has true beliefs.
2 Either he acquired them, or he always had them.

3 He didn't acquire them during this life, so he must have had them in a
  previous life, when he wasn't a human being.
4 So he has had true beliefs both when he was a human being and when
  he was not.
5 For all time, he has had the true beliefs.
6 Therefore his soul is immortal.

If Socrates only wanted to establish immortality, it would not matter which
version of the argument he used. What I suggest has happened is that he
starts the immortality argument thinking of the projected case, as if he
is going to pursue version [A], but then switches to version [B] because
that constitutes a more secure argument, based as it is on the boy's actual
achievement.

But the fact that he switches to the less risky version [B] should not
be taken to mean that he has retracted the first premise of version [A], a
premise that he so clearly endorses. The boy does now have latent knowledge. Socrates is just following a less risky strategy to achieve the objective
currently in his sights, a proof of immortality. And it is no accident that in
the conclusion he distances himself from the more modest conclusion of
version [B], back to a claim that is consistent with version [A]: 'the truth
of all things is in the soul' (86b1–2). He deliberately chooses an expression
that smoothes over the difference between versions [A] and [B] precisely
because he still endorses the thesis that we all have latent knowledge, no less.

Of course, Socrates would have presented his argument much better
by sticking clearly to either version [A] or version [B] throughout. But
my aim has been not so much to redeem the argument, but to provide an
explanation as to why we find three quite different statements of his thesis –
that knowledge, true belief and the truth is latent in us.

CHAPTER 10

The conclusion: 86b6–c2

RECOLLECTION AS METAPHOR?

Socrates rounds off this whole passage (80–6) on a note of caution, followed by a strong exhortation:

> As for the other points, I wouldn't absolutely insist on the argument. But I would fight, both in word and deed, for the following point: that we would be better, more manly and less lazy if we believed that we ought to inquire into what we do not know, than if we believed that we cannot discover what we do not know and so have no duty to inquire. (86b6–c2)

The first few words suggest a disclaimer of some sort; but we should be careful about what we take them to imply. In saying that he would not insist on the argument too strongly, he is acknowledging that it needs further support. We have noted at various points how the *Phaedo* attempts to do this, in regard to both recollection and immortality. But Socrates' words cannot be used as evidence that he only proposed recollection as a metaphor for something else. Of course, many modern readers may feel a deep unease with the whole recollection episode. On the one hand they might admire Plato's insights into the nature of learning and see his theory as a landmark in the theory of knowledge to which later theorists have, to a greater or lesser extent, been returning ever since. On the other, they feel embarrassed to think that the same philosopher might also have signed up to some sort of fairytale about reincarnation and purification. So any excuse to demythologise or 'sanitise' this passage would be very welcome. But there is no evidence, at least from 86b, that Socrates is signalling to us not to take his theory literally. The difference between believing something literally and believing it metaphorically is a difference in kind; but in these lines, Socrates is talking about a difference in degree: how much confidence he feels in his theory. So we should take it literally, but view it as in need of stronger proof.

121

Perhaps one might argue that Socrates means recollection and immortality to be taken literally but discards his predecessors' references to multiple reincarnations, expiation and redemption at 81b–c. But for one thing 86b does not distinguish between different elements of the *logos*, let alone say that some claims are to be taken more seriously than others: they all appear on a par and contrasted with the claim that we shall be better for believing in the duty to inquire. Secondly, although we may have reasons for taking specific elements of the original *logos* with caution, or even discarding them altogether, on my interpretation the religious theme of expiation is important to Socrates and remains at work in the argument right up to 86a: it is because the soul is immortal that we should do everything to recollect (and so live piously).[1]

THE DEFAULT POSITION

In the rest of his speech (86b7–c2), Socrates talks of the moral benefits of believing in the duty to inquire. Here he adopts a rather subtle position, one that has not received much attention from commentators. For the sake of clarity, I shall use 'P' for the proposition that one ought to inquire into what one does not know, and 'P*' for the proposition that believing P will make one less lazy, braver and better. Socrates says that he will do battle 'in word and deed' for P*. This is in effect to advocate P not on logical grounds, as following from an argument considered to be sound, but on pragmatic grounds.[2]

Such an approach may remind us of an earlier point in the recollection passage:

So one shouldn't be persuaded by that eristic argument. It would make us idle and is pleasant for the faint-hearted to hear. But this one makes us hard working and eager to inquire. Trusting it to be true, I'm willing to inquire with you into what virtue is. (81d5–e2)

In both passages, Socrates seems to be more concerned with the moral effects of adopting a certain belief about inquiry. There are, however, important differences. In the earlier passage it was recollection that was being praised for its beneficial effects, whereas now it is simply the belief that we can

---

[1] See above, pp. 93–4.
[2] The most famous example of a pragmatic approach to belief is the 'noble lie' in *Republic* III, 414b8–415d5, a myth that will morally improve the citizens of the ideal state. Here of course the belief is known by Socrates to be false, rather than not known to be true, as in the *Meno*. For a different kind of parallel, see *Phaedo* 91a7–b7 where belief in immortality is recommended pragmatically: if true, we are right to believe it; if not, at least belief in it will make a dying man more agreeable to his friends.

discover and so ought to inquire. Furthermore, the position that Socrates opposes in each passage is different. In the first it is the eristic dilemma, which tried to show that inquiry is impossible. But as I have already argued, 86b6–c1 is not concerned with someone who thinks inquiry is impossible, but with someone who thinks that, since we cannot discover what we do not know, we have no duty to inquire.[3]

It seems, then, that at 86b–c Socrates is not repeating quite the same exhortation directed to Meno at 81d. Rather, he is addressing those troubled by the problem of discovery (or, to be more precise, announcing his intention to address them, if he is allowed to – a possible reference to his future trial and execution: cf. also 94e3–95a1 and 100b7–c2). The point of these closing lines (86b7–c2) is to give such people a second line of defence – should the theory of recollection fail to convince them.

But how robust is this fallback position? Socrates' talk of doing battle in argument suggests that he would be prepared to argue for P* forcefully. In the *Meno* itself, however, he simply asserts the proposition without argument. One part of what he says is uncontroversial: believing P will certainly make us less lazy. But the same cannot be said of the other two effects mentioned. As far as manliness is concerned, an interlocutor might refuse to accept Socrates' claim that this quality applies in the intellectual sphere as it does, for instance, on the battlefield.[4]

One can also dispute the claim that believing P will make us better. The point of 86b–c is that we are better off believing that discovery is possible, even if this is something that we do not know (having failed to solve the problem of discovery directly). Now if discovery really is impossible, those who believe P may waste their own and others' efforts in fruitless labour. If so, they will be beneficial neither to themselves nor anyone else. Hence they are not better for believing P (cf. 87e1–2). This objection could also be targeted against Socrates' claim that believing P makes us 'more manly', if he is using the expression evaluatively, i.e. to mean 'more courageous'. At 88b3–6 he argues that true courage must be beneficial, otherwise it is merely some form of endurance, which on its own is as likely to harm as to help us. So in order to claim that believing P will make us more courageous, he must show that it will make us better – which, as I have just argued, he has not.

---

[3] See above, p. 82.

[4] For other allusions to intellectual manliness or its opposite, see pp. 81 and 89 above with *Euthyphro* 15c11, *Laches* 194a1–5, *Charmides* 166d2–e2 and *Phaedo* 85c6 and 90e3. One interlocutor who would dispute the application of courage to philosophy is Callicles: see *Gorgias* 485d4.

We might take an even harder line against Socrates: not only has he failed to support P*, but we can construct an argument for rejecting it outright. At 88b3–6 he argues that we can only be virtuous, i.e. beneficial to ourselves and to others, if we have knowledge. Whatever resources are available to us – external goods (such as money), skills and character traits – it is only knowledge that can guide us in using them to a beneficial outcome. Being good therefore requires knowledge: indeed virtue, so he concludes, just is a form of knowledge. Turning back to 86b–c, we can see a problem looming for Socrates' fallback position: how can we be better if we lack any knowledge of where our efforts will lead? (As before, this argument can also be used against the claim that believing P makes us more courageous in an evaluative sense.)

There are a couple of replies available to Socrates here. First, he does not actually say that believing P will make us good, i.e. virtuous, only that it will make us better than if we do not. Second, at the end of the dialogue he appears to soften his stance about the relation of benefit and knowledge, and allow that one can be beneficial (to oneself and others) merely by having true belief. This answers the objection that P* is false: if P is in fact true we shall be better for believing it.

Nevertheless the problem remains that Socrates has not justified his confidence in P*. Perhaps he would have been better off using a different type of pragmatic argument, along the lines of Pascal's wager. We do not yet know if discovery is possible. If it is, we shall of course be better – more useful to ourselves and to others – if we endure. But if it is not, although we shall have laboured in vain, this loss is considerably less significant than the loss we would incur if we did not endure and yet discovery is possible. In fact, in the light of the religious aspect of recollection, we could pursue this Pascalian theme a step further. If you put your trust in the priestly *logos* and it is true, you set yourself on the road to expiation and redemption; if you do not, you are on the road to further punishment and misery. If the theory is false, you have merely wasted your efforts, but that is a small loss in comparison to what awaited you on the other scenario.

In the *Phaedo*, Socrates does edge towards a pragmatic approach when addressing the misologists who despair of any argument ever being sound (cf. p. 73 above). He says:

Then, Phaedo, wouldn't it be a lamentable event if there were in fact a true, solid argument capable of being discerned, and yet as the result of encountering the sort of arguments we were speaking of, which seemed true at one moment and false the next, one were not to find the fault in oneself or one's own lack of address, but to find a welcome relief for one's distress in finally shifting the blame on to the arguments, and for the rest of one's life to persist in detesting and vilifying all discussion, and so be debarred from knowing the truth about reality?[5]

The misologists are not the same as the defeatists whom Socrates has in mind at *Meno* 86b9–c1: the latter do not claim that no argument could be sound; merely that we cannot discover what we do not already know. Unlike the misologists, they put the fault in human nature. Yet the *Phaedo* does lean towards the pragmatic approach that would help Socrates in his battle to support P*: as long as there is a chance that discovery is possible, it is better to believe so and to take what steps we can to avoid the tragedy of which the *Phaedo* warns. Perhaps this is one place where Plato has Socrates actually fight the battle in argument that he promises us at *Meno* 86c2.

[5] 90c7–d7, trans. Hackforth 1955.

PART THREE

CHAPTER II

The method of hypothesis: 86c–87c

INTRODUCTION

By 86c, Socrates appears to have removed the obstacles put in his path at 80b–e. Meno approves of recollection, and certainly accepts that he has a duty to inquire. If Socrates were to have his way from now on, they would immediately resume their search for the definition of virtue.

Before we go any further, it is worth pausing to consider what this inquiry would be like in the light of the methodological and epistemological claims made between 81b and 86c. The problem of discovery required us to start with a known specification of the object of inquiry. In the case of a definitional inquiry, however, there is nothing we can know about virtue without knowing the definition itself. Socrates' solution is to say that we have knowledge unconsciously, but at the conscious level we have to start from mere conjecture. There will be no 'hard rocks of certainty' from which to work,[1] and assumptions made at the outset or along the way will be subject to revision. But appearances aside, this inquiry is actually being guided by latent knowledge gradually returning to consciousness.

How in more detail will this process work? We can take our cue from a remark made at 81c9–d3:

Since all nature is akin, and the soul has learnt everything, nothing prevents some- one from recollecting just one thing (which people call 'learning') and so discov- ering everything else . . .

Reality is structured, as was our prior awareness of it. The continued pres- ence of this structure in our memory enables us to use each newly recollected item to progress to the next. So there may be one act of recollection at the beginning of the inquiry, which results in the formation of a true belief.[2]

---

[1] For the expression see Vlastos 1994: 72 n. 19 discussing Burnyeat 1977: 384ff.

[2] Socrates does not say what prompts the initial act of recollection. An analogous lacuna appears in the cave allegory of the *Republic* VII, where we are told without any explanation that one of the

The holding of this belief is not experienced atomistically: that is the point of 81c9–d3, where each recollected belief comes with an associative link (however indistinctly felt) leading us on to the next stage in the process of re-discovery. Gradually we extend our network of true beliefs, increasing the number of explanatory inter-connections.

This interpretation is broadly correct, except in one important respect, where it over-simplifies Socrates' conception of discovery. It assumes a process in which the network of beliefs extends smoothly and consistently towards knowledge. But true beliefs lack stability (97d9–98a8), which makes it much more likely that, having recollected a sequence of true beliefs, we shall sooner or later renounce some of them (e.g. under the pressure of counter-argument). Later still, we can hope to recover them after reconsidering the arguments that led us to renounce them earlier.[3] In other words, we shall follow a pattern of zetetic stop and start – *aporia* and *euporia* – while all the time achieving more and more sophistication in our treatment of the arguments. So although there is not a simple accumulation of true beliefs in the course of the inquiry, there can still be an increase, albeit erratic, of cognitive stability over time.[4]

In all this, Socrates is advancing a model of inquiry in which the true specification may only emerge incrementally in the course of the investigation. It is not as if we start by drawing the map and then head for our destination. Instead, like someone who has forgotten the route but still has it latently within them, we are able to draw the map only in the course of making the journey. We reconstruct it haltingly, etching and erasing all the time. But even though we may take many wrong turns, there is still something all along in our minds that can act to guarantee success.

So this is the process upon which Socrates expects Meno to embark at 86c. Once it is completed and they have recollected knowledge of what virtue is, only then will they turn to the question of what it is like – i.e. how it is acquired.

But this is not quite how the dialogue proceeds. When asked to resume the inquiry into the nature of virtue (86c5–6), Meno proves to be less pliant and instead wants to return to his original question about the acquisition of virtue. This leads Socrates to protest:

prisoners might be released from his chains and turn round to face the fire (515c6–8). In this work, however, Plato seems to give this role to the senses, whose conflicting evidence throws up puzzles for the intellect, 'summoning' it to reflection (523a10–524b6).

[3] The fleetingness of true beliefs is presumably what Socrates is illustrating at 85c9–d1, when he says that the boy's true beliefs have just been stirred up in him 'as if in a dream'.

[4] Again, we should think of Socrates' claim at 85c10–d1 that the path to knowledge will require us to go over the same topics on many occasions and in many different ways. See above pp. 106–7.

If I had control not just of myself but you as well, Meno, we wouldn't inquire whether or not virtue is teachable before we had first examined what it is. But since you don't even attempt to control yourself (for the sake of your own freedom, presumably), but try to control me – and succeed – I'll give in to you: what else am I to do? So it seems we have to investigate what something is like when we don't yet know what it is. But at least relax your hold over me a little, and agree to investigate whether it is teachable, or whatever, by way of a hypothesis.

(86d3–e4)

We have already discussed these lines when assessing Meno's character above (pp. 63–4). But the same passage is also of central importance for understanding the philosophical method of the *Meno*. Socrates begins by repeating some methodological strictures from earlier in the dialogue, but then announces that he is prepared to make a concession for Meno, which in turn heralds the introduction of a new method, the 'method of hypothesis'.

This is a topic that has doubly exercised the commentators. First, in the lines immediately following the quotation, Socrates 'illustrates' the method with a geometrical example whose opacity has baffled modern scholars for more than a century. Second, he quickly goes on to apply the method in a distinctively philosophical context, using it to answer the question about the acquisition of virtue. In doing so, he sends out conflicting signals about how the method is to be applied, and even about what it actually is. Again, the result has been a protracted scholarly debate.

In my view, we have made as much progress as we can on the first issue. Among all the different solutions to the riddle of Socrates' geometrical example, I shall describe what seems to me the best available on pages 133–7 below. As far as the second is concerned, we can make a great deal of headway if we clarify exactly what methodological concession Socrates is making to Meno in the lines quoted.

THE METHOD

Hypothesis as compromise

Socrates expresses his preferred method with the words 'we wouldn't inquire whether or not virtue is teachable before we had first examined what it is' (86d4–6). A few lines later, when he starts to suggest a compromise method, he adds: 'so it seems we have to investigate what something is like when we don't yet know what it is' (86d8–e1). So his preferred method involves the requirement that they must know what virtue is before they investigate how it is acquired.

There is no doubt that this requirement has been at work from the beginning of the dialogue: between 71a and 79e Socrates will accept nothing less than knowledge of the definition from Meno before allowing him to proceed to the question of how virtue is acquired. This comes closest to the surface with the collapse of the third definition at 79a7–e3. By this point they have amended the definition into the claim that virtue is action accompanied by a part of virtue. What is striking is Socrates' stated reason for rejecting this answer. He does not say that it is false. The problem is that neither he nor Meno can know it to be true. Since he immediately asks Meno to try again, it is beyond doubt that he requires a known specification of virtue to precede their inquiry into the question of its acquisition.

It is important to realise that this methodological requirement incorporates two distinct components. One of them is the priority of definition over attributes (PDA): we cannot know whether virtue is teachable without knowing what it is. But there is another. On its own, PDA merely tells us that we cannot know one thing without knowing another. It does not say that we have to know the definition *before* the attributes; it leaves open the possibility that we might discover them together. (All it does rule out in this context is the possibility of knowing the attributes before the definition.) So when Socrates says that they must start with knowledge of the definition, he is adding in a further assumption over and above PDA. In effect, this is a specific application of the principle that knowledge must derive from pre-existent knowledge, the 'foreknowledge principle', as I called it above. Our inquiry into the attributes of virtue must have a starting point, a specification of which we have knowledge. Socrates believes that the appropriate starting point is the definition.[5] To put the matter another way, PDA is a principle about logical, not chronological priority. Only when we combine it with the foreknowledge principle do we get a claim of chronological priority, viz. that knowledge of the definition must temporarily precede that of the attributes.

If this is his preferred method, what is the compromise that he goes on to offer?[6] The exact point at which he throws his hands up in despair is 86d8–e1: 'so it seems we have to investigate what something is like when we don't yet know what it is'. This indicates that he is going to yield on the principle that their inquiry into the acquisition question starts out from knowledge. But in asking Meno to relax his hold a little, he must be expecting him to accept some element of the preferred method. The compromise is that

---

[5] Cf. Aristotle *Met.* XIII 4, 1078b23–5 with p. 21 n. 29 above.
[6] On this question see Robinson 1953: 53 and Bedu-Addo 1984: esp. 2 n. 2.

they will investigate the attribute question, whether virtue is teachable, but will still do so by referring back to its nature. The difference with the preferred method is that they base their investigation only on a conjecture about the nature of virtue rather than knowledge. It is this point that will be crucial for understanding how the method of hypothesis is applied in a philosophical context, and what indeed the method is.

That Socrates offers Meno this compromise is surprising. Where definitional discovery is concerned, they have no choice but to proceed on the basis of conjecture or belief: as I have stressed, at the conscious level, there can be no knowledge about virtue without the definition. But where the discovery of attributes is concerned, the position ought to be quite different. Once they have acquired knowledge of the definition, they will have a firm foundation from which to proceed.[7] Why should Socrates give up on this?

This question becomes more pressing if we think of what Socrates will say later about the instability of true belief. At 97d9–98a8 he claims that true beliefs run away from the mind unless tied down by explanation, by which he means that someone who merely has a true belief is always liable to give it up in favour of a false one. What he has in mind is the way in which someone can be persuaded to renounce a belief under the influence of various factors, e.g. fresh considerations that emerge in the process of inquiry, counter-arguments or just plain rhetoric. So the danger of pursuing the compromise method of 86d–e is that we cannot rely on our beliefs about virtue to be stable, even if they happen to be correct. (The same goes for any true beliefs we may acquire in the process of the inquiry.) The only cognitive state that would have the stability to guide our inquiry reliably is knowledge – hence his statement of the preferred method. So why does Socrates compromise with Meno? Apparently, it is just because Meno cannot control his impatience to return to the question of whether virtue is teachable. Whether that is in fact the whole story is something to which I shall return below.

The geometrical example

The way Socrates goes on to develop the compromise method – the method of hypothesis – is to characterise it as a matter of 'reducing' one problem

[7] Benson (2002: 100–4) claims that the method of hypothesis is not a second-best method at all, and that Socrates is not really conceding anything to Meno. I agree that, when we are searching for a definition, the method of hypothesis is not a second-best method: it is all we have. But the same does not apply when we are investigating how virtue is acquired.

to another.[8] Confronted with the question of whether a proposition, *p*, is true, we avoid tackling *p* directly, but find another, *q*, that is equivalent to it. This allows us to argue that if *q* is true, *p* is true, and if *q* is false, *p* is false. What Socrates is doing in this passage is borrowing a pre-existent method from geometry and adapting it to his own concerns in the dialogue: *p* is a proposition about an attribute of virtue; *q* is one about its nature.

As already indicated, Socrates' presentation of the method of hypothesis has raised difficult problems, the most notorious of which concern his geometrical example:

By 'from a hypothesis' I mean the way in which geometers often investigate when someone asks them about an area, for instance, whether it can be inscribed in this circle as a triangle. One might reply: I don't yet know whether it can, but I think I have to hand a hypothesis to deal with the problem, of the following sort: if the area is such that, when placed along its given line, it falls short by an area like the one placed alongside, one result follows, and a different one if this cannot happen to it. Using this hypothesis, I'm willing to tell you about the result of inscribing the area in this circle, whether it's impossible or not. (86e4–87b2)

This passage is one of the most perplexing in all the works of Plato. The language is so opaque, the example so under-determined, that scholars have long struggled to find the geometrical problem to which Socrates is alluding. There are at least three points where it is difficult to establish what a particular expression refers to: 'this area' (87a3–4), 'its given line' (87a4), and 'falls short by an area like the one placed alongside' (87a5–6). Despite well over a century of debate, there is still no agreed interpretation of this passage. In what follows, I shall describe the one that appears to me the least problematic available, although it is not free of difficulties.

This interpretation has been defended by Cook Wilson and Heath, and adopted by many, though by no means all, scholars subsequently.[9] A geometer is initially asked a question about an area, X (see diagram p. 135), which could be any rectilinear figure. The question is whether X can be inscribed as a triangle in a given circle (86e5–87a1). In reply, the geometer makes the following claim: if the area X can be placed as a rectangle ABCD on the diameter of the circle BH, such that it 'falls short'[10] of the length of the

---

[8] Vlastos 1991: 123 and Lloyd 1992: 166.

[9] Cook Wilson 1903 and Heath 1921: I, 298–303; see also Knorr 1986: 71–3 and Menn 2002: 209–11.

[10] The term 'falls short' is usually taken to be unproblematic. Bluck (1961: 442) comments: 'If a rectangle ABCD is applied to a line BH which is greater than the base of the rectangle, it was said to "fall short" by the area enclosed when DCH is completed as a rectangle.'

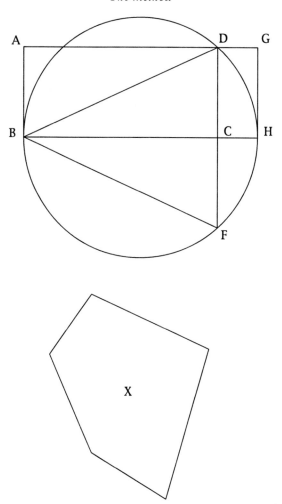

The geometrical example at *Meno* 86e6–87a2

diameter by another rectangle DCHG proportionately similar to ABCD, the answer to the original question is 'yes'; if not, the answer is 'no'.

In this interpretation, the various indeterminacies of the text have to be filled out as follows:

1 'This area' (87a3–4) refers to the rectilinear area X.
2 'Its given line' (87a4) has to be read as the diameter of the circle, BH – i.e. 'its' means 'of the circle'.

3 In the expression, 'it falls short by an area like the one placed alongside' (87a5–6), the term 'like' is here taken to mean 'similar' not 'identical'. (The similarity in question is geometrical proportion: BC : CD = CD : CH.)

4 We have to expand the text of 87a3–5, which translates literally as: 'if this area is such that, when placed on its given line . . .'. On this interpretation we have to add that the area is placed on the line *as a rectangle*.

It has to be admitted that, where 2 and 3 are concerned, there is plenty of room for debate as to whether these readings are philologically the most plausible.[11] The advantage of this interpretation, however, is that it maps well onto the ensuing argument about whether virtue is teachable. Socrates will shortly argue that, if virtue is knowledge, it is teachable. He then gives an argument to show that virtue is knowledge. In following this procedure, he has replaced Meno's original question, whether virtue is teachable, with the question whether it is knowledge. It is not difficult to see how this corresponds to the geometrical example as interpreted above:

Virtue is teachable = Area X can be inscribed as a triangle in the given circle.

Virtue is knowledge = Area X can be placed as a rectangle ABCD on the diameter of the circle BH, such that it falls short of the length of the diameter by another rectangle DCHG which is proportionately similar to ABCD.

A closely related advantage of the interpretation is that it does justice to the following feature of the method. In reducing the examination of *p* to that of *q*, we are saying that, if *q* then *p*, and if not-*q* then not-*p* (i.e. that *p* and *q* are logically equivalent). This feature is clearly present in both the geometrical and ethical arguments (87a6–7 and b5–c9). Some interpretations prior to Cook Wilson's foundered on this point. They only showed what would happen if *q* was true, and said nothing about the case where *q* is false: *p* might or might not follow.[12]

Even if we can find a satisfactory interpretation of the geometrical example, there is a further question: what makes it so difficult to understand? One answer is that Plato himself did not fully understand the example he was describing, perhaps because the mathematicians of his day were not sufficiently advanced. Alternatively, he might be faulted only for failing to describe the example clearly.[13] Here it is important to note that, although the description of the geometrical problem is indeterminate and imprecise, it is very difficult to prove that Plato has actually misunderstood anything.

---

[11] For objections to 2 and 3, see Bluck 1961: 450. In my view, these objections are not fatal.
[12] See Bluck 1961: 442–8 and Lloyd 1992: 168–70.
[13] This explanation is offered by Heath 1921: I, 300 n. 1 and Knorr 1986: 71.

If this is the correct explanation, one might then try to blunt the criticism by saying that Plato was writing for a readership familiar with the geometrical problem in question, and is allusive because he can expect his readers in the Academy to fill in the details. This suggestion, however, would still leave us with a problem about the relation between Socrates and Meno: even if Plato was communicating with a well-informed and esoteric readership, does Socrates really expect Meno to understand what he is saying? Perhaps Meno knew enough about geometry to follow the opaque references in the example, but it seems unlikely. Plato, it seems, has suffered a rare lapse of dramatic realism, momentarily transporting Meno into the ranks of his own Academy.

Yet, with a little more ingenuity, even this complaint can be answered. Although the example may have made sense to the Academy, Plato might deliberately make Socrates talk in terms that Meno cannot fully understand. Perhaps Socrates is attempting to satisfy – as well as mock – Meno's desire for the exotic and technical.[14] He is after all in the process of driving a bargain with him. We have already seen a clear instance of this when he gave the Empedoclean definition of colour (76d4–5): here Meno was also presented with something that, deep down, he did not really understand. By 86e, this combination of bargaining and mockery has become a familiar part of the *joie de vivre* of the dialogue. So although it is possible that the difficulty of this passage is due to Plato's failure to explain (or even understand) the geometry in question, there is a perfectly plausible explanation that permits a more favourable verdict.[15]

The ethical application of the method

I mentioned above that the method of hypothesis is one of 'problem reduction'. We substitute a question about p with one about its logical equivalent, q. In what follows, p is 'virtue is teachable', q 'virtue is knowledge'. In other words, the claim that virtue is knowledge serves as the basis from which we can deduce the truth of the claim that virtue is teachable. This established, Socrates sets about arguing that virtue is indeed knowledge (87d–89a), and so puts himself in a position to deduce that virtue is teachable at 89c.

Socrates' application of the method to the ethical questions of the *Meno* has also been the subject of intense scholarly interest over the

---

[14] See Weiss 2001: 133 for this approach.
[15] Lloyd (1992) also attributes to Socrates a strategy of deliberate opaqueness, but with a quite different rationale. See Appendix 3, pp. 225–6 below.

last few decades.[16] Within this literature there are two principal views about the nature and significance of the method of hypothesis. In what follows I shall endorse one of them, and then discuss the other in Appendix 2 (pp. 000–00).

There are two things upon which most scholars are agreed: one is that a hypothesis is a proposition posited as the basis for drawing a conclusion; the other that in using the hypothetical method Socrates uses a pattern of argument in which a particular proposition counts as 'the' hypothesis.[17] Given what I have said about the context in which the method of hypothesis is introduced at 86d–e, I would add two further points, which I mentioned briefly above. First, a hypothesis is something entertained tentatively, not something of which we have knowledge.[18] This is a consequence of saying that Socrates is temporarily renouncing the chronological priority of definition in concession to Meno at 86d8–e1. Second, one of the main points of dispute in the scholarly literature is the identity of 'the' hypothesis in the ethical argument of 87–9. One side thinks it is the proposition 'virtue is knowledge';[19] the other that it is the bi-conditional 'if virtue is knowledge it is teachable, and if it is not knowledge it is not teachable'.[20] In my view, the context in which the method is introduced points strongly in favour of the first interpretation. Socrates is attempting to compromise with Meno. He is giving up the chronological priority of definition (the demand that they investigate the acquisition question on the basis of explicit knowledge of the definition), but still insists on starting from a hypothesis about the nature of virtue. This makes it natural to take 'virtue is knowledge' as the hypothesis. In effect, we are given the genus of virtue, and hence the beginnings of a definition. Further support for this view as to what constitutes 'the' hypothesis can be found at 89c2–4 where Meno expresses his agreement with the whole argument by saying, 'it is clear, Socrates, according to the hypothesis, if virtue is knowledge, that it is teachable'. The most

---

[16] I.e. since Richard Robinson published the first edition of *Plato's Earlier Dialectic* in 1941.
[17] One scholar, Rose (1970: 1 and 5–7), has denied that we should be looking for a single 'dominant' hypothesis at all. However, the evidence is against her. At 86e3–4, Rose announces that he will investigate ἐξ ὑποθεσέως. Rose translates this as 'from hypothesis', rather than 'from *a* hypothesis' which would of course immediately count against her interpretation. But when he introduces the mathematical example to explain what he means by ἐξ ὑποθεσέως, he talks of the geometer presenting his questioner with 'a hypothesis . . . of the following sort' (87a2–3). This clearly favours the second reading of ἐξ ὑποθεσέως in 86e3–4, and shows that the method of hypothesis involves highlighting a particular dominant hypothesis, not merely that we are arguing on the basis of a number of premises.
[18] For the significance of this see pp. 140 and 224 below.
[19] See Friedländer 1945: 255, Cherniss 1947: 140, Robinson 1953: 116–20, Bluck 1961: 86, Sharples, 1985: 167 and Vlastos 1991: 124.
[20] For references see Appendix 2, p. 221 n. 3.

plausible reading of this sentence is to take the words 'if virtue is knowledge' in apposition to (and hence explaining) 'the hypothesis'.

In outline, then, what Socrates is doing at 87b–89a is to treat 'virtue is knowledge' as 'the' hypothesis, a claim of which he cannot be sure, but from which he is prepared to infer an answer to the original question of how virtue is acquired.

There is a complication for this view. At 87d2–3, just at the beginning of his argument that virtue is knowledge, Socrates lays down the premise that virtue is good, and calls *it* a hypothesis. If there is only one dominant hypothesis per argument, and if we have already assigned this role to the proposition that virtue is knowledge, how are we to accommodate the reference to another hypothesis at 87d3?

Cherniss has given an elegant solution to this puzzle.[21] The method, we should remember, is one of problem reduction: we find a proposition equivalent to *p*, *q*, and investigate that instead. This proposition, *q*, is 'the' hypothesis. So in the first, brief, stage of Socrates' argument, we hypothesise 'virtue is knowledge' and agree that 'virtue is teachable' follows from it. However, we then need to determine the truth of *q*, and at this point, because we are embarking on a new argument, we apply the method again. So we posit another proposition, *r*, (apparently) equivalent to *q*, from which we then derive *q*.[22] This proposition is 'virtue is good'. Thus, at one level of argument we posit a hypothesis and derive conclusions from it; but when it comes to determining the truth of the hypothesis itself, we posit a 'higher' one, from which the first can be derived. So, as long as we separate 87b–89a into two levels of argument, we can treat both 'virtue is knowledge' and 'virtue is good' as dominant hypotheses.

As described, this method anticipates what we find in the *Phaedo* (100a3–102a2). Here, Socrates attempts to answer one set of questions, about causation (or explanation) and particulars, by making the hypothesis that the forms exist as causes. He posits this hypothesis as something probable, using it as a premise from which to deduce answers to the questions that originally perplexed him. If someone then challenges him about the forms, he would make a fresh hypothesis, choosing the most probable from 'those above' (101d7). This seems like a development (in certain respects) of the *Meno*, at least on Cherniss' interpretation of 87d3. A further anticipation is that, in the *Phaedo*, we check the viability of our hypothesis by seeing if there are any inconsistencies among its consequences; in what follows in the *Meno*,

---

[21] Cherniss 1947: 140, accepted by Robinson 1953: 118. See also Bluck 1961: 90.
[22] Socrates retracts the equivalence later on in the work (97a6–7).

Socrates will find an apparent inconsistency between the consequence of the hypothesis, viz. that virtue is teachable, and the fact that there are no teachers and learners of virtue.

In the light of this, the method of hypothesis emerges as an important innovation and, like the theory of recollection, was to be taken up, developed and modified in later dialogues. But this merely exacerbates a problem I raised above. Overtly, Socrates introduces the method as a second best, and does so purely because Meno is too impatient to follow the preferred method. Yet, if this were all that was going on, why would Plato refine the method and reintroduce it in later works? Is there a more serious reason for introducing it over and above accommodating a particular interlocutor's impatience?

There is. The real importance of the method in the *Meno* is that it represents a compromise between what were for Plato two very powerful forces. On one hand there was a pressing need to get an answer to a question of practical importance – how virtue is acquired. The urgency of this question for Plato is clear from the number of his dialogues in which it appears: *Alcibiades I, Laches, Protagoras, Euthydemus, Republic* and *Laws.* On the other hand, I would suggest that Plato is strongly attracted to a certain methodological purism: where possible, an inquiry should proceed on the basis of an explicitly known specification, or set of premises. But to follow the purist route in this case runs the risk of postponing practical questions indefinitely in favour of more abstract inquiries – indefinitely, because the search for moral definitions has proved so elusive. Yet to launch too soon into the practical question runs the risk of sliding into assumptions – possibly erroneous – without even being aware of what they are. Following the method of hypothesis allows us to construct rigorous deductive arguments, all the time being aware of what we are taking for granted. This much can be conceded to the old purist methodology. At the same time we can start to address important practical questions, having acknowledged that we are doing so on the basis of a provisional assumption that we need to revisit at some later point and possibly overturn.

A good parallel for this can be found in the *Republic*, whose own pressing question is whether justice benefits the agent, a question intimately bound up with the issue of how one should lead one's life (344e1–3). To answer the question, however, we must find out what justice is. But it turns out that a truly adequate answer to this question would involve a very long inquiry into the Form of the Good (cf. 504b1–4 with 435d1–5). Methodological purists would postpone the original question until they had completed the inquiry into the Good, a process that might take many years (thirty, in the case of the rulers of the ideal state: cf. 540a4–9). But for Plato the original question is too pressing and needs answering, even if only in a provisional way. Accordingly, he has Socrates take a shorter route. They will define justice in the individual by seeing whether it has the same structure as the state, which they have agreed to be just in virtue of the harmony between its three parts. If they can show the soul also has three parts, then they can provisionally define its justice along the same lines. What is particularly interesting for our purposes is that the main argument for dividing the soul is based upon a mere hypothesis (437a6): nothing can experience contrary states (e.g. desires) in the same respect at the same time. As the soul can be both attracted and repelled by the same thing, it must have different parts. Such is the basis upon which the argument proceeds, and Socrates explicitly acknowledges that it may yet be overturned.

It is in the same spirit that I would argue the method of hypothesis is advanced in the *Meno* – as a way of making progress on a topic of pressing concern whilst being clear-eyed about the fallibility of one's reasoning. If so, it shows that Plato has constructed this section of the *Meno* to operate on two levels, very much in the same way as we found in earlier parts of the dialogue, especially the recollection passage. At both 80d and 86c–d, Meno prompts Socrates to introduce an important epistemological or method-ological innovation. At one level, Socrates makes his response merely as a way of engaging with Meno's wayward motivations – in the recollection pas-sage to re-energise him, in the hypothesis passage to accommodate his impa-tience. At the deeper level, however, Plato is using each episode to bring to the reader's attention a serious difficulty, as is evidenced by the importance of the solutions, both of which continue to be prominent in other works.

Seen in this light, the hypothesis passage joins the other three that I have discussed as an example where Plato puts the historical Socrates on trial. The pattern, as we have seen it emerging, is that Meno (in spite of himself) issues a challenge to a specifically Socratic assumption. In this case, the assumption is that we should achieve knowledge of the definition of virtue before we examine whether it is teachable.

There is good reason for believing this assumption to be Socratic, at least on the evidence of the *Laches* and the *Protagoras*. In the *Laches* Socrates asserts that, in order to know how virtue is best acquired, one must first know what it is.[23] The relevant passage from the *Protagoras* comes right at the end. At 360e, Socrates points out the odd state of affairs they have reached. Protagoras thinks virtue is not knowledge, but is teachable; Socrates thinks

---

[23] 190b7–c2. On this passage see Benson 1990: 38 and 41–3.

that it is knowledge but is not teachable. Yet, if it is knowledge it is teachable, and if it is not knowledge, it is not teachable. He then adds:

> And I should like to work our way through this matter until at last we reach what virtue is *and then* go back and consider whether it is teachable or not, lest perchance your Epimetheus beguile and trip us up in our investigation as he overlooked us in your account of his distribution. I like the Prometheus of your fable better than the Epimetheus; for he is of use to me, and I take Promethean thought continually for my own life when I am occupied with all these questions.[24]

One might think that this just makes knowledge of the definition sufficient for knowing whether virtue is teachable.[25] But this fails to explain the urgency with which Socrates seeks the definition. If there is another way of determining whether virtue is teachable, why does he not even mention it? Nor should we ignore the reference to Epimetheus and Prometheus. This harks back to Protagoras' myth in the earlier part of the dialogue, where Zeus ordered the two of them to distribute different qualities among all the animals that would enable them to survive. But by the time Epimetheus came to the human race, he had nothing left to give them, leaving Prometheus to intervene and steal for mankind the gift of fire. The point of the back-reference is that Epimetheus omitted what was *necessary* for human survival (321c1–3), which Prometheus, by contrast, seeks to provide. Similarly, Socrates takes forethought for what is necessary for resolving their question.

   The other features that make this passage in the *Meno* an instance of Socrates on trial fall readily into place. The Socratic position is clearly being challenged, but again Meno does so in spite of himself: we learn through, rather than from him. Certainly, his motives and attitude are open to question, for the episode is triggered because he is undisciplined, just as he was obtuse in the first episode, resentful in the second and obstructive in the third. Finally, Plato does present an emendation to the Socratic view – though this time within the dialogue itself (as well as in the *Republic*). In this respect, 86d–87b is closer to the recollection episode than it is to the stingray passage, where Socrates refuses to concede that the elenchus might be anything other than beneficial.

IN WHAT SENSE IS KNOWLEDGE TEACHABLE?

Before we go any further, we need to pause over the claim that knowledge can be taught (87c1–3). Clearly, this is central to the argument of the dialogue as a whole; for combined with the thesis that virtue is knowledge,

---

[24] 361c4–d5, trans Lamb 1924, emphasis added   [25] So Vlastos 1994: 83.

it yields an answer to Meno's original question about the acquisition of virtue.

But there is something puzzling about the claim and the way it is introduced:

. . . if [virtue] is similar or dissimilar to knowledge, is it teachable or not – or, as we were saying just now, recollectable? Let's not dispute over which word to use. But is it teachable? Or is it not clear to all that only knowledge can be taught to someone? (87b6–c3)

In commenting on the slave-boy examination only a few pages earlier, Socrates had insisted that he was not teaching the boy, only asking him questions (82e4 and 85d3; cf. 82b6–7). Although this point concerns the boy's recovery of true belief, it also applies to the recovery of knowledge, which is a continuation of the same process (85c9–d4). It may therefore come as a surprise that Socrates so soon after announces that knowledge, and only knowledge, is capable of being taught. What he also says, almost as a parenthesis, is that the expression 'recollectable' can be used inter-changeably with 'teachable' – the difference is merely one of terminology (87b8–c1).

To remove any inconsistency in his various remarks about teaching and knowledge, we need to distinguish different conceptions of teaching. I take it that at 87b–c 'teachable' means something quite specific: knowledge can be recollected with the aid of questioning. It is only in this sense, where the teacher acts as a catalyst working with the innate resources of the learner, that knowledge is teachable.[26]

This sense of teaching is to be contrasted with the approach epitomised in Gorgias' dealings with Meno. Although Gorgias did not claim to teach virtue, he did (in Meno's eyes) teach him what virtue is. But the way in which he did so was by transferring information. In the *Symposium* (175c7–e2), the speaker Agathon, who may also have been under the influence of Gorgias (cf. 198c1–2), believes in the possibility of learning by simple transmission, as if knowledge can be passed from one person to another like liquid into a container. It is in this sense that Socrates denies he is teaching the slave boy. If we have interpreted his argument correctly, he is making the plausible claim that the perception of logical relationships can never be imparted by hearsay.

---

[26] See Bluck 1961: 325–6, Devereux 1978: 120 and Desjardins 1985: 276. I agree with Bluck that we should take 'knowledge is recollectable' not merely to mean 'knowledge is something one can remember', but 'knowledge is something of which one can be reminded by someone else'. This sense implies that two people are involved and thus preserves the symmetry with 'teachable'.

One might say that the type of teaching in which Socrates is interested is 'maieutic' – that is, the teacher acts as a midwife, helping the learner to extract knowledge from within. This, however, raises a further question. When Socrates claims the role of midwife in the *Theaetetus* 149a–151d, he is clear that he has no knowledge himself. If we are to talk of teaching in a maieutic sense in the *Meno*, we need to ask whether someone can teach (i.e. make someone else knowledgeable) without having knowledge themselves.

On the transmission model of teaching, the teacher must have knowledge, for what they are doing is to impart something they already have to someone else. But, as Socrates moves to a new model of teaching, does he preserve this aspect of the old? In principle, he need not. For if the learner already has the knowledge latently, all the teacher needs to do is to ask the right questions to arouse it. One might then argue that asking the right questions does not require knowledge on the part of the teacher. True belief might suffice. Indeed one might even prompt the learner to recollect by asking them questions based on false beliefs.

Nevertheless, there are difficulties with the suggestion that the maieutic teacher does not require knowledge. They must ask the right questions in the right order. If they only have true belief, they might start by asking the appropriate questions but, since true belief is unstable, they will sooner or later go off track. This will in turn undermine the process of recollection. This is not to deny that the learner can ultimately recover their knowledge. But what would happen in the scenario just envisaged is that the teacher and the learner would become co-inquirers. There would no longer be any asymmetry between them to justify calling one the teacher and the other the learner. Instead they would both be prompting each other to recollect.

If so, Socrates in the *Meno* ought to insist that even the 'maieutic' teacher needs knowledge. If in the early stages of recollection the learner relies on questions posed by someone who is further advanced, this person is still not a teacher in the strict sense. A true teacher is someone capable of making another like himself, i.e. knowledgeable or, in the context of the *Meno*, virtuous. This point will be important when we consider one of Socrates' arguments below that virtue is not teachable (p. 175).

CHAPTER 12

Virtue is teachable: 87c–89c

In 87c–89c, Socrates pursues the line of argument from the previous section to establish the conclusion that virtue is teachable. Since they have agreed that it is teachable if and only if it is knowledge, he spends most of this section arguing that it is indeed a form of knowledge (87d–89a). But before drawing the conclusion that it is teachable, he also pauses to reject the possibility that it comes by nature (89a–b), something suggested by Meno at the very beginning of the dialogue.

VIRTUE AS KNOWLEDGE (87d–89a)

Socrates begins by laying down the hypothesis that virtue is good. Since all good things are beneficial, virtue must be beneficial. He then turns to consider the sorts of things often considered beneficial, starting with bodily or material assets such as health, strength, beauty and wealth. Although these sometimes benefit us, they only do so when used correctly; otherwise they harm us. Next he considers qualities of the soul, e.g. temperance, justice, courage, mental agility and magnificence. If any one of these is not some sort of knowledge, it may be either beneficial or harmful. If courage, for example, is not actually knowledge, it amounts to some sort of 'daring' (*tharros*), which results in good or harm, depending on whether it is used wisely. In sum, all qualities of the soul apart from knowledge itself end in happiness when guided by knowledge, but in the opposite when guided by ignorance. On their own,[1] they are neither beneficial nor harmful. He then concludes that, as virtue is something beneficial, it must be a form of knowledge (88d2–3).

Finally, he returns to consider the role of material assets such as wealth. It is the soul's correct or incorrect guidance that makes material things beneficial or harmful. But, in turn, it is knowledge that makes all other qualities

---

[1] I take this to be the meaning of αὐτὰ καθ' αὑτά (88c6). See Vlastos 1991: 305–6.

of the soul beneficial. Knowledge is therefore the cause of everything else becoming beneficial: it is 'the beneficial', as he puts it at 89a1–2, which again leads him to conclude that virtue is knowledge, or at least a species of knowledge.

How much does Socrates want to prove?

Let us start by focusing on an objection that seems to go straight to the heart of the argument. Consider the discussion of psychological qualities at 88b1–8:

soc. Now consider: among these qualities, do those that seem to you not to be knowledge but different from it sometimes harm us and sometimes benefit us? For example, courage – if it is not knowledge but something like daring: when a person is daring without intelligence, isn't he harmed, whereas when he does so with intelligence he's benefited?
men. Yes.
soc. And isn't it the same with temperance and quickness at learning – whatever is learnt and controlled with intelligence is beneficial, whatever without it is harmful?

Here Socrates allows that qualities such as courage or temperance might be considered distinct from knowledge. But his next move is to insist such qualities can only be beneficial if coupled with knowledge. But this, so goes the objection, does not show that virtue is knowledge. If daring in isolation is not beneficial, the same can be said for knowledge: without daring, it might prove ineffectual, unable to determine action because it is overpowered by fear. So Socrates cannot conclude that virtue is knowledge: he ought to say that virtue is a composite consisting of knowledge and a number of other psychological qualities, such as daring or self-discipline.[2]

Underlying this objection is the following basic assumption: when Socrates says that virtue is beneficial he means that, on its own, it is sufficient to benefit us; hence knowledge, if it is to be virtue, must itself be sufficient for benefit. Yet he has failed to show this. Knowledge may be a necessary condition of benefit: wherever there is benefit, there must be knowledge. But it is not sufficient.

There are two ways of reacting to the objection that both accept this basic assumption. The first is just to admit that Socrates has made a mistake. The second is to challenge the standard interpretation of Socrates' conclusion, and claim that he is not actually identifying virtue with knowledge. Instead,

---

[2] See Santas 2001: 43.

it has been argued, knowledge is only supposed to be a component of virtue. Commentators who take this line focus on an ambiguity in the sentence that expresses the conclusion of the argument (89a3–4). On a neutral translation, this reads:

So do we say that virtue is knowledge – either the whole of it or some part?

I have been taking this to mean that virtue is knowledge, either the whole or a part of knowledge.[3] But the Greek could mean something quite different: virtue – either the whole of it or a part of it – is knowledge.[4] If so, there could be an element of virtue other than knowledge, e.g. a non-cognitive component such as daring or self-discipline.

However, although this reading seems to answer the objection to the argument, it is ruled out both by the context and by textual considerations. To show that virtue is teachable (period), Socrates needs to show that it is no more than knowledge.[5] If it were knowledge plus an affective state, its mode of acquisition would have to be similarly complex – teaching plus some non-intellectual training (e.g. habituation). Furthermore, Socrates has already identified virtue with some kind of knowledge at 88d2–3: 'according to this argument virtue, being something beneficial, ought to be a form of knowledge'. (See also 88c4–5: 'if virtue is one of the qualities in the soul, and if it must be beneficial, it ought to be knowledge'.) The point of the qualification at 89a4 is merely to show that there is a choice between saying virtue is the only (true) form of knowledge and that it is one form among many.

I wish to propose a quite different response to the objection and to challenge its basic assumption that virtue must be sufficient to benefit us. To pave the way, let us first consider exactly what Socrates' argument does in fact establish. Grant him that, on their own, neither assets that are external to the soul nor the internal ones (apart from knowledge) benefit us; and that, to do so, they need the addition of knowledge. What does this actually prove about knowledge? Not that it benefits us on its own: that is the point of the objection.[6] But this does not place knowledge exactly on a par with the other psychological qualities. There are in fact two asymmetries. First, it is not true to say of knowledge that, lacking other assets, it may as well harm us as benefit us. If we lack daring, for instance, our knowledge will not actively harm us; it will just fail to benefit us. If our cowardice or acrasia causes harm, we cannot say that our knowledge caused that harm; it played

---

[3] For this reading see e.g. Bluck 1961: 336, Irwin 1977: 301 n. 57 and Sharples 1985: 165.
[4] See Thompson 1901: 161; cf. Irwin 1995: 139.   [5] Cf. Irwin 1995: 138.
[6] There may in fact be occasions when knowledge does produce benefit on its own, but the argument does not establish this, let alone that knowledge is always beneficial on its own.

no causal role at all. The second asymmetry is that, unlike any other quality of the soul, knowledge must always be present if there is to be benefit.[7] Nothing in the argument shows that daring, for instance, is necessary on each and every occasion for benefit.

My contention is that this is all Socrates wishes to say about knowledge. It was never his aim to prove that knowledge is sufficient to produce benefit. This is because he never endorsed the basic assumption that virtue is sufficient to benefit us. We should always have been wary of accepting this claim in the first place, especially when Socrates was thinking about the role of external assets. It is noteworthy that in the argument as a whole he is thinking of virtue as a quality that will benefit both the individual and the city that he leads (cf. 87d8–e1 and 98c5–9). When he talks about external assets sometimes harming and sometimes benefiting in this context, he is most naturally taken to mean that a rich person might use their money for good or evil. In the first case, he surely means that the good could not have been produced were there no money available. In a political example, the leader uses the wealth of the city for its benefit. But the city needs some wealth: even the ideal state of the *Republic* needs resources to flourish.

What then does Socrates mean by saying that virtue is beneficial? I would propose that it is a cause of benefit in something like the sense in which Socrates talks of causes (*aitiai*) at *Phaedo* 96a5ff. Here, he advocates using forms as causes. If an object becomes large, the cause of this is the form of largeness, rather than, for instance, the fact that the object exceeds another by three feet. The cause of something's beauty is the form beauty, not its particular colour, for example (100c10–d8). It is important that, in the run-up to this passage, Socrates has been expressing dissatisfaction with materialist accounts of explanation. Anaxagoras, in particular, promised to reveal intelligence (*nous*) as the cause of everything, on the basis of which Socrates expected him to explain natural phenomena by reference to the good: an object is in such and such a state because that is best for it. But instead Anaxagoras talked only of the material conditions for phenomena being as they are. This, says Socrates, is to confuse the true cause of something with those pre-conditions without which it could not be a cause (99b2–4). Returning to the previous examples, Socrates would say that features such as overtopping another object by three feet or being made of gold are not causes, but merely pre-conditions of largeness or beauty on specific occasions.

Leaving aside the commitment to forms here, or the interest in teleology, I wish merely to focus upon two features of the concept of a cause and on

---

[7] This is the claim that Socrates later retracts when reconsidering the argument (97a6–7).

the distinction made between causes and their pre-conditions. For something to count as a cause, certain things must be true of it: first, it could never be the cause of the opposite condition (largeness could never make something small); second, it must always be present when that condition obtains. Socrates uses these two points to differentiate causes from their pre-conditions. What is a condition of beauty on one occasion, e.g. being gold, could be present where there is ugliness, and need not be present on other occasions where an object is beautiful.

This notion of a cause, together with the distinction between cause and condition, helps to make sense of the argument that virtue is knowledge at *Meno* 87d–89a. My claim is not that the thought of this passage is exactly the same as the causal theorising in the *Phaedo*, but that it is structurally analogous. Thus knowledge is to be seen as the cause of benefit, but this only means that (a) it must be present whenever benefit is produced and (b) it can never produce the opposite of benefit, i.e. harm. By contrast, the other psychological qualities are mere conditions, fulfilling neither of these two criteria. Where producing benefit is concerned, knowledge has a salience that other assets lack.

The argument therefore should be seen in the following light: it starts from the assumption that virtue is a cause (in something akin to the sense of the *Phaedo*) of benefit, not that virtue is on its own sufficient to produce benefit. Knowledge then turns out to be the only quality of soul that can be a cause of benefit in this sense; thus virtue is knowledge.

So once we withdraw the assumption that virtue must be sufficient for producing benefit, we can set the whole argument in a much better light. This is not to return to the interpretation that sees knowledge as a mere part of virtue. It is the whole of virtue. What that interpretation saw as the other parts, e.g. daring and endurance, are not causes of benefit but conditions. Hence they cannot count as parts of virtue itself.

Socrates' underlying moral psychology

In developing the argument as he does, Socrates seems to espouse a moral psychology that may surprise some readers. He allows that, in addition to knowledge, there exist in the soul non-rational affective states such as daring. What he does not say explicitly, but nevertheless implies, is that if we are to call daring 'courage' and self-discipline 'temperance', neither courage nor temperance should count as virtues.

In the *Euthydemus*, he offers a closely parallel argument to show that virtue is a form of knowledge (278e–282d). We find exactly the same division of assets – external and internal – and the same point being made, that on their own they are neither beneficial nor harmful, but require the guidance of knowledge. In describing the internal assets, the qualities of soul, he explicitly talks of 'courage' and 'temperance' as assets that are neither good nor bad on their own (281c6). 'Temperance' presumably refers to some quality of will power or self-discipline that enables one to pursue a resolution despite pleasures tempting one away (cf. *Meno* 88b6 and c2). As in the *Meno*, therefore, Socrates is entertaining a moral psychology that allows the existence of affective dispositions acting as conditions for virtue to cause benefit on particular occasions.

Now compare this position with that of *Republic* IV 439e–442c. The division of the soul into different parts seems to lead us to a very similar position: the benefit associated with courage results when knowledge resides in the rational part and the spirited part provides some sort of affective quality. Even though not explicitly termed 'daring', this acts as a boost and enables the agent to persevere with the decisions of reason even in the face of danger. This position seems similar to that of *Meno* 88b–d.

Yet there seems to be a difference. In *Republic* IV, the quality that results when the spirited part makes its contribution is not only called courage, but is also a species of virtue, whereas the position suggested by the *Meno* and the *Euthydemus* in effect disqualify it from being described in this way. In fact, however, the *Republic* may go on to refine its position and to draw closer to the other two dialogues. In book VII 518d9–519a1, Socrates hints that the only true virtue is knowledge; courage and temperance are merely 'so-called' virtues.[8]

At any rate, whether or not the *Republic* ultimately classifies courage as a genuine virtue, there does seem to be a general similarity with the position articulated at *Meno* 87d–89a in terms of underlying moral psychology. However, it is unclear whether Socrates in the *Meno* is advocating this position as his own preferred view. Recall again the point where he starts to contrast knowledge with other qualities of the soul:

> Now consider: among these qualities, do those that seem to you not to be knowledge but different from it sometimes harm us and sometimes benefit us? For example,

---

[8] 'Then the other so-called virtues of the soul do seem akin to those of the body. For it is true that, where they do not pre-exist, they are afterward created by habit and practice. But the virtue of reason, it seems, is certainly of a more divine quality, a thing that never loses its potency, but, according to the direction of its conversion, becomes useful and beneficent, or, again, useless and harmful' (518d9–519a1, trans. Shorey 1930, modified). (This does not imply that the virtue itself can lead to harm; only that reason, the faculty from which it derives, could be wrongly directed.) On this passage see Sedley 1999: 322–3 with n. 20.

courage – if it is not knowledge but something like endurance: when a person endures without intelligence, isn't he harmed, whereas when he does so with intelligence he's benefited? (88b1–6)

The idea that courage is not a form of knowledge but an affective state is offered as the second of two alternatives. But imagine he had developed the first and said that it is a form of knowledge – specifically, knowledge of what pertains to happiness (cf. 88c2–3). Obviously, he would have moved a step closer to fulfilling his overall task, viz. to show that virtue is knowledge. But what would this alternative consist in, and how exactly would it differ from the one that he actually follows?

I would suggest that this alternative has already been adumbrated by the argument of 77b–78b, which I interpreted as helping to support the thesis that virtue is knowledge: if I know that x leads to my overall good, whereas y leads to unhappiness, I shall have no desire for y at all, only for x. Knowledge is thus sufficient for virtue, as there will be no conflicting desires to be overcome (see above p. 53). Courage, for instance, is just a matter of knowing that it is better to stand firm on the battlefield; temperance, that it is better to abstain from pursuing a pleasure. This is the so-called 'intellectualist' account of virtue, which is often attributed to the historical Socrates.

In the light of this, we can now represent the two options suggested at 88b as follows. In both cases, virtue is the cause of benefit. In neither is Socrates claiming that it is sufficient to produce benefit, since at the very least external assets will be conditions of its doing so. The positions differ of course, when it comes to the internal assets, the qualities of soul. On the intellectualist conception, there are fewer internal assets that act as conditions: because courage and temperance are forms of knowledge, there is no need for the affective qualities of daring and endurance, although there will still be a need for other cognitive qualities that do not count as knowledge, such as having a good memory (in the standard, rather than Platonic) sense and being quick at learning (88a8).

So what is going on at *Meno* 87d–89a, specifically at 88b? We have two versions of the thesis that virtue is knowledge: one intellectualist, the other closer to the psychology of the *Republic*. The text suggests that Socrates is taking a dual track approach to prove that virtue is knowledge. For those who already accept that psychological qualities such as temperance and courage are forms of knowledge, his conclusion that virtue is knowledge follows easily. So, for the sake of argument perhaps, he takes on a more difficult challenge. Many people conceive of the virtues as consisting in non-cognitive qualities such as daring or self-control[9] and, in doing so, assume a non-intellectualist moral psychology. In response to such a conception, Socrates replies that knowledge is still required and that it, rather than the quality alleged to be a virtue, is the source of benefit, and hence true virtue itself.

But which version of the overall thesis does Socrates himself endorse? There is nothing in the text to suggest that Socrates is tentative about the argument of 77b–78b. So it seems that he himself adopts the intellectualist alternative mentioned in passing at 88b, but pursues the other to convince even those who adopt a different moral psychology to agree with the overall thesis that virtue is knowledge. Nevertheless, it is striking that Plato should consider it worth having Socrates develop a line of thought that was later to be espoused in the *Republic*. Perhaps he was already tempted to move in that direction while writing the *Meno*.

Finally, we need to consider an objection to the position that Socrates develops for the sake of argument at 88b–89a. Knowledge as the cause of benefit is virtue, while 'daring' is merely a condition of knowledge producing benefit, just as money or health might be. Suppose, however, that someone who has knowledge lacks daring. Since they have the knowledge, they are virtuous; yet they will not stand fast in battle, and may indeed act acratically. But surely acrasia and virtue are incompatible.

Interestingly enough, the same problem arises for the view expressed *Republic* VII 518d–e. Here only knowledge counts as true virtue. But what if someone had knowledge but lacked daring (perhaps because they had been trained or habituated in the wrong way)? Would not the same paradoxical mixture of virtue and acrasia obtain? In principle, it would. But the way in which the *Republic* stops this result is by adding in a number of further assumptions about moral psychology, including the claim that one could not properly develop knowledge of the good if the non-rational parts of the soul had not already been adequately prepared by a long process of education involving the arts and physical training to instil the requisite habits and character.[10]

In fact, Plato has already prepared the way for such an approach in the *Meno*. Knowledge will only come through patient dialectic of the kind

---

[9] This might be what Plato calls 'demotic' or 'civic' virtue at *Phaedo* 82a11–b3 and *Republic* IV 430b6–c4 and VI 500d4–8.

[10] See e.g. III 401e2–402a4 and VI 485a4–487a8. This point was taken over by Aristotle, who thought that anyone lacking the correct habits would have their rational judgement distorted by wayward passions or desires (*N.E.* VI 12, 1144a29–b1).

we see exemplified in the slave-boy demonstration. Learning of this kind requires certain qualities that Socrates highlights throughout the dialogue. Endurance is one of them: in response to Meno's desire to give up in the face of *aporia*, Socrates reminds him of the need to show intellectual staying power (81d6–7; cf. 86b8–9). But to follow the inquiry in the right way also requires self-discipline – again something that Socrates has to bring to Meno's attention (86d6). Furthermore, if learning requires co-operation, it also requires mildness and a sense of justice between the interlocutors, such that they keep to their agreements (75d4; cf. 76a9–c2).[11] In other words, discovery does not come out of the blue, morally speaking, and someone who lacks endurance and self-discipline and certain other moral qualities is no more likely to have acquired knowledge in the *Meno* than in the *Republic*.

So the argument of 88b–89a can escape the objection that it makes virtue and acrasia compatible. For the very qualities that, according to the objector, might make someone act against their knowledge would actually have stopped them acquiring that knowledge in the first place.

A final word of clarification on this point: although Socrates develops a non-intellectualist psychology at 88b–89a, his own position is intellec-tualist, as 77b–78b suggests. However, on either theory he thinks that the acquisition of the knowledge in which virtue consists requires such qualities as endurance and mildness. On the non-intellectualist theory, these qual-ities will be non-cognitive, on his preferred view, cognitive. In the second case, however, it is important to stress that these qualities are not the fully developed virtues, otherwise a vicious circle threatens: one would not be able to acquire knowledge without already possessing it – shades of Meno's challenge. However, Socrates need only be saying that discovery presup-poses qualities *en route* to virtue – e.g. a state of mildness that consists in true belief. As one advances in the process of inquiry, the necessary conditions to sustain it will also develop into knowledge. (See further p. 212 below.)

THE VALUE OF KNOWLEDGE

Instrumental goods

Any adequate understanding of this passage needs to probe the notion of 'good' at work in it, in particular by introducing the distinction between something being good instrumentally and good as an end (or as a final

---

[11] See above p. 37. Given the close association between recollection and religion (see above pp. 93–4), Socrates would also argue that dialectic requires a religious attitude – a willingness to be initiated, again something that Meno is too impatient to do (76e7–9).

good).[12] When Socrates talks of virtue and knowledge as being good, or of the assets becoming good when guided by knowledge, what sense of 'good' is in play?

To clarify the issue, we should start with the sense of good that is applied to virtue (and to knowledge, with which it is eventually identified). Is Socrates arguing that virtue is instrumentally good, good as an end or both? He must have the instrumental sense in mind, if not exclusively. This is required by a remark made towards the beginning of the argument. Having said that anything good is beneficial, he adds that virtue 'makes us beneficial' (87d8–e2). In a clear back-reference to this passage later on in the dialogue, he claims that virtue makes us beneficial to our city (98c5–9; cf. also 89b6–7). Throughout this final section of the dialogue he is giving virtue a political, other-regarding dimension: it is the quality by which the great Athenians such as Pericles have improved the city. This in turn tells us about the meaning of 'good' in the argument of 87d–89a: virtue is beneficial because it enables us to produce some further good for the city; it must therefore be instrumentally good.

But what of the benefit that virtue brings to the individual who has it? Does Socrates mean that it is an instrumental good, good as an end or both? The idea that virtue is a final good is of course very familiar in ancient philosophy. In the *Republic*, for instance, Socrates defends the claim that justice is good as an end, and the idea has been attributed to the historical Socrates and was later developed by the Stoics. But I doubt very much whether it is in play in *Meno* 87d–89a. In other texts – Platonic, Aristotelian or Stoic – the goodness of virtue is in part that it constitutes the perfection of human nature, or even approximates to the divine. Accordingly it makes sense to see it as being good as an end. But in *Meno* 87d–89a, the only value it is explicitly said to have is that it produces happiness (*eudaimonia* 88c3) by showing how to *use* one's assets correctly. This renders it instrumentally good, and the passage gives us no reason for attributing to it any other kind of value.

When he talks of knowledge guiding our assets in this way, he says that they too become good (88d1–89a1). Here again, he has in mind the instrumental sense: the goal is happiness and these assets are all deployed as means to attain that goal. For the sake of argument, however, suppose that Socrates was interested in final goods when discussing the value of the assets.[13] Consider what his conclusion would have to be. He would be saying that money, for example, on its own is not valuable as an end but

[12] This distinction appears explicitly at the beginning of *Republic* II (357b4–d2).
[13] As Vlastos does in 1991: 305

becomes so when guided by knowledge; the same would apply to internal assets like daring.

We can make sense of this position, but only by keeping two distinctions clearly apart: that between instrumental and final goods, and that between intrinsic and extrinsic value. This point comes out clearly in Kant, for whom happiness is valuable as an end, but only when accompanied by good will. Happiness is an extrinsic but final good, for it depends for its value on something else (good will) rather than possessing that value in itself.[14] (The happiness of a successful villain, for example, will not be good.) Nevertheless, when it does have the value granted to it by good will, that value is not instrumental but final.

It is within the realm of possibility that a distinction of this kind is at work in *Meno* 87d–89a, but highly unlikely. If it were, we would have to add another refinement, this time of an Aristotelian variety. At 88c2–3, Socrates says that the assets, when correctly used, result in happiness. This would have to mean not that money, daring and so on are instrumental in producing happiness as something quite distinct from themselves but that, once turned into final ends, they become components of happiness. Again, this is a coherent theory. Yet to read so recondite and sophisticated a position into such a brief argument is to strain the limits of plausibility too far. For one thing, how can Meno possibly be expected to understand all this? Is he familiar with such niceties, and fully in control of the distinction between intrinsic and final goods? For this reason, it is far more plausible to take the more intuitive reading of this passage, and maintain that throughout Socrates is discussing the instrumental value of all the different assets available to us.

The regress objection of the Euthydemus

The notion of a final good is not only absent from the *Meno*, it is conspicuously absent from it; and the fact that Socrates only considers instrumental goods in this argument leads to an important problem, one that he raises explicitly in the *Euthydemus*. In this work there are two discussions of virtue: I have already referred to the first, 278e–282d, which establishes that virtue is knowledge. Though longer, this reaches a similar conclusion to *Meno* 87d–89a. But, very interestingly, at a later point in the dialogue, 288d–292e, Socrates takes up this conclusion and subjects it to criticism. In an attempt to find the content of this knowledge, he dismisses crafts like carpentry

---

[14] *Groundwork of the Metaphysic of Morals*, 392–6. See Korsgaard 1983.

and medicine, because they produce outcomes that are on their own neither good nor bad; hence the knowledge that produces such assets must
be correspondingly neutral. He then tries to identify the benefit produced
by the knowledge in which virtue consists. Because it has been agreed that
only knowledge is good, this further benefit must be a form of knowledge.
So what makes this new knowledge good, except that it in turn produces
a further good, which also has to be a form of knowledge? Faced with the
prospect of an infinite regress, Socrates throws his hands up in despair.

Returning to the *Meno*, we can see how the same problem arises. The
seeds of trouble are sown in the very first steps of the argument. In saying
that all good things are beneficial (by which he turns out to mean that
they are all instrumental goods), he implies that each good thing produces
some further good. Since this further good is itself instrumentally good, it
is productive of yet another instrumental good, and so on *ad infinitum*.

As in the *Euthydemus*, we can generate a specific version of this regress
by deploying the claim that knowledge is the only good:

(a) Knowledge alone is good.
(b) All good things are instrumental goods.
(c) Therefore knowledge produces a further good.
(d) That good must be a form of knowledge.
(e) It must produce a further good, i.e. more knowledge – and so on *ad
    infinitum.*

To stop this regress, Socrates would need to introduce the concept of a
final good explicitly into the argument. In fact he has opened up a place
for the concept at 88c3 by saying that assets guided by knowledge lead to
happiness (*eudaimonia*). This presumably is doing the work of a final good,
since happiness is in itself not beneficial, but explains why other things,
which lead to it, are beneficial. But this merely raises the further question
of what *eudaimonia* itself consists in.

To pursue this question would take us too far afield. My purpose here is
merely to show that the notion of the good is very underdeveloped in the
Meno. In particular, the claim, 'virtue is good', obvious though it may sound,
needs much greater exploration. The argument of 87d–89a only entertains
the proposition that virtue is instrumentally good; from the perspective
of the *Euthydemus*, this position, taken together with other assumptions,
generates a vicious regress; from the perspective of the *Republic*, where virtue
is also good as an end, the proposition represents only a partial truth. But
all this is to be expected: at 87d3 Socrates called the proposition, 'virtue is
good', a hypothesis. However obvious it may appear, it is in fact far from
clear, and to understand it better we need to start by making the distinction

between instrumental and final goods. Having done that, we need then to consider what might count as the final good – the most profound question raised by the *Republic*.

Our analysis of the argument of 87d–89a, especially of its shortcomings, dovetails in one very important respect with the specific interpretation I gave of the hypothetical method in the *Meno*. I claimed that the method has an important similarity to its use in the *Phaedo*: a hypothesis is a proposition tentatively held, which may be challenged by an investigation of its consequences.[15] Within the *Meno* itself, the hypothesis that virtue is knowledge is challenged and found to generate a contradiction with the claim that there are no teachers and learners of virtue. What we can now see is that the 'higher' hypothesis, virtue is good, also generates unpalatable consequences in the form of an infinite regress, as set out in the *Euthydemus*. The problem with the hypothesis is not that it is false, but that it is inadequately understood. Ultimately, the only solution will be to ascend the upward path towards the Good recommended in the *Republic*.

VIRTUE DOES NOT COME BY NATURE (89a–b)

Now that Socrates has argued that virtue is knowledge, he is in a position to conclude that it is teachable. He does this at 89a3–4, and then continues:

SOC. If so, people would not be good by nature.
MEN. I think not.
SOC. And in addition, there would be this point: if good people came into being
   by nature, we would have people who recognised those of the young who
   had good natures; and once those people had revealed them to us, we would
   set them aside and guard them in the Acropolis, placing a seal on them even
   more than if they were gold, so that no one would corrupt them; but when
   they came of age they could be useful to their cities.

(89a5–b7)

Socrates' first statement constitutes an argument that virtue does not come by nature, though it is so brief that it might pass by unnoticed. If spelt out, the argument is that whatever is a case of knowledge cannot come by nature; virtue is a case of knowledge; therefore it cannot come by nature. What follows in the rest of the passage quoted is a separate argument: this is clearly sign-posted with the words 'and in addition' (89b1).

In the second argument Socrates claims that, if virtue did come by nature, there would be people who could recognise the qualities in the young; and

---

[15] See pp. 138 and 139 above.

further that we would follow their advice and set the young apart in some safe place; yet none of this obtains, so virtue does not come by nature. This argument is easily challenged. One objection is that it may be very difficult to detect the quality in the young. In turn this may be because there is no agreement as to what virtue is. Thus, even if some people are accurate talent-spotters, the rest of us might not accept their judgements. So it seems very unwise of Socrates to mount an argument based on common practice, or the lack of it.[16] This objection is exacerbated if one looks ahead to the *Republic*. In books VI–VII Socrates is very clear that in the ideal state one generation of rulers will talent-spot the next generation, set them apart and ensure that they are not corrupted. In III 415a2–c7, he even talks of the naturally talented as the 'gold' class, as if developing the imagery of the *Meno*. Yet what the rulers are able to do is no ordinary task. It requires exceptional insight to know who will be best suited to rule.

What then of the first argument? We find it repeated – and somewhat amplified – at 98c8–d5. By this point he has argued that true belief, no less than knowledge, is useful to the city. But since neither knowledge nor true belief comes by nature, people do not become good by nature.

This point, though stated briefly, is of considerable philosophical interest. To some readers, Socrates' claim may come as a surprise. Earlier in the work, he has argued that knowledge (and, *en route* to it, true belief) comes by recollection. That is, it is born with us and waits to be aroused by the appropriate catalyst. I have called this theory one of innate knowledge, and most commentators and writers on the *Meno* see it as an innatist theory of some sort. But then why does Socrates deny that knowledge comes by nature? The answer lies in the specific conception of nature that he is using. The first argument (89a5–7 and 98c8–d5) only makes sense if we contrast 'nature' with any process that requires attention and effort. Exactly the same sense is at issue in the *Protagoras*:

> That people do not regard virtue as natural or spontaneous, but as something taught and acquired after careful preparation by those who acquire it – of this I will now endeavour to convince you.[17]

If something comes 'by nature', it appears without any effort, just as certain physical characteristics might.[18]

The reason that this is philosophically important is that it shows a sharp distinction between Plato's brand of innateness and later varieties. For him,

---

[16] Klein 1965: 219–20.   [17] 323c5–8, trans. Lamb 1924.
[18] The same conception of nature is at work in the second argument (89b1–7). If virtue comes by nature, all that seems necessary for its development is that those who have it are kept free from corruption. No mention is made of any effort or labour in the process. See Weiss 2001: 137–8.

what is innate to the soul is not aroused spontaneously and without effort. Rather, it has to be elicited through sustained questioning ('teaching'), a process that will require some determination and staying power. But later thinkers, some of whom styled themselves 'Platonists', espoused versions of innatism that involve the sense of 'natural' dismissed as an option at *Meno* 89a and *Protagoras* 323c. Typically, they thought that certain principles and maxims, both moral and logical, manifest themselves at an early stage in our thought, without any attention or learning. The same applied to certain concepts, such as cause, substance or identity. These theories do not deny that there are further stages in the arousal of innate knowledge that require careful attention and effort, but they still insist that the early stages of the process are spontaneous.

Elsewhere, I have argued at length that Platonic recollection is not to be assimilated to such theories.[19] Plato did not think that any stage of recollection is automatic or spontaneous. In fact, he thought that most people do not even begin to recollect at all. To put the point in the context of the *Meno*, recollection only begins once one has started on the road to *aporia* – or even after that point. I shall not rehearse the arguments for that position here, except to say that the way in which Socrates dismisses nature as a route by which virtue is acquired lends it clear support.[20]

However, this does reveal a gap in Socrates' argument. Even if he is right that virtue is knowledge (or true belief) and that it comes by recollection, he does not consider the possibility that the early stages of recollection might happen 'naturally' or spontaneously, without effort or attention. In other words, many of his commentators have (wrongly) thought that the early stages of recollection are spontaneous and happen in everyone. If that really had been Plato's view, he could have said that virtue comes partly by teaching (i.e. questioning) and partly by nature. The fact he dismisses nature may show that these commentators are wrong in their interpretation. But it could be said to be a fault on Plato's part not to have Socrates consider the possibility.[21]

---

[19] Scott 1995: chs. 1, 2 and 9.
[20] See also *Phaedrus* 237d6–9, where the desire for pleasure is described as 'innate' (ἔμφυτος) and distinguished from acquired judgements about the good. It is interesting that Socrates nowhere uses the word ἔμφυτος in describing recollection. On my view this is no anomaly: unlike the arousal of appetitive desire, the process of recollection does not happen naturally or without effort.
[21] A possible response is that Plato was rather sceptical about the evidence for this more optimistic variety of innatism. In the seventeenth century, thinkers were quite confident that most people had tapped into a common source of moral truth, and used innateness to explain this fact. Plato, I think, kept his optimism for the thought that we can discover moral truths if we persevere, rather than claiming that we have already made some headway in establishing the right foundations for moral knowledge.

This relates to a more general problem in the work, one that was detectable from the very opening lines. Meno asks whether virtue comes by teaching, nature or in some other way. Socrates, as we saw on p. 16 above, does not appear to challenge the assumption that virtue must come exclusively by one route. In the end, he does consider the possibility that it might come by one of two routes (teaching or divine dispensation), but he still does not consider the possibility that it might come by two or more routes combined, e.g. nature and teaching.

There is another sense in which nature might have figured in Socrates' own theory. This relates to a point made in the conclusion of the slave-boy passage, 85c9–d1, where he asserts that the slave boy will achieve as good a knowledge as anyone, as long as he continues to be questioned about geometry. As we saw (pp. 107–8), this assumes that everyone has equal ability or, in terms of the theory of recollection, that the latent knowledge is equally (though not at all *easily*) accessible to all in their present incarnation. In the light of this, of course, it is not so surprising that Socrates then proceeds to dismiss nature even as a partial answer to the question of how virtue is acquired. By contrast, the *Phaedrus* allows for differences between people's specific natures: even though they all have the same knowledge latent within them, some may perhaps not be able to retrieve it in their current incarnation. If the *Meno* had done the same, it would have had to conclude that virtue comes by a combination of nature and teaching.

CHAPTER 13

Virtue is not teachable: 89e–96d

INTRODUCTION

Having argued that virtue is knowledge and hence teachable, Socrates begins to express some doubts:

soc. I'm not retracting the statement that virtue is teachable if it's knowledge. But see whether you think I'm right to doubt that it *is* knowledge. Tell me this: if something is teachable, not just virtue, isn't it necessary for there to be teachers and learners of it?
MEN. I think so.
soc. And conversely, if there were no teachers or learners of something, wouldn't we be right in surmising that it isn't teachable?
MEN. That's true. But do you think there are no teachers of virtue?

(89d3–e5)

The assumption that there must actually be or have been teachers and learners of something if it is to be considered teachable is crucial for what follows: throughout 89e–96d, Socrates scours the scene to find teachers of virtue, first with the new character Anytus, then with Meno; and when the search proves to be unsuccessful, he concludes that virtue is not after all teachable (and hence not a form of knowledge). But this assumption is easily questioned: the fact that there happen to be no teachers of virtue does not rule out the possibility that it might in principle be taught.

One might think that Socrates has covertly changed the subject at issue. In discussing the opening of the work, I said that Meno's question could be read in three different ways.[1] He might be asking whether it is in the nature of virtue to be teachable, i.e. whether it is in principle teachable; whether, as things stand, it is teachable; or whether it is in fact taught. I argued that, from the way Socrates responds to Meno at 71b1–7, it is clear that he is addressing the question of whether virtue can in principle

---

[1] See above p. 22.

be taught: he immediately proceeds to the definitional question, thereby showing that he wants to know whether it is in the nature of virtue to be teachable, regardless of contingent circumstances. Yet, one might claim that after 89e he ceases to be interested in this question and instead focuses on an empirical one – either whether it is teachable as things stand, or indeed whether it is actually taught. This, one might argue, explains why he introduces the question of whether there are any teachers or learners of virtue.

But it is possible to explain Socrates' strategy in 89e–96d without accusing him of changing the subject. Notice the exact terms in which he phrases the question of whether there are any teachers or learners of virtue: 'if there were no teachers or learners of something, wouldn't we be right *in surmising that it isn't teachable?*' (89e1–3: emphasis added). Clearly Socrates sees their task as making an inference, but only a tentative one. This immediately shows that he is not raising the purely factual question of whether virtue is in fact taught, because that is exactly the same question as whether there are any teachers and learners of virtue.[2] Were he asking the purely factual question the tentativeness of 89e would make no sense. Nor do we need to say that he has abruptly turned to the question of whether virtue is teachable as things stand. Rather, his point is that, if no one has succeeded in teaching or learning virtue, this is *probably* to be explained by something in the nature of virtue itself. So I shall assume that between 89e and 96d Socrates continues to ask whether it is in the nature of virtue to be teachable, i.e. whether it is so in principle.

THE ARGUMENT WITH ANYTUS

As Socrates starts on this line of inquiry, Meno takes a back seat and a new character is introduced in the form of Anytus: an extremely prominent politician at the dramatic date of the dialogue, famous for helping to restore Athenian democracy in 403, which had been replaced by the rule of the thirty tyrants a year before after the city's defeat in the Peloponnesian war. He was also one of the two people most active in bringing about Socrates' trial and execution, a role not unconnected with his position as a leading democrat: one of the charges he brought against Socrates was that of corrupting the young, doubtless a reference to his association with such aristocrats as Charmides and Alcibiades, both of whom had revealed themselves to be hostile to Athenian democracy. Charmides had actually

---

[2] See Brunschwig 1991: 595.

been one of the thirty tyrants; Alcibiades was accused of plotting against the democracy as early as 415, before going on to commit a string of offences against his native city.

The appearance of Anytus raises the question of why Plato chooses to introduce a new character just at this point in the work. But before addressing this, we need to analyse the actual content of the argument. The passage consists in a search for teachers of virtue, conducted in two stages: first, an examination of the sophists' claim to teach virtue, then of four Athenians particularly renowned for their virtue.

The sophists

Socrates and Anytus first agree that, if we wanted someone to learn a particular craft such as medicine, cobbling or flute-playing, we would send him to people who profess to be teachers and take money for their services. We would never refuse the services of such people, nor turn to those who neither claimed to teach nor had ever had any pupils (90d7–e8).

But when it comes to identifying those who claim to be professional teachers of virtue, the conversation turns nasty. Socrates suggests that the sophists might fit the bill and, when Anytus is appalled at the idea, rather disingenuously comes to their defence, focusing on Protagoras in particular, who held on to a good reputation for forty years and commanded enormous fees. If, as Anytus and others claimed, he really corrupted the young, like a shoe repairer returning the articles in a worse state than they had been given to him, he would surely have been found out long ago. This provokes a further outburst from Anytus, who lambasts those who go to the sophists for tuition, their relatives who allow them to do so and, most of all, those cities that allow the sophists to enter in the first place.

Like Anytus, Socrates also took a negative view of the sophists. His confrontations with Protagoras and Hippias in the dialogues named after them succeed in exposing the hollowness of their claims to teach virtue. The problem with Anytus, however, is not so much what he believes as why he believes it. The continuation of this exchange is worth quoting in full:

soc. Has one of the sophists done you an injustice, Anytus – or why are you so hard on them?
an. By God, I have never associated with any of these men, nor would I allow any of my people to do so.
soc. So you've had absolutely no experience of them?
an. Nor would I want any.

SOC. So how could you know about this – whether there's either good or bad in it – when you've no experience of it at all?
AN. Easily: I know these people for what they are, whether or not I've had any experience of them.
SOC. Perhaps you're a seer, Anytus. From what you say, I'm amazed how else you can know about them.

(92b5–c7)

Anytus' verdict on the sophists, even if correct, is reached only by hearsay and prejudice. He has never met one of them, a fact of which he is actually proud. Socrates ironically calls him a seer or prophet for 'knowing' all this without any experience. In reality, of course, such a verdict requires a firmer basis. Contrast the way Socrates in the *Euthydemus*, *Hippias Major*, *Protagoras* and *Republic* I carefully and patiently cross-examines the sophists. What is so disconcerting about Anytus' reaction in this context is the way he is prepared to accuse someone of corrupting the young without any serious argument.

The great and the good

The sophists rejected, Socrates asks Anytus to suggest who else might be teachers of virtue. He replies that anyone who possesses virtue can perform the task. To test this out, Socrates goes through a list of four Athenian statesmen, all of them paradigms of virtue, and asks if they were successful in transmitting their virtue to their own sons. His selection probably constitutes a standard list of great Athenians, striking a balance between conservatives and reformers. The first mentioned is Themistocles, a statesman noted for his decisive action in securing the Greek victory over the Persians in the wars of 490–479; he was also important for his opposition to the old aristocratic constitution. Next comes Aristides, roughly contemporary with Themistocles, and renowned for his honesty, who was instrumental in repulsing the Persian threat and afterwards in building up the Athenian empire. Pericles, the most powerful of Athenian democratic leaders, rose to power after helping to dismantle the old aristocratic constitution in 461–2. He was responsible for leading the building programmes at Athens that resulted in, among other monuments, the Parthenon. Thucydides was a rival of Pericles, and a conservative 'leader of the rich' until he was ostracised in 443.

The 'father argument' goes as follows. For each eminent Athenian, Socrates argues:
(a) X was virtuous.
(b) X would have been a good teacher of virtue, if anyone was.

(c) X wanted his son(s) taught virtue.
(d) X's son(s) did not succeed in acquiring virtue.
(e) X didn't succeed in teaching them any virtue. Hence:
(f) Virtue is not teachable.

(a) is a premise that Anytus is keen to accept, as does Socrates. (b) is also accepted without demur. (c) is supported by the fact that most of the fathers mentioned went to great expense to teach their sons other skills, such as throwing a javelin while standing upright on horseback. They would surely have wanted to teach their sons the most important thing of all, virtue. Anytus accepts (d) and (e): the sons in question, although not actually wicked, did not distinguish themselves in the city's affairs.

By the time Socrates draws the conclusion (f), Anytus has become so incensed that he withdraws from the argument altogether.[3] It is far from clear, however, that he is actually defeated, for the argument seems vulnerable to a very simple objection: the fact that the sons did not become distinguished says nothing at all about their fathers' ability to teach virtue; there could surely have been something wrong with the sons.

WHY DOES PLATO INTRODUCE ANYTUS INTO THE DIALOGUE?

At this point we should pause to ask why Plato includes the Anytus episode at all. Overtly, it is meant to contribute to the overall argument of the dialogue by showing that virtue is not teachable. But this cannot be the whole answer. This is obvious in the case of the first phase of the discussion. Having played devil's advocate for the sophists in general (and Protagoras in particular), Socrates abandons his defence (92c6). What he conspicuously fails to do, however, is to endorse Anytus' negative conclusion about the sophists, even though he himself would have had a wealth of direct evidence to support it. He merely says: 'we aren't asking who Meno should go to in order to become bad – let that be the sophists if you want' (92c8–d2). Socrates cannot therefore think they have done anything at all to show that the sophists are not teachers of virtue. The argument, such as it is, is purely *ad hominem*.

One might say the same of the father argument. Bluck has argued that Anytus is in no position to make the objection that the sons lacked the requisite ability to become virtuous because, as a democrat, he would have downplayed differences in natural abilities. Everyone, so long as they have

---

[3] The text does not explicitly say whether Anytus walks away from the company or merely remains silent, but I agree with Bluck (1961: 432–3) and Sharples (1985: 178 and 188) that the former is more plausible.

sufficient exposure to other decent citizens, ought to be able to acquire virtue.[4] This is what justifies democratic practice. Against Anytus, at least, the argument is successful.

On this view the whole of the episode is *ad hominem*, and Socrates cannot be said to endorse any of it, even if he happens to agree with its conclusions. Another reason for doubting that Socrates would be satisfied with the father argument as it stands is that it represents only a fragment of the evidence that he has amassed in other inquiries. This is clear from the way in which he first introduced the proposal to look for teachers and learners of virtue:

Although I've often inquired whether there are any teachers of it, for all my efforts I'm unable to find any. And yet I make this search with many people's help, especially those who I think are most experienced in the matter. (89e6–9)

Thus, although he lays a few cards on the table (unlike in the attack on the sophists, where he reveals none), he still has many more up his sleeve. Also, in the *Protagoras* he hints at a much broader inductive base than that offered to Anytus in the *Meno*:

And there are a great many others whom I could mention to you as having never succeeded, though virtuous themselves, in making anyone else better, either of their own or of other families.[5]

According to this line of thought, therefore, the function of the Anytus episode is not to further the argument of the dialogue as a whole. Instead, Plato must have some special interest in the figure of Anytus himself, and it is here that the real purpose of the passage is to be found.

Although I think this is in the main correct, the situation is not quite so clear cut. Certainly the first phase of the argument is *ad hominem*. But in the context of the dialogue, the father argument is not as weak as it may sound, for Socrates himself has already downplayed differences in natural ability earlier in the dialogue. First, at 85c10–d1, he claimed that the slave boy could come to have as a good a knowledge of geometry as anyone else, so long as he undergoes continued questioning. The same should apply to virtue, if it really is a form of knowledge. Second, just before Anytus came on the scene, Socrates had argued that virtue does not come by nature (89a5–b7). We noted that he did not even allow nature to be a partial explanation of how people become virtuous. This implies that everyone is equally capable of being taught knowledge, and so has important

---

[4] Bluck 1961: 27–8.   [5] 320b1–3, trans. Lamb 1924.

implications for the father argument. For, if the sons of the virtuous failed to acquire their fathers' virtue, this cannot be blamed on their lack of ability, and so it looks increasingly unlikely that virtue is teachable or a form of knowledge.

However, even if Socrates believes that the father argument can be defended, there is still a question hanging over the purpose of the passage as a whole: does he really think it proves that virtue is not teachable? The fact remains that the first phase of the episode, the critique of the sophists, is merely *ad hominem*. Even after the father argument, when he draws the conclusion that virtue is not teachable (94e2), he does so in very cautious terms.[6] Also, the discussion with Anytus ends not because Socrates now thinks the conclusion has been firmly established, but because Anytus becomes annoyed and disengages. When Socrates and Meno are left on their own, they do not take it as established that virtue is not teachable, but see themselves as having unfinished business on their hands: the following passage (95a6–96c10) consists in yet another attempt to establish the conclusion. So even if Socrates thinks that the father argument inclines him towards believing that virtue is not teachable, he still sees it as only a part of what needs to be done.

Besides, even if we thought that Socrates was fully convinced by the argument with Anytus, we would still not have explained why Plato introduces a new character into the dialogue. Why not simply conduct the argument with Meno? I now wish to explore three possible answers to this question.

The defence of Socrates

In a number of works, Plato is keen to defend Socrates from the charges laid against him at his trial. The *Apology* of course is the most conspicuous example, but there are others. At the end of the *Symposium* Alcibiades, often thought to have been a prime example of Socrates' ability to corrupt the young, gives a speech partly in praise of Socrates, in the course of which he confesses that it was his own love of popularity that led him astray; Socrates' influence had been nothing but positive (cf. 210a ff.). *Republic* vi paints a similar picture (cf. 490e–495b): without mentioning Alcibiades by name, Socrates himself claims that those who corrupt the young are certainly not the philosophers, nor even the sophists, but the *demos* itself, on the grounds that it makes ambitious young men accommodate themselves to its own corrupted values and desires.

---

[6] The Greek construction μὴ οὐκ ᾖ . . . shows that the conclusion is being drawn only tentatively.

In the *Meno*, it could be that Plato is yet again defending Socrates, this time by lambasting his principal accuser. The real indictment in the first argument is not against the sophists, but against Anytus himself, who is prepared to accuse the sophists of corrupting the young without any acquaintance of them (92b9–10); when faced with a counter-argument, he is unable to make any cogent reply (92a7–b4). In his reaction to both phases of the argument, he shows himself unable to engage in any sustained dialogue, and eventually disengages altogether. Moreover, he probably misunderstands the point Socrates is actually making, which is not that the men lacked virtue, but that they failed to pass their virtue on to anyone else (cf. 95a2–4 with 93a3–4).

It is possible, even plausible, to see this passage as contributing to Plato's *apologia* for Socrates. But it is worth pointing out, if only in passing, that the critique is not all sound and fury, and that there is as much humour as bitterness. When Socrates first introduces Anytus, he does so as someone ideally suited for the inquiry:

For to begin with, Anytus here is the son of a father who was both rich and wise – Anthemion – and who didn't become rich by luck or inheritance, like the Theban Ismenias, who has just inherited the wealth of Polycrates, but acquired it by his own wisdom and hard work. Also, in other respects he didn't seem to be an arrogant, conceited or offensive citizen, but orderly and well behaved. Furthermore, he gave this man a good upbringing and education – so it seems to the Athenian people, who elected him to the highest offices. (90a1–b3)

A closer look at this deliberately confusing sentence shows that almost all the praise is being heaped not on Anytus but on his father, Anthemion. A self-made man, he did not have *his* father's wealth as a starting point in life. He was also moderate and well tempered. The only 'compliment' paid to Anytus is that Anthemion brought him up sufficiently well for the Athenian people (or 'mob': *plethos*) to consider him worthy of high office. Anytus is introduced from the start as the son of a successful father and throughout the discussion reveals himself as worse than mediocre. We are given not four examples of fathers with unsuccessful sons, but five.

At any rate, one reason for the introduction of Anytus into the dialogue may be Plato's ongoing concern to provide an *apologia* for Socrates. Yet, plausible as it may sound, I do not think it gives a full explanation of Anytus' appearance. The justification for introducing him would be that he is the friend of the character whom (for other reasons) Plato wishes to use in this work; the discussion is about moral education (and hence the issue of corrupting the young comes easily to mind); so it makes sense to include a critique of Anytus. This still leaves his connection to the dialogue somewhat tenuous. So I would like to suggest two further functions for the episode, both of which tie it much more satisfactorily into the work as a whole.

Anti-intellectualism

Whatever Plato may have thought of Anytus as a person, he also represents an anti-intellectual tendency that goes to the heart of Plato's concerns about contemporary Athens. Recall the point that the argument had reached just before Anytus' appearance. Virtue is a form of knowledge that comes by teaching, in a special 'maieutic' sense. Attaining this knowledge requires a long and arduous process of recollection, involving rigorous self-scrutiny and frequent bouts of *aporia*. One is also likely to subject the views of one's fellow citizens to similar examination.

Remember that Plato is having Socrates prescribe this educational process for anyone who aspires to political leadership. But for this prescription to be practicable, it would have to be accepted by the city's current leaders and, in Athens, by the people at large. Anytus might feature in this passage partly because he is representative of the attitude that many Athenians would have held towards the intellectualist stance taken in the dialogue. (When Anytus is introduced at 90b1–3, he is hailed as having met with the approval of the Athenian people.) The reaction that Socrates draws from Anytus might therefore be illustrative of a more general response to the intellectualism implicit in the dialogue.[7]

If so, the importance of the Anytus episode is that it gives us an important layer of commentary on Socrates' views about the acquisition of virtue – in particular on their practicability. Such an interpretation obviously ties the episode in with the dialogue as a whole. I shall return to this theme when discussing the very end of the dialogue, which talks ominously of the need to engage with Anytus and, for the benefit of the Athenians, to allay his anger.

An object lesson for Meno

But there is one more reason Plato might have for including the Anytus episode in the *Meno*. The most dramatic point in the confrontation between Socrates and Anytus comes at the end of the episode. He complains that Socrates is apt to be too critical of his fellow-citizens and issues a warning:

---

[7] This interpretation is similar to that of Taylor 1926: 141.

My advice to you, if you'll take it, is to be careful. In any city, perhaps, it's easy to do a man harm or good – and that's especially true here. But I think you realise that. (94e4–95a1)

This should remind us of an earlier point in the dialogue at the end of Meno's stingray speech:

I think you are well advised not to set sail from here or travel abroad: if you did such things as a foreigner in another city, you'd probably be arrested as a wizard.

(80b4–7)

In each case, the interlocutor appears to be giving Socrates useful advice. But in both contexts, the 'advice' sounds distinctly menacing. While this is obvious in Anytus' case,[8] it is difficult not to find a sinister undertone in Meno's words as well.[9] Of course, Plato is not putting a *verbatim* quote from Meno into Anytus' mouth. But there are undeniably similarities: the same reference to advice; the mention of possible ill treatment – explicitly arrest in the first case; but the same comes to mind when one thinks of Anytus.

What are we to make of these similarities?[10] My claim is that Socrates is using a pedagogical technique that has already appeared twice in the work: he stages a dialogue within the main dialogue with the aim of getting Meno to look at himself from a distance. The first example came at 74b–75a, where Socrates imagined a particularly obtuse interlocutor failing to understand the difference between talking about surface or colour in general and a specific surface or colour. But the most striking example of the technique comes in the interview with the slave boy, and it is worth pausing to review the way in which this passage acts as an object lesson for Meno. The crucial text is 84a3–d2, which I called the second stage of the meta-dialogue between Socrates and Meno.[11] First of all, Socrates gets Meno to see from the outside the benefit the boy has received by losing his false pretensions to knowledge (84a3–b7). But there is an associated point: the elenchus can make the interlocutor take pleasure in inquiry. In stark contrast to Meno's defeatism, the boy is apparently quite undeterred and shows no signs of weakness in the face of *aporia*. Unlike his master, he is eagerly inquisitive (84b10–11).

---

[8] For other references to Anytus' anger, see 95a2 and 99e2; cf. also 100a8–c1.
[9] He had prided himself on his ability to talk about virtue, but has just been reduced to silence on the topic (presumably in front of a crowd of onlookers). He is annoyed and, just at this point, would no doubt take pleasure in seeing Socrates maltreated. See Klein 1965: 89, 'Meno is angry and he utters something that amounts to a threat . . . there is an ominous ring about this remark . . .'
[10] For a (somewhat idiosyncratic) comparison between Meno and Anytus, see Brague 1978: 212–20.
[11] See above pp. 98–100.

Through this technique, Socrates tries to shame Meno into inquiry. Certainly, the staged interview must have been humiliating for him, especially if there were onlookers present: he is being shown up in front of them all as (intellectually) so much feebler than his own slave. The slave-boy dialogue also throws into relief another of Meno's faults. The boy gives answers that are all his own; he answers for himself and would continue to do so, if the examination were prolonged (cf. 84c11–d2, 85b8–9 and 85d4–6). Obviously, this claim is crucial if Socrates is to have any chance of supporting recollection. But it also stands in direct – and embarrassing – contrast to Meno's own habit of relying on hearsay in the first part of the dialogue. Finally, the boy is seen to follow a sequential chain of reasoning (82e12), rather than accept each proposition piece-meal. Again, this stands in sharp contrast to Meno's refusal to think synoptically.[12]

The dialogue with Anytus is yet another example of this technique at work. Socrates stages a mini-dialogue to act as an object lesson – only with one obvious difference: whereas the slave boy throws some of Meno's faults into relief, Anytus shows some of the same faults in exaggerated form. In this respect, the Anytus episode is closer to the imaginary dialogue about definition (74b–75a). Here the imaginary interlocutor fails to grasp the difference between colour and a colour, something that Socrates says would be 'amazing' (75a2–4). His point is that the same criticism could be made of Meno himself, for failing to grasp the difference between virtue and a virtue. What all three instances of the technique have in common, however, is that Meno has the opportunity to learn something about himself and to acquire a greater degree of self-consciousness by witnessing a dialogue sufficiently similar to the one he has been having with Socrates.

The most obvious point of comparison between the behaviour of Meno and Anytus is the similarity between the passages quoted above, 80b and 94e: what Meno does rather tentatively, Anytus does more openly. But this is only part of a broader set of similarities. First, both interlocutors wish to absent themselves from further inquiry. Anytus shows this by walking away; Meno does so by raising his challenge to the possibility of inquiry and discovery, whose essential purpose is obstructive. Underlying both cases is an unwillingless to engage in inquiry, specifically co-inquiry. I have already discussed this as far as Meno is concerned,[13] but the fault is even more marked with Anytus. Notice how Socrates introduces him at 89e6–90b6: he mentions the project of shared inquiry no less than five times, thereby preparing us for the very feature that will be lacking from the ensuing dialogue between them.[14] Anytus seems incapable of any sustained inquiry. For instance at 92a7–b4, after Socrates has put up a defence of Protagoras, he makes no attempt to construct a counter-argument, but merely repeats the same themes of his previous speech (91c1–5), only with greater vehemence. He certainly makes no attempt to investigate *with* Socrates. His responses are explosive rather than co-operative; he fails to engage in any friendly exchange of dialogue. It is very relevant that when describing Anytus' lack of mildness at the very end of the work, Socrates uses the same word (πρᾳότερος: 100c1) as he used when describing the mildness of dialectic at 75d4.

Anytus' lack of co-operation is particularly obvious in the following exchange, when Socrates asks him to name an Athenian who might teach Meno virtue:

AN. Tell him yourself.[15]
SOC. But I've mentioned the people I considered to be teachers of it, though you claim I'm talking nonsense. And perhaps there's something in what you say. But now it's your turn: tell him which of the Athenians he should go to. Give him the name of anyone you like.
AN. Why does he need anyone's name in particular?

(92d6–e3)

The unwillingness to engage, and the attempt to throw Socrates' questions back in his face seems like a more extreme version of Meno's attitude, as epitomised when he is asked to define surface: 'No, Socrates, *you* tell me' (75b1). At 93b7, despite asking Anytus twice to name someone who can teach virtue, Socrates has in the end to suggest one himself: he is even less able to keep control of Anytus than he was of Meno (cf. 86d3–8).

It is also relevant that Anytus admits to having no experience of the sophists himself, though he claims to know that they corrupt the young. He is relying purely on hearsay (92b7–c7). Relying on hearsay is part of the same syndrome that includes a resistance to active inquiry: inquiry (of the Socratic kind) and hearsay represent opposing methods of arriving at one's beliefs. In his laziness and his resistance to inquiry, it never occurs to him to do what Socrates did – to examine the sophists for himself. It is also no coincidence that, like Meno, he thinks it easy to acquire the knowledge that he claims for himself (cf. 92c4 with 71e1–72a5).

---

[14] Another way in which this passage anticipates Anytus' faults is by congratulating Anytus' father for not being arrogant, conceited or offensive, all of which Anytus will manifest: for the first two see 95a4, for the third 95a2 (cf. 99e2).
[15] Literally translated Anytus' words are: 'why didn't you tell him?' But I agree with Bluck (1961: 366) that they are best read as implying an imperative.

In short, Anytus manifests some of the same faults as Meno in a more extreme form. I am not claiming that the two characters are portrayed as identical. There are clear differences between the two: Meno is intellectually curious (to an extent) and reasonably deferential towards Socrates. But often the differences are a matter of degree rather than kind. For instance, it is true that, unlike Anytus, Meno at least acknowledges that he is unable to defend his previous views. But he still shows that in the past, at least, he has been conceited, and is resentful at being shown up rather than eager to make good his deficiencies.[16] Again, although the atmosphere created by the stingray speech is certainly less heated than in the Anytus episode – Meno conveys his feelings by means of a joke (80a4–5) – the resentment is still there. So despite the differences, there are still crucial points of similarity that make it plausible to see this whole episode as an object lesson for Meno.[17] The most significant of these similarities is that, deep down, both characters feel the same antipathy towards co-operative inquiry.

If this interpretation is right, we need to address the question of whether Meno actually improves as a result of Socrates' efforts. I think there are grounds for optimism here, based on Meno's behaviour in the last part of the dialogue, but shall wait until I have reviewed the conclusion of the work before answering this question.

The discussion with Meno (95a–96d)

After Anytus' departure, Socrates mounts a fresh argument to show that virtue is not teachable based on the very existence of disagreement over the issue. First, they focus upon the virtuous people of Meno's own country, Thessaly. He admits that they are individually in two minds on the question.[18] This then prompts Socrates to ask:

So are we to say that people who don't even agree on this point are teachers of virtue? (95b5–6)

---

[16] Cf. 80b3 with 95a4.

[17] Recall how Socrates gives Meno advance warning of Anytus' principal failings – arrogance, conceit and offensiveness (90a6–7). That he does so ties in well with the suggestion that he is about to use the dialogue as an object lesson for Meno, as who has already started to show signs of the same qualities himself. For arrogance see 76a9, conceit 71e1 and 80b2–3, and offensiveness 80b4–7.

[18] According to Meno, sometimes they talk of virtue as teachable, sometimes as not (95b4–5). On its own this might mean that some of them say that it is teachable, some not. But I take it to mean that they are all in two minds about it because at 95c9–d1 Socrates (with Meno's tacit consent) goes on to assimilate their type of disagreement to that of Theognis, who is in two minds himself.

Next he asks whether Meno considers the sophists teachers of virtue. Although he (instinctively) starts reporting Gorgias' view (95c1–4),[19] Socrates presses him to declare his own, which turns out to be different. He is like the majority of people, he says, sometimes believing that they are teachers, sometimes that they are not. Finally, Socrates cites a third case of indecision, the poet Theognis, who in one place appears to say that virtue is teachable, but in another contradicts himself. He then sums up the argument:

[1] Can you mention any other thing where those who profess to teach are not only not agreed to be teachers of others, but not even agreed to be experts themselves – in fact are considered defective in the very thing they claim to teach? [2] Or any other thing where those who are agreed to be good sometimes say it's teachable, and sometimes that it's not? Would you say that people who are so confused about something are teachers of it in the strict sense?[20]

As my numbering indicates, there are two arguments in this passage. The first is inductive: in all the other cases in our experience, a teacher is someone who is recognised both as a teacher and as an expert in their field. (One could imagine Socrates, if he were in a more expansive mood, following his usual inductive procedure of listing doctors, cobblers, flute-players and the like.) Since the sophists fail to conform to this regularity, they are not teachers. The second argument could also be read inductively. In all other cases, a teacher is one who is clear in his own mind that his subject can be taught. As the virtuous fail to conform to this regularity, they are not teachers either.

Both arguments are open to objection. As for [1], why could there not be an unrecognised teacher? A parallel objection can be made against [2]: why should we assume that to be a teacher of something one has to be confident that it can be taught? At this point we have to take account of the third question in the passage: 'would you say that people who are so confused about something are teachers of it in the strict sense?' This is meant to support [2], perhaps by repeating the inductive approach assumed in it. The point may be that, any teacher who kept changing his mind as

---

[19] Complete with the repetition characteristic of Gorgias' style: ἀκούσαις ὑπισχουμένου and ἀκούσῃ ὑπισχουμένων in c2–3, and the four occurrences of -ειν in c4. I am grateful to Myles Burnyeat for pointing this out.

[20] 96a6–b4. The Greek of this sentence is extremely difficult. Some translators treat ἄλλου ὁτουοῦν πράγματος as if it were in the accusative (or at least appeal to the 'genitive of mentioning', if there is such a thing). Thus Day (1994), Grube in Cooper (1997), Guthrie (1956) and Lamb (1924) all take Socrates to be asking: 'can you name any other subject in which . . . ?'. In an effort to make sense of the question I have reluctantly followed their lead. For some objections see Thompson 1901: 210–11 and Bluck 1961: 396–7.

to whether a subject was teachable would stand out as an anomaly; if the virtuous are teachers, they are so only in an abnormal sense. Yet this invites the same objection against the use of induction in this context: an abnormal teacher is still a teacher.[21]

There is, however, another way of reading the argument. Instead of saying that the final question merely repeats the same type of inductive argument in [2], we could claim that it adds fresh support by explaining why the very indecision as to whether a subject is teachable undermines one's claim to have expertise in it. Socrates could do this by using premises from elsewhere in the dialogue. If someone vacillates between thinking that virtue is teachable and that it is not, they do not know that it is teachable: knowledge requires stability, as we shall shortly be told (cf. 98a1–6). Next, if they do not know that virtue is teachable, this has consequences for whether they know what it is. At 87c1–3 Socrates declares it obvious to everyone that only knowledge can be taught: this is the bi-conditional claim that if something is knowledge it can be taught, and if it can be taught it is knowledge. Thus if someone sees this as obvious, yet vacillates as to whether virtue is teachable, they must also vacillate over the question of what virtue is, in particular whether it is a form of knowledge or not. If they vacillate on the nature of virtue, they do not know what it is (cf. again 98a1–6). Now on page 144 above I claimed that, for Socrates, a teacher needs to have knowledge of their subject matter. If so, someone who fails to know what virtue is will also be unable to teach it.

At any rate, Socrates now thinks he has established that neither the sophists nor the virtuous are teachers. At 96b6–c10 he then infers that, in the absence of any other suitable candidates, there are no teachers of virtue to be found at all. If there are no teachers, there are no pupils, and so virtue seems not to be teachable.

---

[21] Grube in Cooper (1997) translates 96b3–4: 'would you say that people who are so confused about a subject can be effective teachers of it?' This is in effect to render κυρίως (96b4) not as 'strictly speaking', but as 'authoritatively'. However, if Plato had meant this, he would have used the adjective κύριοι rather than the adverb κυρίως. The fact that he uses the adverb shows that the point is not whether the teachers are authoritative, but whether we can use the word 'teachers' of them authoritatively.

CHAPTER 14

Virtue as true belief: 96d–100b

When Socrates tentatively concludes that virtue is not teachable, Meno replies:

It seems not, if we've considered the matter correctly. So I wonder, Socrates, if there are any virtuous men, or what might be the way in which good men come into being. (96d1–4)

In response, Socrates revisits the argument that virtue is knowledge to show that they overlooked an important distinction. They were correct to say that virtuous people are beneficial, and that to be beneficial one must guide one's affairs rightly. What they failed to notice was that there are two ways of giving the right guidance. One is by knowledge, the other by true belief. True belief, so long as one has it, is as useful as knowledge. The problem is that it is not stable, and people with mere true belief are apt to change their minds. Only by chaining belief down with explanatory reasoning will they achieve the stability of knowledge (97e2–98a8). Returning to the political context of the dialogue, Socrates claims that Pericles and the other virtuous men guided the city's affairs correctly by true belief. Because they lacked any knowledge, he compares them to prophets and soothsayers who, under the influence of divine dispensation, say much that is true without any understanding. Similarly, the virtue of the eminent Athenians comes not by teaching but by divine dispensation (99e6).

Such in bare outline is the conclusion of the dialogue. Before we go any further, we ought to consider how this passage relates to the argument of 87d–89a that virtue is a kind of knowledge. One point is very clear: by conceiving of virtue as a quality beneficial to the city, the conclusion bears out the instrumentalist conception of virtue that we found in the argument of 87d–89a. But in another respect – by revising the thesis that virtue is knowledge – the conclusion is at odds with the earlier argument.

However, there is room for debate as to exactly what this revision consists in. On one interpretation, Socrates is rejecting the thesis altogether and claiming that virtue is something else, namely true belief, whose nature is not such as to be teachable. Alternatively, he might be giving a disjunctive account: virtue is either knowledge or true belief; when it is knowledge it is teachable;[1] when true belief, it comes by some other way, rather abruptly characterised as divine dispensation.

There are some indications to suggest that Socrates takes the first approach. Shortly before he embarks on the discussion with Anytus, he suggests that he may be about to overturn the conclusion that virtue is knowledge (89d5–6). There are also some points later on where he states that virtue is true belief rather than knowledge (e.g. 98e7–8 and 99a7–8).

However, it is far more plausible that he takes the disjunctive approach. At both 96e2–3 and 98c8 he says that it is not only knowledge that is useful but true belief as well; at 99a1–2 he stresses that there are two ways of guiding affairs rightly, a point supported by the claim that knowledge is a more valuable means of doing this than true belief (98a6–8).

But if he has not given up on the possibility of a kind of virtue consisting in knowledge, what are we to make of those texts that suggested that virtue is only true belief? These can be read as applying only to the virtue that has been manifested in Athens, by such people as Themistocles and Pericles.[2] It remains in principle possible for someone to have virtue based on knowledge, a point made near the very end, where Socrates talks of the possibility of a statesman who would be able to make another like himself – i.e. to teach virtue (which implies that his virtue takes the form of knowledge). For the time being therefore, I shall assume that Socrates takes the disjunctive view. (Later on we shall see that he begins to retreat from claiming that real virtue can consist in true belief.)

This shows that Socrates continues to be interested in the question of whether virtue is in principle teachable, as I argued he was at the beginning of the dialogue and throughout 89–96 (see pp. 22 and 162 above). However, in taking the disjunctive approach to virtue from 96e onwards, we ought to concede that he also shows a developing interest in the empirical question of how virtue is acquired as things stand in Athens. Thus, between 90b and 96c, he gathered empirical evidence to show that there were no teachers and learners of virtue. At 96c he used this evidence to conclude (somewhat tentatively) that virtue is not teachable in principle. After this point he uses the distinction between knowledge and true belief to argue

---

[1] In the 'maieutic' sense: see above pp. 142–4.   [2] See Bluck 1961: 23–5.

for a different answer to the conceptual question – that virtue is in principle teachable – and redeploys the evidence gathered between 90b and 96c to establish the empirical conclusion that virtue is not teachable as things stand.

The ending of the dialogue raises two major questions. First, we need to ask exactly how Socrates understands the distinction between knowledge and true belief, a distinction that went on to play an important role in other of Plato's works and has been a central issue in recent epistemology. The other question concerns the sincerity of Socrates' tribute to the prominent political figures of Athens. Although they acted without understanding, they apparently had virtue and guided their city rightly on the basis of true belief. Furthermore, they acquired their virtue by divine inspiration. Whether this tribute is sincere or whether the whole passage is laced with irony is a question that has been a subject of long-standing disagreement.

KNOWLEDGE AND TRUE BELIEF (96d–98c)

The distinction in outline

Socrates first introduces the distinction with an example:

> SOC. If someone who knew the road to Larisa (or wherever you like) went there and led others, wouldn't he guide them correctly and well?
> MEN. Of course.
> SOC. But if someone had a true belief about what the road is, without having gone there or knowing it, wouldn't he also guide them correctly?
>
> (97a9–b3)

Knowledge and true belief are both as useful as each other. Once Meno has grasped this point, he asks two interrelated questions (97d1–3). First, if true belief really is as useful as knowledge, why is one held in higher esteem than the other? Second, what is the difference between knowledge and true belief? In reply, Socrates draws an analogy with the legendary statues of Daedalus:

> It's not worth a great deal to have acquired one of his works unbound: like a runaway slave, it doesn't stay put. But once tied down, it's extremely valuable: his works are very fine. Why am I telling you this? Because it's relevant to the question of true beliefs. True beliefs are also a fine thing and produce every kind of benefit, so long as they remain. However, they aren't willing to stay put for long, but run away from one's soul. So they're not worth much until one ties them down with

explanatory reasoning. This, Meno, is recollection, as we agreed before. When they are tied down, in the first place they become knowledge and, second, they are stable. This is why knowledge is more valuable than true belief; and it differs from true belief by being tied down. (97e2–98a8)

The tendency of one of these statues to run away is a metaphor for the way in which someone who merely has a true belief may stop believing it in favour of a false one. Socrates thinks that we can achieve stability by finding the explanation for a belief, which in turn involves the process of recollection.

How do these different points – explanation, stability and recollection – fit together? By appealing to the notion of explanation, Socrates makes the distinction between knowledge and true belief turn on the difference between grasping that something is the case and understanding why it is so; and it is the concept of understanding that gives the epistemology of the *Meno* its distinctive flavour, a concept that suggests grasping a body of propositions and seeing how they interrelate.[3] This is especially clear if we think of mathematics, prominent in the *Meno* as a model for philosophy. Here the expert is one who has the ability to see how an entire body of propositions fits together into a system. Someone who lacks such understanding altogether would merely grasp isolated propositions in a piece-meal way.

As we have seen, the importance of grasping interrelations ties in well with recollection: this involves following an ordered sequence of reasoning (82e12–13), which of course requires that one grasp the connections between different propositions. Recollection will culminate in the synoptic mastery of a whole domain, as was suggested when the theory was originally introduced:

Since all nature is akin, and the soul has learnt everything, nothing prevents someone from recollecting just one thing (which people call 'learning') and so discovering everything else . . . (81c9–d3)

The interest in synoptic understanding dovetails with Socrates' emphasis on stability. One will have a greater commitment to holding a proposition if one understands how it connects with a number of others. To cease holding it would have considerable knock-on consequences for one's epistemic commitments elsewhere. By contrast, someone who only grasped a proposition in isolation has little to give up if, under persuasion (for instance),

---

[3] As Myles Burnyeat has observed. He has explored this issue in a number of articles on ancient philosophy, including Burnyeat 1980, 1981 and 1987.

they decide to change their minds. Their less systematic approach allows for greater fluidity.

The value of stability

Socrates' concern with stability is striking. He talks as if the problem is not so much hitting the truth, but maintaining a grip on it. In fact this has already been highlighted in the *Meno*, which is a good example of the instability caused by philosophical cross-examination. For instance, although they seemed to be making real progress after the recollection episode, Socrates has apparently been unravelling their own conclusion that knowledge is necessary for virtue; and the argument of 95a–96c referred repeatedly to people's vacillation on the question of whether virtue is teachable.[4] The problem of doxastic instability also finds echoes in other dialogues, most notably in the *Euthyphro*, where the interlocutor complains that all his beliefs about piety have become destabilised under cross-examination, prompting Socrates to make an allusion to Daedalus (11b6–d6). Another relevant text is *Timaeus* 51e4, which distinguishes knowledge from true belief by saying that the latter can be changed by persuasion.[5]

In making stability a hallmark of knowledge, Socrates had his antecedents. Alcmaeon seems to have distinguished knowledge from belief by stability,[6] and Parmenides contrasts the 'wandering' opinion of mortals (DK 28 B6, 4–6) with 'the unshakable heart of well-rounded truth' (B1, 29). Another important figure to mention in this context is Gorgias. In his *Encomium on Helen* §§11–13, he describes the power of rhetoric, claiming that it feeds off the volatility of true opinion. Were an orator to face an audience of experts, he would have no power at all to move them. As it is, however, instability is rife. As examples he cites the arguments of philosophers and meteorologists, and also alludes to debates in political assemblies and law courts.

Clearly, there was something of an epistemological tradition behind the stability requirement in the *Meno*. But tradition aside, the bald statement that knowledge is stable, while true belief is not, should give us pause. Surely people might hold on to their beliefs obstinately – out of faith, upbringing, habit, or because of their character. It has to be said that Socrates offers no explicit defence for the generalisation that all true belief is unstable.[7]

---

[4] See also pp. 69 and 73–4 above on one of the criticisms implicit in the stingray speech.
[5] A thought echoed by Aristotle at *Posterior Analytics* I 2, 72b3–4.
[6] Cf. *Phaedo* 96b3–8 with DK 24 A5. Cf. also Aristotle, *Posterior Analytics* II 19, 100a6–9.
[7] It is important to distinguish two senses of instability here. In the *Meno*, the point is that someone who merely believes that *p* is likely to stop believing it in favour of not-*p* (under the influence of

But if he were to concede that beliefs can be stable, would this under-mine any of the other claims made in the *Meno*? Consider again Meno's question about the distinction between knowledge and true belief. If Socrates' reply is that it consists merely in stability (i.e. knowledge is sim-ply stable true belief), there clearly is a problem. But this is not Socrates' view in the *Meno*. Knowledge is true belief stabilised in a specific way – by explanatory reasoning. In other words, explanation is necessary for knowledge.

Meno's other question was about the value of knowledge. If Socrates con-cedes that some true beliefs are as stable as knowledge, he faces a problem: why should a stable true belief be any less valuable than knowledge? The seriousness of this problem depends on whether all the value of knowl-edge lies in its stability. If it does, knowledge and stable true belief may be distinct, but Socrates cannot claim that one is more valuable than the other.

Yet does all the value of knowledge lie in its stability? What status does explanation have? There are two options here. It could be that explanation is merely a means towards stability and has no value beyond that, in which case the problem remains unresolved (as long as there are other ways to stabilise true beliefs without explanatory reasoning). On the other hand, it is possible that, quite apart from serving as a means towards stability, explanation has a value in itself. To be sure, nothing in the text requires this reading, but neither is it ruled out. If it were Socrates' view, he would again be following in an epistemological tradition, at least as Aristotle reports it. In *Metaphysics* I.1, 981a30–b2, where he surveys some epistemological intuitions prior to developing his own theory, he says that 'we' consider those who grasp the explanation to be 'more honourable'[8] than those who do not. Knowledge based on explanatory reasoning wins our admiration, quite apart from any utility it may have (cf. 981b13–17). If Socrates in the *Meno* is appealing to the same intuition, we can see why he claims knowledge is always more valuable than true belief.

counter-argument or persuasion, for instance). That this is the sense at issue is clear from 98a2: true beliefs 'run away from one's soul'. This is a psychological point, concerned with the changing contents of the mind. But if we look ahead to the *Republic*, we find a different analysis of instability. The belief, 'it is just to return what is due', for example, is true in many contexts, but not in all (e.g. where one borrowed a weapon from someone who has since gone mad). Here we can imagine someone who holds a belief and retains it, while the truth of the belief varies from one context to another (cf. v 479a5–c5). Only someone who has grasped the underlying explanation, through knowledge of the form of justice, would consistently hit the truth in different contexts. This approach would vindicate the claim of the *Meno* that knowledge is always superior to true belief in terms of stability; but I do not think that this conception of stability is being considered in the *Meno*, which is concerned with changing states of belief, not changing truth-values. On this see Irwin 1995: 143–5.

[8] τιμιωτέρους: cf. *Meno* 97d1 and 98a7.

Nevertheless, it remains the case that he offers no explicit argument for this position.

Some inconsistencies

If all knowledge requires explanation, we run into a problem with the one example of knowledge that Socrates gives in this passage, the road to Larisa (97a9) – at least if this is understood in the most natural way, i.e. one gains knowledge of the road by actually travelling there. For the text says that the person who merely has true belief has not travelled there and does not have knowledge (97b1–2); and this most probably means that he has not been there and *therefore* does not have knowledge, while the other person has knowledge *because* he has been there. In this case, therefore, first-hand evidence, rather than explanation, is sufficient to convert true belief into knowledge.

The best way of restoring consistency to the passage is to claim that the Larisa case is not ultimately to be seen as an example of knowledge in the proper sense. Socrates uses it as a handy and intuitive way of showing that true belief and knowledge can be as useful as each other. We have come across another case where, for pedagogical purposes, Socrates uses a point that he himself would not fully endorse: at 71b4–8, his argument for the priority of definition over attributes rested on a rough and ready analogy (knowledge of who Meno is), illustrating a point about understanding with an example of knowing a particular. In this case, I suggested that we should not take Socrates' preliminary remarks on the topic as beyond revision.[9]

A quite different set of inconsistencies seems to arise if we compare this passage with the slave-boy examination, which ended with the claim that he had achieved true belief but not yet knowledge (85c6–7). At 98a3–5 Socrates seems to identify the process of tying down true beliefs with explanatory reasoning, which he in turn identifies with recollection. This has two implications. First, it suggests that the distinction between knowledge and true belief is clear cut. True belief is upgraded into knowledge when something previously lacking is added: explanatory reasoning. Second, by identifying recollection with such reasoning Socrates implies that no recollection is involved in the formation of mere true belief – otherwise true belief would also have to involve explanatory reasoning.

---

[9] See above pp. 21–2. One might also say that the Larisa case is an analogy used to bring out the difference between understanding and true belief. Understanding must involve 'seeing' something for oneself, not relying on hearsay. See Nehamas 1985: 27. We should, however, be cautious here: this is surely not the immediate or main point at issue in this passage.

But this creates tensions with the conclusion of the slave-boy passage, where Socrates had already referred to true belief as something distinct from knowledge. (At 85c2–7 he insists that the boy does not yet know the answer to the problem, but only has true beliefs.) At the same time, he tried to show that the boy was engaged in a process of recollection, which means that in this case true beliefs as well as knowledge are the result of recollection.

Furthermore, the boy comes to form the true beliefs by a process of sequential reasoning. As we stressed, he was beginning to see the interconnections between his answers (in contrast to Meno, who simply grabbed at different views piece-meal). This is beginning to sound like the first stages of the explanatory reasoning required for knowledge, a point also suggested by Socrates' remark at 85c10–d1:

. . . if someone questions him about the same matters on many occasions and in many ways, you can be sure that he will end up with as exact a knowledge of them as anyone.

This implies that the path from true belief to knowledge will be continuous with the process that elicited the true beliefs. Of course, someone with understanding will have grasped a great many more interconnections between propositions and traced everything back to the most basic principles. Nevertheless, the process that leads to this is of the same kind as has begun in the slave-boy demonstration.[10] He is already beginning to trace interconnections between propositions, to follow through a proof. In other words, he has already embarked on a process of explanatory reasoning, however rudimentary that might be.[11]

One might try to resist this conclusion by saying that not all sequential reasoning is explanatory reasoning. Thus, although there will be some continuity between the earlier and later stages of learning, explanation proper might only come in at the end. But this is difficult to square with the text, which both identifies recollection with explanatory reasoning at 98a4–5 and states that the slave boy is recollecting (cf. 82e12–13). Taken together, these imply that he engages in some sort of explanatory reasoning.

[10] What the slave boy needs is to be taken through the same kinds of problem, but to be questioned from different angles. This will help to draw him away from the specific features of the original puzzle to see the underlying explanation (which in this case has to do with Pythagoras' theorem). If the slave boy is tied to the specific case and can only give the right answer there, he is likely to be thrown off course the moment someone changes the inessentials of the problem. This would show that he does not really understand the correct answers he gave.

[11] See Vlastos 1991: 118 n. 54, with references to Nehamas 1985: 24–30 and Burnyeat 1987: 8–24.

The problem, therefore, is that in the later discussion of knowledge and true belief, Socrates talks as if the difference is one of kind, in the earlier as if it is one of degree. Also, the two passages seem to differ on the question of whether recollection is involved in the formation of true belief. In response, I would suggest that we should not expect the later discussion to map too neatly onto the earlier one. It is important to realise that there will be many different types of true belief, distinguished by their different processes of formation. Some, like the slave boy's, arise through a sequential but incomplete process of recollection; perhaps there could be others formed by haphazard recollection. But recollection and explanation need have nothing at all to do with the formation of many of our beliefs: they may come by perception, induction, hearsay, or (as we find at the end of the dialogue) divine dispensation, i.e. supernatural hearsay. The epistemological discussion at the end of the dialogue should be seen as applying to true belief in very general terms, not as picking up the very special case of the slave boy. Of all the varieties of true belief, this is the one to which the later discussion applies least well. In this case, we would have to modify the clear-cut distinction stated at 98a, and see the slave boy's true beliefs as something of an exception, where the difference between knowledge and true belief is more blurred than in the other cases.[12]

Explanation and justification

The fact that the *Meno* focuses on explanation and understanding has been used to open up a gap between Platonic and modern epistemology. Since the 1960s, there has been an enormous literature on the question of how knowledge differs from true belief, and a very common approach is to make justification a necessary condition for knowledge. Exactly what justification consists in is, of course, a matter of intense debate. But there is no doubt that the concept is central in modern epistemology. Yet, Socrates' interest in the Meno seems to lie in explanation, and explaining why *p* is true is quite different from justifying that it is so. By giving the notion of explanation centre stage, Socrates in the *Meno*, it has been argued, is not really interested in justification at all. Indeed one might go further and claim that he is not

---

[12] Not everything said in the later passage fails to apply to the slave boy: his true beliefs would be as useful as knowledge, while they remain; also they have a dream-like quality and so may be unstable, liable to 'run away' under future cross-examination. In distinguishing different types of cognitive state that fall short of knowledge, we should look ahead to the *Republic*. In v 476e–480a, Socrates makes a very sharp distinction between knowledge and belief, but then in book VI 511d–e introduces *dianoia* as an intermediate state between empirically formed belief (*pistis*) and philosophical understanding (*noesis*).

even talking about what we now call knowledge, which is the function of justification, but understanding, the function of explanation.[13]

In my view, this line of interpretation is exaggerated: there is greater continuity between the concept of knowledge adumbrated in the *Meno* and modern epistemology. A justification consists in a good reason for believing that *p*. According to the interpretation sketched in the previous paragraph, Socrates is concerned with establishing why a proposition is true *rather than* that it is true. Yet in the *Meno*, as elsewhere, the latter is surely at the forefront of his mind. He wants good reasons for believing that virtue is a form of knowledge, teachable and so on. And even if, as I have said, the emphasis of 97d–98a is more on maintaining our grip on the truth rather than simply hitting it in the first place, this is still enough to show that he is deeply interested in justification: for a justification also gives one reason to continue maintaining *p* rather than to renounce it – hence his talk of tying beliefs down.[14] (This is particularly important in the political context of the *Meno*, with its emphasis on giving successful guidance in the city's affairs.) Socrates is interested in knowledge and justification, but thinks that knowledge requires understanding and justification requires explanation: as we have seen, this is because understanding a belief helps to tie it down within a wider system, thereby giving it stability. Through explanation, one acquires a reason to continue holding a belief.

So although the concept of explanation is distinctive of the approach in the *Meno*, we should not take this as evidence that it was not concerned with justification or with the concept of knowledge in something like the modern sense.[15]

Irony in the Meno

Very broadly stated, the conclusion of the *Meno* is that there is a form of virtue consisting in knowledge, which is teachable in a very special sense: it can be recollected with the right kind of questioning. Alongside this kind of virtue is another, consisting in true belief, which has actually been found to exist in Athens. It comes by way of divine dispensation. The argument of 87d–89a, coupled with the recollection thesis, gives us the ideal or Utopian

---

[13] See Burnyeat 1980: 187 and Nehamas 1985: 25; cf. Annas 1981: 192–3 and 200–1.
[14] See 89c8–10, where Socrates suggests that his concern is to achieve a stable position on whether virtue is teachable.
[15] In general, I agree with the approach taken by Fine (1990: 106–7, 114–15, and 2004: 64–71). See also Barnes 1980: 204.

answer to Meno's original question. What the last ten pages add is an assessment of the actual achievements of Athenian politicians.

But is this assessment seriously meant? It is essential to realise that there are really three questions at issue here. This is because Socrates may be making three distinct claims about the Athenians: first, that they guided the city rightly by holding true beliefs; second, that they had virtue; third, that they were divinely inspired. It is not difficult to see how these might come apart. Socrates might be sincere in saying that they had correct beliefs, and even virtue, but not in attributing divine dispensation to them. Of course, if he is not sincere in attributing either true belief or virtue to them, he is unlikely to be serious when he refers to divine dispensation. But our best course is to examine each point in turn: it is common in the literature for scholars to adduce a reason for treating one claim as insincere and assume, without further argument, that the other two are thereby undermined as well.

Real and shadow virtue

When giving an outline of the conclusion of the dialogue, I provisionally accepted that, in response to the arguments purporting to show that virtue is not teachable, Socrates proposes a disjunctive definition of virtue: virtue can be knowledge or true belief. Both of these, it appeared, counted as *bona fide* cases of virtue. (I shall call them virtue$_k$ and virtue$_{tb}$ respectively.) Thus, Socrates uses virtue$_{tb}$, which is still a *bona fide* type of virtue, to account for the quality that distinguished the likes of Pericles. But does he really think that such men were genuinely virtuous? True, throughout much of the final part of the dialogue he explicitly attributes virtue to them. So it does appear as if virtue$_{tb}$ is just another form of virtue, and that true belief is sufficient for making someone a genuinely good person. (In other words, Socrates has retreated from the claim that knowledge is necessary for virtue.)

But this appears to be qualified at the end of the dialogue:

But for now, if we have been right in our investigations and in what we've said throughout the whole of this discussion, virtue comes neither by teaching nor by nature but by divine dispensation without intelligence to those to whom it does come – unless there were some statesman capable of making another like himself. Were there to be such a man, he would be called among the living what Homer said about Teiresias among the dead, when he said that, of those in Hades, 'he alone kept his wits'; 'the rest were flitting shadows'. In the same way, here on earth *such a man would be the real thing in comparison with shadows as far as virtue is concerned.* (99e4–100a7; emphasis added)

At first sight, this passage only repeats a point already made, viz. that true belief is unstable compared to knowledge. But the last sentence clearly goes beyond this and adds that virtue$_{tb}$ is not exactly another form of virtue, but a shadow of virtue, i.e. a defective type: henceforth 'virtue'$_{tb}$.[16]

Richard Kraut, who thinks that Socrates does mean to make true belief sufficient for virtue, objects to this reading: 'Plato is not saying that the political expert would be to the rest of us as a flesh-and-blood man is to a ghost. For Teiresias is no flesh-and-blood man in *Odyssey* 10.493–5 (from which the *Meno* quotes); he is just one shade among many.'[17] But even if this were true of what Homer says, we have to look to the moral that Socrates himself draws, and this is clearly enough stated in the last sentence of the quotation: in respect of virtue, true belief is not the real thing. Besides, Kraut may not be quite correct even when it comes to Homer: the contrast between Teiresias and the rest suggests that they are shadows in a way that he is not: 'he alone kept his wits; the rest were flitting shadows'; i.e. he does not act as a shadow.[18] The point is most likely that, although all the mortals in Hades are shades, those apart from Teiresias are also intellectual shades in a way that he is not.

It is still not clear, however, why Socrates retreats from the claim that the great Athenians had true virtue. The best explanation is probably to be found in the unitarian assumption that was so conspicuous in the first part of the dialogue.[19] If Socrates has insisted so emphatically that Gorgias and Meno must give a single account of virtue running through all the different types, it would be very surprising if he went on to breach his own principle and claim that different accounts of virtue can apply to different people.

True belief and the eminent Athenians

Nevertheless, even if the eminent Athenians lacked genuine virtue, this in itself does nothing to undermine the claim that they had true beliefs.

---

[16] In fact Socrates had subtly anticipated this move at 97a–b when comparing knowledge and true belief. His point there was to say that someone who had true belief about the road to Larisa would be as useful as someone with knowledge. Talking of the latter, he had said: 'if someone who knew the road to Larisa . . . went there and led others, he'd guide them correctly *and well* (εὖ)' (97a9–11). The person with true belief will also guide them correctly, but Socrates fails to add the words 'and well' (97b1–2).

[17] Kraut 1984: 302 n. 82. Contrast Irwin 1977: 317 n. 22.

[18] Even if we read αἱ rather than τοί or οἱ in 100a5 (cf. Bluck 1961: 437), the fact that Teiresias is distinguished from 'the shadows' is suggestive: in some sense he is not really a shadow.

[19] See above, pp. 25–7.

And, on the face of it, Socrates is quite clear about attributing 'virtue'$_{tb}$ to Themistocles, Aristides, Pericles and Thucydides, as well as to many other Athenians. Even though they lacked the capacity to give an account of their beliefs or to impart them to anyone else, they apparently still had true beliefs about *the same matters* (cf. 97b5–6) as someone with virtue$_k$; consequently they managed to steer their city in the right direction.

But does Socrates really believe this? Let us look back to the relevant texts more closely. When he asks Anytus whether virtue is teachable, he starts by questioning him about those who claim to teach and receive fees for their services – the sophists. After Anytus' hostile reaction, he turns to those whom Anytus considers teachers of virtue – the virtuous Athenians (92e3). As Socrates asks where they in their turn acquired their virtue, Anytus becomes concerned and asks whether it really seems to him that there are many good men in Athens (93a3–4). Socrates replies as follows:

There also seem to me, Anytus, to be men here who are good at politics, and to have been no less of them in the past than in the present. But were they also good teachers of their virtue? This is what our discussion is about. For some time now, we've been asking not whether there are good men here or not, or whether there have been in the past, but whether virtue is teachable. In asking this question we are asking whether the good men, both past and present, knew how to pass on to someone else the virtue by which *they themselves were good* . . . (93a5–b4; emphasis added)

This paragraph shows Socrates himself endorsing the claim that the great Athenians had virtue. Sceptics of this interpretation, however, might seize upon the word 'seem' (δοκοῦσιν) in the first line of the quotation. On its own, however, this cannot be used to undermine Socrates' sincerity here. First, Socrates may just be using the word in response to Anytus' use of it in 93a3. If it signals anything, it may signal not that Socrates is being ironic, but that he is tentative, and this could be because he is hesitating over the issue of whether the Athenians had virtue in the fullest sense, as he does at 100a1–7. We have to be very careful not to assume that, if the use of δοκοῦσιν signals hesitation on Socrates' part, this hesitation concerns whether the Athenians had true beliefs, rather than whether they were genuinely virtuous.

At 95a1, Anytus ceases to argue with Socrates, and Meno takes over the discussion of whether virtue is teachable. By 96d4 they have concluded that it is not, prompting Meno to ask his question of whether there are any good men, or whether there is another way of becoming good. Still assuming that the Athenians were good, Socrates concludes that their virtue consists in true belief:

So it is not by any kind of wisdom, or by being wise, that such people guided their cities – those like Themistocles and the ones Anytus was talking about just now . . . If it is not by knowledge, then, it can only be by true belief (εὐδοξίᾳ).

(99b5–c1)[20]

He does not merely rely on Anytus' or Meno's beliefs and then draw out the consequences. In other words, it is not as if his arguments can be dismissed as being purely *ad hominem*.

So why should we, in the face of this, doubt Socrates' sincerity in attributing true belief to the Athenians? A number of scholars adduce the evidence of the *Gorgias*, where Socrates launches an extended critique of Themistocles and Pericles and their like, claiming that, far from guiding their citizens on the right path, they failed to benefit them at all and only tried to gratify them. Assuming that the *Gorgias* pre-dates the *Meno*, and that Plato has not changed his mind between the two, these scholars infer that the *Meno* must be ironic in its claim that the Athenian leaders guided their city successfully.[21]

For the time being, however, I wish to leave the *Gorgias* on one side and instead continue to examine the text of the *Meno* itself. Are there any internal grounds for not taking Socrates at his word when he attributes true belief to the Athenians?

Some interpreters point to 99e1–2.[22] Socrates has just concluded that the politicians, like soothsayers, say many fine things without any understanding. He adds that we should also be prepared to call them divine as women and Spartans do (99d7–9). At this point Meno agrees, but warns Socrates that Anytus will be angry. Surely, then, Socrates cannot be paying any compliment to the politicians whom Anytus so admired.

Certainly, to make sense of the reference to Anytus' anger, we have to assume some implied criticism in Socrates' remarks. But this need not mean

---

[20] See also 96b7 for the assumption that there are virtuous people around. Hall (1981: 37) has claimed that Plato's use of the word εὐδοξίᾳ (whose usual meaning is 'good repute') supports the sceptical interpretation: the leaders merely succeeded by winning popular acclaim. See also Weiss 2001: 164–5. In reply, Calvert (1984: 10–11) rightly points out that this would make nonsense of the argument: that these men guided their city by good repute does not follow from anything that has preceded in the argument. Besides, even after this point, Socrates continues to insist that the Athenians guided their city *rightly* (ὀρθοῦσιν and κατορθῶσι , 99c1–2 and d4: there is no philological case at all for claiming, as Weiss (2001: 165) does, that these verbs imply merely the reputation for acting rightly). As Bluck (1961: 424) and Sharples (1985: 187) rightly note, εὐδοξίᾳ is used 'etymologically' to mean 'true belief' rather than 'good repute', as it usually does.
[21] Among the sceptics are Klein (1965: 238), Bluck (1961: 38–9 and 368), Sharples (1985: 15), Kraut (1984: 302 n. 82) and Weiss (2001: 168). Those who think that Plato is genuinely positive about the Athenian statesmen include Gomperz (1905: II, 375), Hackforth (1952: 149 n. 3), Dodds (1959: 360), Calvert (1984: 11) and Vlastos (1991: 125 n. 75).
[22] E.g. Irwin 1977: 317 n. 22

that he intends to deny them their success. It could as well be the reference to their lack of understanding that will cause offence. Alternatively, Meno may take the reference to divine inspiration ironically, and assume that Anytus will do the same. But this is not to the point: we are discussing whether Socrates is sincere in attributing *success* to the Athenian leaders, in the sense of genuinely correct guidance. Whether he is ironic about divine dispensation is something we shall discuss separately in the next section.[23]

But aside from the fact that there is no internal evidence for the sceptical interpretation, there is strong evidence against it. The claim that the Athenians did guide their city correctly and by true belief is essential to the logical structure of the dialogue's conclusion. Without it, most of the last ten pages of the dialogue would be redundant. In 89–96 Socrates sets up a problem which he then solves in the remainder of the dialogue. The problem arises essentially out of two claims: (a) that the Athenian leaders were successful and (b) that they were unable to pass on their qualities to anyone else. In the face of this problem he introduces the distinction between true belief and knowledge as the solution. Yet, if all along (a) was never meant seriously, what is he doing in the last ten pages of the dialogue?

This question is particularly pressing when one thinks of Socrates' attitude to his distinction between knowledge and true belief. At 98b1–5 he makes it clear that this is something to which he attaches great importance. Now the success of the Athenian leaders (along with their inability to teach) is the *raison d'être* for introducing this distinction in the first place. On the sceptical interpretation, he appears to have no reason to be serious in his quest for an alternative route to virtue, and the whole discussion of the distinction between knowledge and true belief becomes redundant.

One of the sceptics, R. S. Bluck,[24] attempts to preserve the importance of what is said in the conclusion of the *Meno* as follows: although Socrates does not mean to attribute true belief to the likes of Themistocles, he does think that, in principle, someone with true belief could emerge who would benefit the city.

Notice how this interpretation differs from the one that I have been defending, viz. that, in principle, it is possible for someone to be virtuous by having virtue$_k$, while in actuality the success of politicians in guiding the city is explained by their having 'virtue'$_{tb}$. The sceptical interpretation adds an extra component to the analysis: in principle there could be virtue$_k$; *also*

---

[23] It would also be a mistake to use the passage where Socrates talks about shadows of virtue (100a2–7) to infer that he is ironic in attributing success to the Athenians. I agree that this does show Socrates backtracking, but only on the issue of whether they had genuine virtue.

[24] Bluck 1961: 39–40.

in principle, there could be another form of virtue, 'virtue'$_{tb}$; in actuality, however, those considered by Anytus as possessing virtue had neither form of it.

Now compare this reading with the text:

> But for now, if we have been right in our investigations and in what we've said throughout the whole of this discussion, virtue comes neither by teaching nor by nature but by divine dispensation without intelligence to those to whom it does come – unless there were some statesman capable of making another like himself. *Were there* such a man, he *would* be called among the living what Homer said about Teiresias among the dead. . . (99e4–100a4; emphasis added)

> . . . it is by divine dispensation that virtue appears to us to be present in those in whom it is present. (100b1–4)

There is a deliberate contrast here. In 100a1–3, Plato uses remote conditionals with the optative to allude to the possibility of someone appearing with virtue$_k$; when he refers to 'virtue'$_{tb}$, the grammar he uses – the indefinite construction of 99e6–100a1 and the indicative of 100b3–4 – signals that this quality is not the remote possibility that virtue$_k$ is.[25] Bluck's hypothesis of an 'ideal' true belief has to elide this distinction.

So why should we join him in this? Notice that, in making this move, he only solves part of the original problem. He may have found a reason for Socrates' interest in the distinction between knowledge and true belief, but he still has to explain the presence of 90b–96c, where Socrates sets up the problem that the distinction is meant to solve. On Bluck's interpretation the distinction is still introduced to solve a problem that never existed. Yet Socrates spends some time with Anytus and then again with Meno puzzling about how certain citizens can stand out by virtue of their political success and yet be unable to instruct anyone else. On Bluck's view, Socrates only needed to refer back to the argument of 87d–89a and make an emendation in the light of the distinction: that true belief can also give correct guidance.

Furthermore, if we are not to accept the conclusion at face value that virtue$_k$ is attainable in principle but 'virtue'$_{tb}$ in practice, what leads us to accept Bluck's interpretation, where both virtue$_k$ and 'virtue'$_{tb}$, are

---

[25] There is a disputed reading at 100b3–4 as between an indicative and a subjunctive. Bluck himself at 1961: 439 seems right to favour the indicative, though either variant will make a clear distinction with the optatives used to refer to virtue$_k$ in 100a1–3. (The optative εἴη is used in 99e5, which applies to the whole of the conclusion stated in the lines that follow. But this is used to signal that the conclusion is tentative; it does not undermine the distinction subsequently made between the actuality of 'virtue'$_{tb}$ and the remote possibility of virtue$_k$.)

attainable only in principle? It seems like an *ad hoc* move simply to find
some rationale for the presence of the distinction between knowledge and
true belief. There is no signal in the text that this interpretation is the one
the reader is intended to uncover.

As if to acknowledge the difficulty of drawing his interpretation from the
text, Bluck tries to find a parallel in the *Republic* where, in the ideal state,
Plato is happy for most of his citizens to survive on a diet of true belief.
The fact that he adopts this position in the *Republic* is then used to bolster
the claim that he had already done so in the *Meno*. But this comparison is
misleading. The *Republic* allows that the *subjects* of the ideal state may have
mere true belief; it adamantly refuses to allow anything less than knowledge
for the leaders. The *Meno* is discussing the virtue of the rulers that enables
them to lead their city successfully; it is not discussing the qualities of their
subjects. So if we attribute to the *Meno* the claim that in an ideal world our
leaders could succeed by true belief, we cannot support this interpretation
by appealing to the *Republic*.

So on internal grounds, there are strong reasons for assuming Socrates'
sincerity in attributing true belief to the Athenians. There is one important
qualification to be made here: in denying that the *Meno* is ironic, we do not
have to go to the other extreme and claim that it is giving a ringing endorse-
ment of the Athenians' leadership. A mid-way position is quite possible.
The success of the politicians in guiding their city is accepted as an appearance, though a plausible one.[26] That it is considered plausible is strongly
suggested by the fact that Socrates goes to the trouble of expounding the
theory of true belief to explain it. But this is not to say that he thinks the
success of the Athenians is not open to more scrutiny.

Divine dispensation

Finally, there is the question whether Socrates is sincere in attributing a
divine origin to the true beliefs of the Athenian leaders. The claim arises
out of the comparison with poets and soothsayers: they say many fine things
without understanding, and do so through divine influence. In the same
way, the politicians whose speeches lead to success in many important ways
are divinely inspired (99c11–d5).

There is some agreement among scholars that Socrates is being serious
when he mentions divine dispensation. Vlastos, who claims that Plato is
serious in his evaluation of Pericles in the *Meno*, adds that he also means to

---

[26] This would be my explanation of the use of δοκοῦσιν in 93a5.

attribute divine inspiration to him.[27] But even some sceptical interpreters of the *Meno* take the reference to divine dispensation seriously. This is not, of course, because they think Socrates is attributing it to the Athenian leaders themselves but, just as they allowed him to be in earnest about the *possibility* of 'virtue'$_{tb}$ arising, they also allow that it might arise as a gift of the gods.[28]

It is in fact difficult to find conclusive reasons for doubting the sincerity of Socrates' reference to divine dispensation. Admittedly, the argument he gives for the conclusion is very brief: what goes for soothsayers and poets is applied to politicians in the space of a few lines. So perhaps Socrates should not be seen as investing heavily in the conclusion. Certainly, he does not use it as a premise for any further arguments and goes on to sound highly tentative in the closing paragraph stressing, yet again, the need to investigate the nature of virtue properly before asking how it is acquired. But this does not mean that he is wary of talking about divine inspiration *per se*. It is just a reaffirmation of his methodological stance (the chronological priority of definition), which would apply whatever answer he gave to the question of how virtue was acquired, even if that answer was more mundane. So, although the conclusion may be provisional, I can see no grounds for taking it to be ironic.[29]

---

[27] Vlastos 1991: 125 n. 75. He cites the divine inspiration attributed to the poets in the *Ion* (534b), which he also takes to be sincere.

[28] Bluck 1961: 41 and Kraut 1984: 302–3 n. 82.

[29] *Pace* Scott 1995: 43. There is an ironic reference to divination at 92c6, where Socrates calls Anytus a seer, wondering how he could know so much about the sophists without ever having met them. So the concept has already been stained with irony. But I do not think that on its own this is enough to cast doubt over its use in the rest of the dialogue.

CHAPTER 15

Irony in the Meno: *the evidence of the* Gorgias

In the previous chapter, I went against the trend of many recent commentators who take the conclusion of the *Meno* to be largely ironic. In doing so, I concentrated solely on the evidence internal to the text. This, however, is to overlook what many of these commentators would see as crucial evidence: the trenchant critique of Athenian politicians in the *Gorgias*. If, as these sceptics assume, the *Gorgias* predates the *Meno* can we not assume that Plato's earlier views are in the background when he has Socrates revisit the question of what the Athenian politicians did for their city?

I wish to continue to go against this trend and argue for a different way of relating the two dialogues. I shall begin by rehearsing the essentials of the political critique of the *Gorgias* and then argue that, by comparison with the *Meno*, it operates at a greater level of sophistication where the analysis of political virtue is concerned. It is more likely that the *Meno* represents an earlier point in Plato's career as a political commentator. To support this claim, I shall attempt to undermine the reasons usually given for dating the *Meno* after the *Gorgias*. The upshot will be that there is no longer any reason at all to read the *Meno* in the shadow of the *Gorgias*; and any external evidence for finding the *Meno*'s conclusion ironic fades away altogether.

THE RELATION OF THE *MENO* TO THE *GORGIAS*

Shadows of virtue in the Gorgias

The argument of the *Gorgias* starts by trying to determine the nature of rhetoric (447d1ff.). Gorgias says that orators are able to persuade almost anyone[1] of anything; because they persuade rather than teach, they produce 'conviction' (πίστις) rather than knowledge (cf. esp. 454c7–e9); moreover,

---

[1] Except the expert: 459a4–6. See p. 180 above.

they manage to do this without themselves needing any knowledge of the relevant subject matter (cf. esp. 459b1–c5).

When Polus takes over the argument, he asks Socrates what he takes oratory to be. Socrates says that it is a 'knack' (ἐμπειρία) rather than a craft (τέχνη),[2] and that it aims to please and gratify those whom it addresses (462c3–7). Polus immediately moves on to the question of whether rhetoric is fine (καλόν), but Socrates continues to speak (albeit obscurely) about its nature, saying at 463d1–2 that it is 'an image of a part of politics' (πολιτικῆς μορίου εἴδωλον). Having aroused Gorgias' curiosity, he is persuaded to elaborate at more length.

At 464a1ff., he embarks on a detailed classification of crafts and knacks, starting with the distinction between body and soul. In each case, one can work towards its good or towards its apparent good, its gratification. There are two practices that tend to the good of the body – gymnastics and medicine – and two for the good of the soul – legislation and justice. Each of these four counts as a craft, the last two being grouped under the term 'political'. At 464c5 Socrates turns to flattery and says that for each of the four crafts there is an 'image', a practice that pretends to aim at the good, but aims only at the apparent good, pleasure. Cookery corresponds to medicine (464d3–e2), and cosmetics to gymnastics (465b2–6).

All this goes some way towards explaining the claim that originally perplexed Gorgias, viz. that rhetoric is 'an image of a part of politics' (463d1–2). The relation between a knack and a craft is not simply that one aims at pleasure and the other at the good. Since pleasure is an apparent good (464a3), a knack appears to be aiming at the goal of its corresponding craft – hence the claim at 464c7 that each knack 'impersonates' one of the crafts. Like an actor on stage a knack hides behind the mask of its corresponding craft, deceiving its victims into thinking they are acquiring the good from a true craftsman (cf. also 517e3).

That knacks aim at pleasure rather than the good is one of two ways in which Socrates distinguishes them from crafts. The other is epistemological: a knack has no account (λόγος); it fails to grasp the explanation of the nature of its objects, or of what it is doing to them (465a3–6 and 501a1–7; cf. *Meno* 98a3–4).

So far, most of what I have said about rhetoric comes from the discussion with Polus at 462b–466a. From 466a10 onwards, Polus tries again to move Socrates away from the definition of rhetoric onto its merits, this time successfully. But the nature of rhetoric and of the true political craft re-enters

---

[2] At the beginning of the work, Polus had insisted that rhetoric was a τέχνη (448c4–9).

the dialogue explicitly when Callicles joins the fray. Having distinguished the good from pleasure (499b8), Socrates is able to return to his distinction between flattery (κολακεία) and craft. There then follow two extended discussions that build on the theory set out in 462b–466a: 500a–505b and 513c–522e.

As far as the definition of rhetoric is concerned, these later passages add little to what was said before. What they are concerned with, among other things, is the question of what it is like (ποῖον) – specifically whether it is fine.[3] As before, the answer is resoundingly negative. Rhetoric corrupts not only the souls of its subjects (by feeding them with unwholesome pleasures), but also the orators themselves. Forced to say only what their audience want to hear, they are eventually no longer able to keep a cynical distance between what they say and what they themselves believe (cf. 510d6–8 and 513b3–c2).

More is said, however, about the nature of the craft that marks out the true politician. Even if we are never given what amounts to a full definition, Socrates speaks at some length about the way it imposes order on the souls of its subjects, hinting that such order could be explicated in geometrical terms.[4] In the original discussion with Polus (462b–466a), we were told that, as a political craft, justice is a kind of knowledge involving an account of its subject matter; in the argument with Callicles, we are told rather more about what it actually does (i.e. its function).

Now that we are clearer on Socrates' distinction between true politics and rhetoric, we can turn to the passage that aroused our interest in the *Gorgias* in the first place. Having distinguished the true politician from the rhetorician, at 515c4ff. Socrates names some of the pretenders to the true art of politics: Pericles, Themistocles, Cimon and Miltiades (cf. also 503c1–d3). Although Callicles wants to say that these were great and successful politicians, Socrates replies that they failed as true politicians, because they failed to impose the necessary order on the souls of their subjects. They satisfied all desires indiscriminately rather than those which would be beneficial for their subjects. Pericles, for instance, cannot have improved his citizens because, after being in his care for some time, they took it into their heads to punish him, thereby showing that they had become more brutal while under his charge (515d6–516d3). The same argument is applied to the other three leaders at 516d3–e7.

---

[3] When Socrates chastises Polus for asking whether rhetoric is καλόν (462c10–d2 and 463c3–5), he is doing so not because he objects to the question *per se*, but because the definitional question has not yet been addressed. As the dialogue progresses, Socrates' interest in the ποῖον-question becomes increasingly obvious.

[4] See 503d5ff., esp. 507e6–508a8.

Political virtue in the Meno and Gorgias

All this puts us in a better position to compare the two dialogues. If we start by looking specifically at the two lists of eminent Athenians in *Meno* 93b–94e and *Gorgias* 515d–519b, we can see that the dialogues are using different principles of selection. The *Gorgias* has the more specific criterion for singling out individual politicians, viz. whether or not they were orators. The *Meno* seems to use no other principle than notoriety. Thus only Themistocles and Pericles are common to both lists.[5] And, although the dialogues do have these two figures in common, their assessments of them are quite different, as we have repeatedly stressed. The *Meno* allows that they guided their city correctly: to recall the analogy of 97a, even though they lacked knowledge, they still managed to lead their people to Larisa, as it were. In the *Gorgias*, by contrast, they failed to guide their citizens correctly and achieved only the apparent good for their citizens, not the real one; the Athenians thought they were being led to Larisa when in fact they were being taken somewhere else.

But now look at the relation between the two dialogues from a more general perspective. Despite their diverging assessments of Athenian politicians, there is a significant continuity of topic between them. In both dialogues Socrates acknowledges that certain Athenians stood out from their fellow citizens for some quality that they had. In neither case is he talking about the quality that enables the ordinary citizen to co-operate effectively with others in everyday transactions (cf. *Protagoras* 322c1–323c2 and *Phaedo* 82a11–b8). This is implied in the *Meno* when it says that they had something that they were unable to pass on to others, including their own sons (cf. 99b7–8). What is common to the two dialogues is that they are both trying to determine the nature of some extra-ordinary quality possessed only by

---

[5] Aristides is actually mentioned elsewhere in the *Gorgias* – favourably so. In the course of the myth, describing the treatment different characters receive in the afterlife, Socrates praises him for his justice (526a3–b3). To preserve consistency with the rest of the dialogue, which says that no one, past or present, is or was good at politics (517a1–2), we have to think of Aristides as coming somewhere between the rhetoricians and the true politician. He was not good in the sense implied at 517a1–2, because he failed to make his subjects better: like Themistocles and Cimon, he was ostracised: see Dodds 1959: 382. On the other hand, unsuccessful as he was at improving the people, he always acted justly. I do not agree with Irwin's suggestion (1979: 247) that Plato would have considered Aristides a flatterer. Flattery is condemned as being base (αἰσχρόν, cf. 463d4), and yet at 526a7 Aristides is ranked among the fine.

It is difficult to know what the *Gorgias* would have to say about Thucydides. Although he was a conservative, that may not have stopped Plato classifying him as a flatterer. Conversely, what would the *Meno* have had to say about Cimon or Miltiades? Presumably Cimon would be accused of being unable to pass on his virtue to his son (assuming his son Thessalus was undistinguished). Miltiades presents an interesting problem: Cimon was his son, and so the *Meno* ought to admit that he can count as having virtue based on knowledge. Fortunate for the *Gorgias* that it uses a different argument.

a few, which is still not to be confused with whatever marks out the true politician.[6]

At this point there is an important point of terminology to register. At *Gorgias* 503c4–d3 Socrates uses the terms 'virtue' (ἀρετή) and 'good' (ἀγαθός) when describing the true politician. Given that the true political craft corresponding to rhetoric is justice, it is of course unsurprising for it now to be called virtue and for those who possess it to be considered good politicians. But the terminological point is important, because it means that the *Gorgias*' distinction between justice and its impersonator is that between genuine virtue and its image (463d2).

This makes the task of comparing the dialogues clearer. The *Meno* is dominated by two questions: the question Meno himself wants answered, the question of whether virtue is teachable, which is one about what virtue is like (ποῖον), and the question that Socrates thinks has priority, the definitional question (τί ἐστί). In the event, both questions get an answer (or answers) of a kind. In the *Gorgias*, Socrates himself sets the agenda by asking a definitional question about rhetoric. Polus explicitly shifts the topic to the question of what it is like (a ποῖον-question), viz. whether it is fine. At the end of the dialogue, both questions have been addressed at length.

From a distance, perhaps, one might think these two dialogues are on substantially different topics: one on the nature and acquisition of virtue, the other on the nature and value of rhetoric. But as one looks more closely the similarities of subject matter are striking. Like the *Meno*, the *Gorgias* concerns virtue, and both dialogues end up giving a dual answer to their definitional question. After giving a definition of ideal virtue (87d–89a), the *Meno* moves down a level to define actual 'virtue', later calling it a shadow of virtue. (Remember that 'virtue' here signifies *political* virtue, the quality that will enable one to guide the city rightly.) The *Gorgias* starts by defining rhetoric but, in the course of doing so, moves up a level to the ideal, i.e. to true political craft. Like the *Meno*, it considers true virtue and its shadow in tandem.

Having acknowledged the convergence of interests (as far as the definitional question is concerned) we should also note the fact that the *Gorgias* investigates the question in far more detail than the *Meno*. True virtue in the *Meno* is defined as knowledge, but we know nothing about the content of this knowledge, apart from the fact that it concerns the good of the city.

---

[6] In Scott 1995: 45 and 50–2 I wrongly assimilated the extra-ordinary quality possessed by the Athenian politicians to demotic virtue, a quality widely shared among the citizens at large. See also Taylor 1926: 144–5 and Penner 1973: 40–1.

In the *Gorgias*, we may not have a complete definition of the virtue of the politician but we know that it involves differentiating good and bad desires, and determining the right order to be imposed on the citizens – a theme to be developed further in the *Republic* (cf. vi 500d–501c). Equally, its account of shadow-virtue is, on its own terms, considerably more detailed than the *Meno*'s. There is an elaborate classification situating rhetoric in relation to the other members of the flattery-genus. The content of rhetorical knack is specified, being pleasure rather than the good – a distinction that is not simply assumed, but argued for in some detail (494a–499b). We are also given an explanation for why it is a *shadow* of virtue, based on the claim that pleasure is an apparent good.[7]

In the light of the greater sophistication of the *Gorgias*, one way of putting the difference between the two dialogues is as follows. Once the *Meno* has outlined the nature of virtue and its shadow, it concludes with a claim about how virtue is acquired, but ends with a note of warning (100b4–6): the investigation of the definitional question has not been adequate and must be continued. Since the *Meno* has given a dual answer to this question, I take it that the proposal to return to it is a proposal to continue the investigation into both types of virtue.

The *Gorgias* can be seen as a deeper investigation of the *Meno*'s dual definitional question. However, it departs from the *Meno* in two ways. First, when the *Gorgias* discusses shadow-virtue, it deals with a specific type (rhetoric), rather than any quality that, while falling short of genuine virtue, makes someone stand out from his fellow-citizens. The *Meno* does not discriminate between what, for the *Gorgias*, would be different types of quality (e.g. Themistocles' *vs* Aristides'), but treats all such exceptional qualities together.

Second, there is the fact that the *Gorgias* gives a different assessment of the Athenian politicians, which might now be explained in the following way. The *Meno* had operated more at the level of appearances, taking it for granted that Themistocles and his like did lead the city successfully, and on this basis asked what quality, if not knowledge, allowed them to do so. Once it has fulfilled the promise of the *Meno*'s conclusion to investigate virtue in more detail, the *Gorgias* is in a position to overturn this assumption (while explaining, with its account of pleasure as the apparent good, why it might

---

[7] *En passant*, we are even offered an answer to the acquisition question of the *Meno*. The rhetoricians got their 'virtue' by experience and memory (!) (501a7–b1): 'Through routine (τριβή) and experience (ἐμπειρία), it [sc. rhetoric] merely preserves the memory of what customarily happens, and that's also how it supplies its pleasures.' No divine dispensation here: all we have is an empirical process, which is also unsystematic and perhaps unreflective in nature.

have been an attractive one to make). The *Gorgias* is thus further down the line of inquiry: it has achieved what the *Meno* had left as unfinished business.[8]

In the light of this, I would propose the following hypothesis: Plato wrote the *Meno* at a time when he was prepared to take seriously the thought that the Athenian leaders were in some measure successful, although he felt the need to investigate the nature of political virtue in more depth. Once he has accomplished this task, he writes the *Gorgias* – hence its greater sophistication. Given what I have said, it would be surprising if the chronological order were the other way around. Having written the trenchant critique in the *Gorgias*, why would he then write a work in which he expects his readers to entertain the notion that Themistocles, Pericles and a great many others really did achieve good for their citizens?[9]

Perhaps one might insist that, although the *Meno* is sincere in attributing true belief to the Athenian leaders, it still post-dates the *Gorgias*. This would be because Plato had changed his mind and put his earlier bitterness behind him.[10] Yet the greater sophistication of the *Gorgias* creates a problem for this view. What is unsatisfactory here is not that he changes his position, but that he does so with no explanation. The *Gorgias* has a long and articulate account of why the politicians should be demoted as they are, and yet the *Meno* makes no allusion to it, and cheerfully attributes true belief to them. If Plato were having a genuine change of heart, he would surely attempt to explain how, after all, Pericles and Themistocles do not fall into the hole dug for them in the *Gorgias*. In comparison to the *Gorgias* the analysis of the *Meno* is more superficial. Thus an earlier date of composition remains the more plausible hypothesis.

So much by way of a proposal. Of course, it will be resisted by those who accept the standard view that the *Gorgias* pre-dates the *Meno*. So to help my proposal on its way, let me end by showing that the standard chronology rests on extremely shaky grounds.

Arguments for dating the *Gorgias* before the *Meno* tend to follow a set pattern. The absence of a certain theme from the *Gorgias*, combined with its

---

[8] Although Socrates does disclaim knowledge in the *Gorgias* (509a5), his tone is much more confident than in the *Meno*, and he does not make the type of qualification that we find at the end of the *Meno*.
[9] To repeat from p. 188 above: in the *Meno* the content of the actual politicians' judgements is the same as that of true political expertise (cf. 97b5–7). It follows that they did accurately divine the good.
[10] See p. 189 n. 21 above for those who take this view.

presence in the *Meno*, is construed as evidence for an innovation in Plato's thought. The themes in question are epistemological and methodological: Plato's alleged dissatisfaction with the elenchus, the influence of mathematics, the hypothetical method and the theory of recollection. I shall examine each of these in turn.

Disenchantment with the elenchus

One type of argument, associated especially with Gregory Vlastos, runs as follows. In the *Gorgias*, the elenchus is 'vibrantly alive':[11] Socrates uses his method of cross-examination with Polus and Callicles to prove substantive moral theses. The *Meno* begins in the style of the early elenctic dialogues, but the paradox of inquiry signals Plato's doubts about the method. In effect, he abandons it as a means of proving anything and relegates it to the status of a dialectical preliminary, something that causes *aporia* and so provides the necessary stimulus for further inquiry. This allegedly becomes clear in the course of the slave-boy demonstration, which Vlastos sees as a mini-exemplar of Plato's new approach to philosophical inquiry. The first part of the examination corresponds to the old-style elenchus: the boy makes confident assertions, sees them overturned and reaches *aporia*. But in the passage that follows (82b8ff.), where the boy eventually acquires a true belief, Socrates drops the adversarial role of the elenctic questioner.[12]

Let us look at this argument more closely. At page 119 Vlastos says that the question put to the boy does not admit of an arithmetical solution (i.e. one in terms of rational numbers) and that, up to the point of *aporia*, they have only been proceeding arithmetically. It is only when Socrates moves him in a geometrical direction that the boy is able to emerge from the impasse:

Extending the diagram, he plants into it the line that opens sesame, and *then* the boy 'recollects' that the side of the square whose area is twice that of a given square is the diagonal of the given square.

It is not entirely clear how Vlastos' argument is supposed to work. What does he think happens at the 'open sesame' moment that precludes the use of the elenchus? Socrates certainly does not deliver a lecture about rational and irrational numbers or about the difference between arithmetic and geometry. Rather, he proceeds in terms that the boy can follow and extends the diagram. Crucially, of course, he professes not to lecture the

---

[11] Vlastos 1991: 125.   [12] Vlastos 1991: 118–19.

boy about anything. As far as he is concerned, he asks questions, and all the answers come from the boy himself: it is essential to the experiment that Socrates, as he had always claimed to do, merely draws out answers from his interlocutor. The moment of 'open sesame' is not a moment where Socrates tells the boy something. It is one where he asks a question that the boy would not have thought of asking himself but that, once asked, enables a chain of further questions to be asked which result in the boy recollecting the true answer.[13]

I cannot see why this should be construed as abandoning the elenchus, at least as it is practised in the *Gorgias*. Here Socrates also claims to have achieved positive results by drawing responses from his interlocutors. Again, progress is often made when Socrates asks a question that might not have occurred to the interlocutors, but which helps to set them on the right course.

Admittedly, the slave-boy demonstration is not adversarial like the *Gorgias*: but this is not essential to the elenchus.[14] Polus and Callicles are much more wedded to their prior beliefs than the boy is to his; in both dialogues, however, Socrates refutes these prior beliefs and proves another by drawing the answers from his interlocutors.

In general, one should be wary of seeing the elenchus as being more alive in the *Gorgias* than the *Meno*. True, there is more elenctic argument in the *Gorgias*, but then it is longer. Yet it also contains extended passages where the interlocutors listen in silence as Socrates confidently espouses his own views.

The influence of mathematics

Commentators sometimes point to the *Meno*'s interest in mathematics (especially geometry), and see this as pointing ahead to the middle period, especially the *Republic*. As we have seen, Plato's interest in mathematics in the *Meno* is apparent at three points. In the first part of the dialogue, an arguably geometrical definition of surface is used as an example to help define virtue (73e1ff.); the subject matter of the slave-boy demonstration is geometrical; and Socrates borrows the method of hypothesis

---

[13] In other words, I cannot see how Vlastos' argument is supposed to work unless he thinks Socrates is feeding the boy the answers. Yet ironically, it is Vlastos (1965) who argued so persuasively against the common complaint that Socrates just instils the answers in the boy. See above pp. 101–2.

[14] As Fine (1992: 208–9) points out. I am also in general agreement here with Irwin (1977: 139), who thinks that the elenchus is used throughout the whole of the demonstration.

from the mathematicians (86e1–87b2). All these passages suggest (apparently) that, for Plato, mathematics provides the key for making progress in moral inquiry, a view then developed in the central books of the *Republic*. Although the *Gorgias* does allude to arithmetic (451b7–c5 and 453e1–3) and geometry (465b7, 507e6–508a8), it does so only briefly. This difference is then used as an indication of a later date for the *Meno*.[15]

Let me start with one specific point. At *Gorgias* 507e6–508a8, Socrates makes it clear that mathematics, especially geometry, is relevant to understanding justice:

The wise, Callicles, say that heaven and earth, gods and men, are held together by community and friendship and order and temperance and justice; and for this reason they call the whole the 'world-order', my friend, not 'disorder' or 'intemperance'. But you don't seem to me to pay attention to them, wise as you are in such matters. You've failed to notice that geometrical equality has great importance among gods and men; you think one should practise taking more, because you neglect geometry.

This is an extraordinary passage. The *Meno* only sees mathematical and moral inquiry as methodologically parallel;[16] the *Gorgias* makes the much stronger claim that, in some sense, morals *are* mathematical, a claim that would begin to explain why the *Meno* can treat mathematics as a parallel. It is also the claim that we find developed in the *Republic* and the *Timaeus*.

At any rate, how much can be made of the fact that the *Gorgias* makes less use (in some sense of 'use') of mathematics than the *Meno*? It would be very unwise to treat the amount of mathematics used as some sort of chronometer: how much mathematics is used in the *Phaedo*, or in Diotima's speech in the *Symposium*? In fact, a closer look at the *Republic* is instructive here. Despite the work's claim to fame in this area, it is noticeable that almost all the mathematics occurs in book VII as part of the discussion on the education of the guardians, a digression from the argument of books I–IV and VIII–IX that justice is good for the individual. This argument is started is book I, restarted in book II, brought to a temporary conclusion in book IV, then resumed and concluded in books VIII–IX. Apart from two short passages, 546b–d and 587c–588a, there is almost no explicit use of mathematics made at all. This is not to deny that, ideally, one should seek knowledge of the good *via* mathematics; but in the actual argument of *Rep.*

---

[15] This is the general thesis advanced by Vlastos in 1991: ch. 4. Cf. also Kraut 1992: 6.
[16] Even here one should be careful not to exaggerate Plato's interest in geometry. See above pp. 34–5 and 41–2.

I–IV and VIII–IX, Socrates chooses for the most part to avoid mathematics. To consider here why he does so would take us too far afield. But the central point is that Plato's views on the relevance of mathematics to morals is not straightforwardly related to the extent to which mathematics is actually deployed in any particular dialogue.

I would suggest that whether Plato chooses to use mathematics is to some extent determined by the readiness of his interlocutors to respond. Unlike Meno who, although arguably somewhat shallow, can still be intellectually curious (especially if what is on offer is exotic and technical), Callicles, at least, is impatient with philosophy quite generally (484c4ff.), and would soon have become bored and perplexed by the introduction of extensive mathematics.[17] This is made reasonably clear at the end in the passage quoted above (507e6–508a8): Callicles has no interest in geometry. It is difficult enough for Socrates to persuade him to stay and listen to an argument that has an obvious and straightforward relevance to the topic at hand. Long drawn-out geometrical excursions are surely out of the question.

The method of hypothesis

The method of hypothesis is introduced with a display of geometrical sophistication in the *Meno*; the method, or a development of it, then occurs in the last argument of the *Phaedo*; and in the *Republic*, hypothesis is contrasted with dialectic and made the subject of the guardians' ten-year mathematical studies. The type of argument used by scholars who invoke the method should now be familiar. If the method is introduced in the *Meno*, occurs in the middle-period dialogues, but is absent from the *Gorgias*, then the *Gorgias* is likely to come before the *Meno*.[18]

We should not, however, exaggerate the extent to which Plato uses this method. It is not as if, from the *Meno* onwards, every philosophical argument must be pursued according to the method of hypothesis. It makes no appearance in the slave-boy demonstration, which is significant if one sees this as a paradigm for philosophical inquiry.[19] Nor is it used for all the arguments of the *Phaedo*; let alone by Diotima in the *Symposium*.

Again, we need to take account of the nature of interlocutors and the dialectical context. Where the method is used, it is used on those who,

[17] Admittedly, this might not apply so much to Polus: see 465b7–c1.
[18] See Vlastos 1991: 122ff. and Day 1994: 11; cf. Kraut 1992: 37 n. 24.
[19] According to Vlastos (1991: 120), 'its whole purpose is to illuminate the process by which according to this new, all too-Platonic Socrates, *all* inquiry – and therefore all moral inquiry – must proceed'.

like Meno, have some intellectual curiosity, and some willingness to listen to an excursus about mathematical method. In the *Phaedo*, of course, the Pythagorean inclined interlocutors will be highly sympathetic to the use of a method that derives from mathematics. But why assume that the hypothetical method would cut any ice with Callicles if, more generally, mathematics would not?

The theory of recollection

Perhaps the most commonly used argument is that the *Gorgias* must come before the *Meno* because it makes no use of the theory of recollection.[20]

There is an immediate question to be asked about the assumptions underlying this argument. Are we to believe that, as soon as Plato had thought of a new theory and for as long as he held it, he put it into every dialogue that he wrote? Surely, if we make an inference about dating from the absence of a particular doctrine, we need to demonstrate that the missing doctrine is relevant to the topic and context of the dialogue in question. In this respect, the previous three arguments seem to start on a better footing, because they are all concerned with philosophical method, and this is something whose relevance ought to be easier to demonstrate than that of a particular doctrine.

So why should we expect the *Gorgias* to mention recollection? The *Meno* is concerned with teaching and education, and so the theory of recollection is clearly relevant. But the *Gorgias* is not concerned with how virtue and its shadow are acquired, but with what they are, and whether the shadow is something fine.[21]

Advocates of an earlier date for the *Gorgias* might respond to this by looking once more at Vlastos' work on the elenchus. The method involves a number of stages: extracting an initial answer (p) from the interlocutor, extracting further premises (q, r, s), which are then used to demonstrate -p. The 'problem of the elenchus', as Vlastos sees it, is that Socrates does not just claim to have found an inconsistency in the interlocutor's premise set,

---

[20] Yet again, see Vlastos 1991: ch. 4. (When arguing for the priority of the *Gorgias*, Vlastos uses all four of the arguments I have mentioned. For him they are closely connected, with mathematics providing the common thread.) See also Bluck 1961: 110, Day 1994: 11 and Benson 2000: 257.

[21] Bluck (1961: 111) thinks that the theory of recollection is used by Plato in the *Meno* to solve a problem of moral knowledge: to show 'how there can be fixed standards of conduct when everything here is relative and transient, and how, if there are such standards, we can hope to acquire knowledge of them'. But he does not attempt to demonstrate that the *Gorgias* has such concerns as well.

but actually to have demonstrated -*p*. The clearest evidence for this comes from the *Gorgias*, especially at the following two places:[22]

Has it not been proved (ἀποδέδεικται) that what was asserted is true? (479e8)

These things having become evident in the foregoing arguments, I would say, crude though it may seem to say it, that they have been clamped down and bound by arguments of iron and adamant . . . (508e6–509a2)

For Vlastos, lurking behind Socrates' confidence in the demonstrative power of the elenchus is the startling belief that:

. . . the truth he presses on his adversaries is already *in* them, despite their stubborn resistance to it – that they already 'believe' it and can be compelled by elenctic parley to 'witness' for it; that unless they recognise its truth they doom themselves to a life of unacknowledged self-contradiction.[23]

But how can Socrates justify such strong claims? Vlastos argues that in the *Gorgias* he cannot, but that the theory of recollection was subsequently developed to solve the problem.[24] On this interpretation, then, the theory of recollection would certainly have been relevant to (and hence mentioned in) the *Gorgias*, had Plato already committed himself to it.[25]

In the face of this, let me make an unorthodox suggestion: the theory of recollection is not, after all, absent from the *Gorgias*.

According to Vlastos, Socrates in the *Gorgias* takes it for granted that the truth is already in his interlocutors. Here are the texts that support this claim:

But I know how to produce one witness to my assertions: the man against whom I am arguing. (474a5–6, trans. Vlastos)

I believe that I and you and the rest of mankind believe that committing injustice is worse than is suffering it . . . (474b2–4, trans. Vlastos)

At 482b2–6 he warns Callicles that, if he does not accept the thesis that to commit injustice with impunity is the greatest of evils, he will dissent from himself his whole life long.

---

[22] Both translations are from Vlastos 1994: 19 with n. 57, and 34.   [23] Vlastos 1994: 34–5.
[24] Vlastos 1994: 29.
[25] This brings out a curious feature of Vlastos' work on the elenchus. In Vlastos 1994: 29, he argues that recollection is used to support the elenchus (by providing the epistemology to underwrite the method). Yet in Vlastos 1991: 119, he seems to think that the recollection (at least in the slave-boy example) brings with it the abandoning of the elenchus.

These are indeed extraordinary claims. What can Socrates possibly mean by saying that the truth about justice lurks in the souls of his interlocutors, for as long as they live? Instead of assuming that these claims are made in the *Gorgias* and later justified by recollection in the *Meno*, why not invert the order of the dialogues and say that Socrates is confident of making these claims because he has *already* adopted the theory? It lies in the background, and Plato can expect his readers to pick up the reference. Interestingly enough, there is an allusion to recollection at *Gorgias* 493c2–3 (although the reference is probably to the Pythagorean version).[26]

But if Plato has already adopted the theory of recollection by the time of the *Gorgias*, why is Socrates so coy in his allusions to it, especially given the importance of the theory to solving the problem of the elenchus? Once again, we must keep the dialectical context in mind. First, although the epistemological issues that recollection addresses are of fundamental importance to Plato, they are not directly the point at issue between Socrates, Polus and Callicles. These interlocutors do not raise problems about whether there can be moral knowledge: Callicles seems confident enough in his espousal of natural justice. They are all concerned to determine the content of that knowledge, i.e. what is fine and good.

Second, we saw how uninterested Callicles was in geometry. It is surely very unlikely that he would be any more receptive to the theory of recollection, once brought out into the open. In fact, Socrates gives us a very good hint of this at 493c4. Having alluded to the Pythagorean version of recollection, he himself admits that what he has said is somewhat out of the ordinary (ἄτοπα). Doubtless Callicles finds it absurd, and a little later on says that, however many stories Socrates tells of this kind, he will remain unconvinced.[27] With this kind of reception in prospect, and enough on the agenda already, it is not surprising that Socrates keeps the theory only in the background.

* * *

In sum, the arguments for dating the *Meno* after the *Gorgias* based on method and epistemology are weak. By contrast, comparing the political and ethical theory of the two works is a surer way of determining their order,

---

[26] See Dodds 1959: 297 and 303, Carcopino 1927: 287 and Canto 1987: 338–9 n. 137.
[27] Similarly, at the end of the final myth, Socrates says that Callicles will probably pour scorn on it as an old wife's tale (527a5–6). For the claim that reincarnation is implicit in the myth (esp. at 525b1–526d2), see Friedländer 1958: 185 and Dodds 1959: 381.

the greater sophistication of the *Gorgias* suggesting that it was written later than the *Meno*.²⁸

---

²⁸ Another area in which the *Meno* might be thought to be more sophisticated and hence later than the *Gorgias* is in its analysis of knowledge and true belief. According to Calvert (1984: 5–7), although the *Gorgias* briefly acknowledges that belief (πίστις) can be either true or false (454c7–e2), it then suppresses this insight by refusing to allow that the belief of the Athenian politicians (called 'knack', ἐμπειρία) might have been true; the *Meno* corrects this oversight, re-establishes the possibility of true belief and so allows that the great Athenians might have had true belief after all. If true, all this could be used to date the *Meno* after the *Gorgias*. However, Socrates' condemnation of the eminent Athenians is not based upon so gross an epistemological oversight, but on detailed political analysis. The correct way of understanding the relation between the two dialogues is that the *Gorgias* investigates belief with a much more specific focus than the *Meno*. It is not interested in belief in general, nor even in the belief that any successful politician may have had (e.g. Aristides), but in the specific mental state of the orators, ἐμπειρία, and, correlatively, in the cognitive state it induces in the audience, πίστις. This ties in with my claim that the *Gorgias* is to be seen as developing the thought of the *Meno* in specific directions, particularly by analysing in more detail what made a certain type of Athenian statesman stand out.

CHAPTER 16

Meno's progress

On pages 60–65 above, I claimed that Plato draws an extremely vivid portrait of Meno's character throughout the work, and has Socrates attempt to reform it as the conversation goes on. One of his main stratagems is to use the slave boy and Anytus as object lessons from which Meno is supposed to learn. I now wish to examine the last section of the dialogue, 96d onwards, to see whether Socrates ultimately has any success.

Let us turn back to the point where Anytus leaves Socrates and Meno to continue the discussion as to whether virtue is teachable. After concluding that it is not (95b1–96c10), Socrates introduces the distinction between knowledge and true belief (96d1–98b6); finally they agree that virtue is true belief, not knowledge, and comes not by teaching but by divine dispensation (98b7–100c2). What I wish to show is that throughout this passage Meno's behaviour as an interlocutor undergoes a marked change, especially in comparison to the first ten pages of the dialogue.[1]

He is much milder and more co-operative. There are certainly no abrupt or peremptory demands, nor any obstructions. At no point does Socrates need to comment on his failings, even light-heartedly. The third section (98b7–100c2) is a particularly striking contrast to Meno's behaviour in the

---

[1] Whether Meno actually improves is an issue that divides commentators quite sharply. Thompson (1901: xx) ('he certainly was a bad pupil') and Guthrie (1956: 11) think he remains essentially unchanged, and throughout her book, Weiss (2001) is particularly severe on Meno as a character. On the other side, Brumbaugh (1975: 112), Seeskin (1987: 125–7) and Gordon (1999: 108–11) think he improves in the second half of the dialogue. They also all agree that Socrates uses the slave boy demonstration to achieve this. Given the explicit connections that Socrates draws between Meno and the boy at 84a3–c11, there can be no doubt that they are right here. However, they do not confront the fact that, even after the demonstration, Meno is still criticised by Socrates for his unruly behaviour (86c7–e1). This is why it is so important to see the Anytus episode as providing additional support in Socrates' attempts to educate Meno. None of these commentators take this extra step: although Meno may have learnt something about good dialectic from the slave-boy episode, the message needs further reinforcement.

first part of the dialogue: in all his answers he agrees straightforwardly with Socrates.[2]

One might think that Meno has simply collapsed and become wholly submissive. However, there is clear evidence from 96d1–98b6 against this explanation. When Socrates concludes that virtue is not teachable, Meno comments:

> It seems not, if we've considered the matter correctly. So I wonder, Socrates, if there are any good men, or what might be the way in which they come into being. (96d1–4)

This cues the distinction between knowledge and true belief. Socrates' initial point in making the distinction is to stress that true belief is just as useful as knowledge. But Meno picks him up:

> MEN. Except that the person who has knowledge will always be successful, while one with true belief will sometimes be successful, sometimes not.
>
> SOC. What do you mean? If someone always has true belief, won't he always be successful, so long as he has true belief?
>
> MEN. That does seem necessary to me. So I wonder, Socrates, if this is so, why knowledge is so much more valuable than true belief, and what makes one different from the other. (97c6–d3)

Both these texts show that Meno is not submissive, but can take the initiative when he feels it necessary. In the first case, he does so by considering where the inquiry has to go in the wake of the conclusion that virtue is not teachable. Notice that this also requires some sequential reasoning, because he needs to think about the way this new conclusion relates to what they have agreed before. In the second case, he is even more obviously taking the initiative by raising an objection to Socrates. We should not therefore be deceived into taking his agreement in the third section 98b7–100c2 as submissiveness. It is possible for someone to agree with a chain of reasoning while thinking for themselves. This, after all, is the point of the slave-boy demonstration. In other dialogues we have interlocutors who agree extensively with Socrates, even though they are still thinking for themselves, as is evidenced by the way they will interrupt the agreement with an objection: think of Simmias and Cebes in the *Phaedo*, or Adeimantus and Glaucon in the *Republic*.

---

[2] Of course, it is not uncommon for an interlocutor to give up resisting Socrates as the dialogue proceeds and just agree with everything he says. This happens at various points with Polus, Callicles and Thrasymachus. But in all these three cases the agreement is just an appearance. They are merely agreeing with Socrates to end the argument as soon as possible. At heart they are adamantly opposed to the conclusions he reaches. Meno is clearly not in this camp. See Scott (1999: 15–25).

Meno's interest in knowledge and true belief (97c6–d3) is also important for our purposes because, although it involves a challenge to Socrates, it is not in any way obstructive or eristic. The expression 'so I wonder, Socrates . . .' (also used at 96d2) suggests a healthy curiosity, of the kind that attempts to move the inquiry forward rather than stall it.[3] It also stands in marked contrast to his much more aggressive curiosity, as expressed earlier in the dialogue: there, a question would be a demand for information – Meno wanting to *extract* something from Socrates (hence the need for bargaining: cf. 75b4 and 86e2). Meno now seems genuinely more co-operative.

There are two qualifications to make here. First, I am not saying that Meno only starts to improve after the Anytus episode. He is relatively well behaved during the argument of 87d–89a that virtue is knowledge. Perhaps the implicit message in the slave-boy demonstration has started to do some work. My point is that the change in him is more marked after he has witnessed the Anytus episode. Second, we should not exaggerate Meno's improvement. Given the time-span of the dialogue, there is no opportunity to effect a deep-rooted or long-lasting improvement. (To judge from Xenophon's testimony, of course, he went very seriously downhill.[4]) Nevertheless, there is no reason to be entirely cynical. Socrates' technique of using dialogues within the dialogue as object lessons for Meno has had some success.

This way of reading the dialogue does give rise to an objection.[5] Meno has certainly not attained full virtue, but he has moved a little way towards it and started on the path of moral education. The objection is that, if virtue comes by sequential recollection prompted by a process of questioning, we ought to expect that Meno has himself recollected in this way and that this is what is responsible for his improvement. Yet the use of object lessons to induce a sense of shame in Meno is quite different from sequential recollection prompted by questioning.

There are two components to this objection. One is the assumption that what progress Meno has made is a purely cognitive achievement; the second is that all cognitive progress is made by sequential recollection. The first assumption is plausible for anyone who takes an intellectualist view of the dialogue's moral psychology, as I have done (cf. pp. 151–2). Thus, by

---

[3] Here I agree with Gordon (1999: 109). Roslyn Weiss has put to me the objection that Meno changes just because he has now got what he wanted all along: a discussion of how virtue is acquired. This might explain why he is no longer overtly rude to Socrates, but not why he becomes more active in the inquiry – more inclined to follow a sequential line of reasoning on his own behalf.

[4] See above p. 65.

[5] The objection comes from Tarrant (2003: 438) discussing Gordon 1999.

witnessing the performance of the slave boy and the behaviour of Anytus, Meno has started to realise the benefits of mildness and co-operation, and the harm that can be done by arrogance and irascibility. Furthermore, he realises that these lessons apply directly to his own case. He has learnt something at both general and particular levels. Because his beliefs have changed, his desires will follow suit: that was the point of the argument of 77b–78b. So now that he appreciates the value of mildness, he desires to engage more co-operatively with Socrates, and behaves accordingly.

However, the objection is wrong to assume that every stage of moral improvement consists in sequential recollection. As we have argued (p. 184), there are several ways in which true beliefs may arise. For sure, Meno has learnt something for himself in discovering the value of mildness, but we need not say this is the result of sequential recollection. He could have started to learn about the benefits of mildness by perception – for instance, through observing the progress the boy is able to make when he co-operates with Socrates. It might also be that this episode kick-starts a moment of recollection in him. Were he then to engage in sustained questioning with Socrates, he might ultimately examine the quality of mildness more systematically, i.e. to recollect about its nature and value with the aid of sequential questioning. But there is no need to insist that he has to be doing so here.

A further point: as we learn from 75d4, mildness is a pre-condition of dialectic, and hence of sequential recollection. Mildness is not the only pre-condition. For successful and sustained recollection one also needs staying power and self-discipline (cf. 81d7–e1 and 86b8–9). But if, as the objection assumes, such pre-conditions could themselves only be acquired by sequential recollection, Socrates would be caught in a vicious circle. All the more reason, then, for insisting that such qualities can arise without the need for sequential recollection.

This is not to deny that Meno does engage in some recollection in the course of the dialogue. It may well be that he has started to recollect in the argument of 87d–89a and perhaps beyond. If so, the slave-boy demonstration is to some extent a microcosm of the dialogue more generally.[6] Having reached *aporia* in the first ten pages, he makes some progress in recollecting a true belief in the course of 87d–89a. The result of this *euporia* is his agreement that virtue is knowledge and hence teachable. What happens thereafter takes us beyond anything that happened with the slave boy, because he starts to be subjected to the further questioning alluded to

---

[6] This general approach is taken by Brown 1967, Wilkes 1979 and Bedu-Addo 1984.

at 85c1–11, which results in his newly aroused true belief being destabilised. Thus by 96d1, he reluctantly comes to the conclusion that virtue is not teachable, and so feels himself in *aporia* again. This is the point at which he wonders whether there are any good people around, or how they become virtuous. What follows could be seen as a further stage of recollecting, leading to further *euporia* in the conclusion (still very fragile, and to be revised on some future occasion).

To support this last point, recall how Socrates starts to extract them from the *aporia* of 96d:

Meno, we have not been particularly good ourselves, you and I. Gorgias has failed to train you properly, and Prodicus me. We would do much better to turn our attention on ourselves and find out who might make us better in one way or another. I say this looking back at our previous inquiry because, quite absurdly, it escaped our notice that people can run their affairs correctly and well not just under the guidance of knowledge. Perhaps this is how the knowledge has eluded us of how good men come into being. (96d5–e5)

Instead of listening to their teachers, they should turn *inwards* to themselves (96d8); the difference between knowledge and true belief has 'escaped' them (ἔλαθεν: 96e2) – an expression that could also mean that they have forgotten the distinction and are now recollecting it.[7] It is difficult to be sure whether Meno does start to recollect in the course of the dialogue, but the suggestion is certainly attractive.

---

[7] The same might be said of διαφεύγει ('has escaped us') in 96e4. For this sense of the word see LSJ *s.v.* 2.

Conclusion

THE UNITY OF THE DIALOGUE

Although much of this book has been devoted to examining the arguments of the *Meno* individually, it has also been concerned to read the dialogue as a whole. In the event, this has meant a number of things: sometimes a matter of ironing out inconsistencies between different claims made across the work, sometimes of showing how different passages interrelate or support each other. But one of the main challenges of reading the dialogue as a whole is the question I raised at the outset (p. 3 above): what is the *Meno* about? We are now in a position to address this explicitly. Faced with the large number of different topics covered in the dialogue, some commentators have sought to find a single underlying theme, claiming that is it 'about' virtue, inquiry or knowledge. But in the light of what we have said, it is a mistake to look for a unity of this kind. The fact is that the main protagonists cannot agree on what they should be discussing. Socrates wants to talk about the nature of virtue, Meno about its acquisition. His inability to define virtue leads to a protracted struggle, in the course of which certain methodological and epistemological concerns are aired. So what Plato actually offers us is a dramatised conflict of interests. In a sense, the *Meno* is a dialogue that cannot quite decide what it is about, and that conflict is essential to the work.

In the end, however, it is Meno's question that takes up most of the work. For the whole of the second half (86d–100b) it occupies the limelight and, because Socrates takes virtue to be some kind of knowledge (89a), we realise (in retrospect) that the recollection episode is not just about education, but also moral education. Yet, even if Meno wins his battle, deep down the conflict is never resolved. Moral education is a theme that comes to dominate the work, rather than to unify it.

In answer to the question of why Plato constructs the dialogue in this way, I have suggested that the conflict at issue is something he took very seriously (pp. 140–1). He certainly approved of Socrates' purist methodology, according to which the definitional question must be settled first. Yet the question of how virtue is acquired was one of pressing practical concern, which could not wait upon the successful outcome of a protracted Socratic inquiry. Through his principal interlocutors, Plato worries about these conflicting demands and tries to find a compromise between them.

The fact that he is striking a balance of this kind explains a great deal about the way in which the dialogue concludes. On the one hand we do get an answer to Meno's question – two, in fact. Virtue, the quality by which one will benefit the city, comes by recollection. Since this involves a questioner eliciting the knowledge from within, virtue is 'teachable' in a special sense. At the same time, there is another quality, similar to virtue but of less worth, that consists in true belief. This is the quality by which the noteworthy Athenians have benefited their city, and it is acquired in the same way as poets or soothsayers receive their inspiration: divine dispensation. So much by way of concession to Meno's concerns. On the other hand, and in deference to Socratic methodology, Plato has Socrates flag these conclusions as tentative and provisional: they shall never attain a clear knowledge about how virtue is acquired until they first try to search for the definition (100b2–6).

THE DIALOGUE FORM

Another concern of this book has been to understand Plato's use of the dialogue form – to explain why he could not simply have written a treatise about virtue and its acquisition. In event, I have proposed two quite distinct answers to this question. One is intimately connected to the educational content of the work. Socrates goes out of his way to highlight some of the defects in Meno's character and throughout the work attempts to remedy them. As I have argued, one of his main stratagems is to use the slave boy and Anytus as object lessons. As we saw in the previous section, Socrates actually has some success, as Meno finally becomes much more co-operative. In this way, the dialogue deals with the process of education not only at a theoretical level, but at a practical one as well.

The second use to which Plato puts the dialogue form is also linked to the educational content of the work, though in a different way. It is implicit in the phenomenon that I have called 'Socrates on trial'. In the course of the work, Meno poses a number of challenges to Socrates; even though these may be poorly motivated or only half-understood, they still have serious philosophical force. Plato uses Meno to sow the seeds of doubt and unease in the mind of his reader. As such, his strategy is also very much of a piece with the educational content of the dialogue. He attempts to create in the reader not a simple memory of what Socrates has said, but a dialogue that can be sustained beyond the work itself. As Socrates said of the slave boy at 85c9–d1:

At present, these beliefs have just been stirred up in him like in a dream. But if someone questions him about the same matters on many occasions and in many ways, you can be sure that he will end up with as exact a knowledge of them as anyone.

So too the dialogue between Meno and Socrates becomes internalised and continued in a more sophisticated form in the reader.[1]

Since I have argued that Plato uses the interlocutor in two distinct ways, the question arises as to how they are related. They are in fact complementary. The danger of using Meno as a character in such serious need of improvement is that the philosophical content of the work will be brought down to his own level. Plato solves this problem by having Meno issue challenges that are in fact profound, even though he himself does not really understand their significance; he manages to guide the reader in the right direction in spite of himself. As I have argued, the dialogue consistently operates at two levels. At the lower level, Socrates is engaging with Meno as a pupil who needs close supervision; at the higher level, issues are being broached between them that can engage Plato's most sophisticated readers. The *Meno* is certainly not unique in this respect, but the way Plato combines these two levels is undoubtedly a *tour de force*.

THE END

In the closing lines of the dialogue Socrates casts Meno in the role of intermediary between himself and Anytus:

But now the time has come for me to go somewhere, and you must persuade your guest-friend Anytus of the same things of which you have been persuaded yourself, so that he may become milder. For if you persuade him, you will also be doing a favour to the Athenians. (100b7–c2)

Given Meno's improvement, this makes sense. What he has been persuaded to accept is that even the best of the Athenians lacked any understanding; and that their 'virtue', useful as it may be, will never be stable until they undergo the process of recollection, guided by questioning, or 'teaching'. In addition, Meno has changed his attitude to inquiry, and started to

---

[1] For an elegant statement of this idea see Sedley 2004: 1.

acquire the necessary mildness to engage in further dialectic and recollection. Although his improvement is fragile and has only just begun, he is in a position to mediate between Socrates and Anytus.

The problem, however, is Anytus. Being in an influential position, he holds the key to whether Socrates, or anyone else, will be allowed to act as a 'teacher' to others. He never did become milder towards Socrates – quite the contrary; and, in Plato's eyes, the Athenians paid the price.

In more general terms, the problem is that the *Meno* does have a prescription but, through the figure of Anytus, leads us to worry whether it is practicable. Virtue can be taught, but Socratic questioning is part of this process. Remember that what the slave boy needs to do to regain his knowledge requires a process of questioning continuous with what has gone before.[2] There will be more interrogations of the sort that Socrates recommends, not fewer. Yet his reception in the dialogue has not been good. Even though Meno has been receptive, Anytus – the representative of the *demos* – remains unmoved and unconvinced. The fact is that the patient may be too sick even to take the remedy. The solution that the dialogue proposes may, after all, be impracticable.[3]

Shortly before these concluding remarks Socrates had said that, if someone ever did appear who had virtue and was capable of imparting it to others, he would be as Homer described Teiresias in Hades: he alone kept his wits about him, the others were mere flitting shades (100a2–5). Elsewhere, I have suggested that this reference is pregnant with allusion, much of it pessimistic.[4] One suggestion may be that the philosopher's attempts at education will prove unpalatable to society, just as Teiresias is represented in Greek tragedy as running into conflict with leading political figures: with Oedipus in Sophocles' *Oedipus Rex* (316–462), Creon in the *Antigone* (987–1090) and Pentheus in Euripides' *Bacchae* (266–369). Teiresias may also be a symbol for the fate of Socrates himself at the hands of the Athenians, and an anticipation of the philosopher who returns to the cave (likened to Hades at *Rep.* VII 521c2–3): when he does so he is blinded, despite his wisdom; and when he attempts to educate the prisoners by leading them out to the light, he is threatened with death (*Rep.* VII 517a4–6).

So the *Meno* ends teetering on the brink of pessimism: whatever help Socrates could have given the Athenians was ultimately forestalled by Anytus and his like. This concern is developed extensively in the *Republic*, whose central books argue for essentially the same proposal: that political leaders require an education only philosophy is able to give. While

---

[2] See 85c10–d1 with p. 107 above. [3] See above p. 169 [4] Scott 1995: 48–50.

articulating this idea and trying to soothe his critics, Socrates worries that philosophy will prove too controversial for any actual city to accept.[5]

Such comparisons, however, are for another occasion. The aim of this book has been to read the *Meno* not under the shadow of other works, but as a source of interest in its own right. As for the result – whether the dialogue is indeed a philosophical gem – I now leave that to the reader to decide.

---

[5] *Rep.* VII 501c4–502a4 contains some striking similarities to the ending of the *Meno*. Socrates talks of the need to persuade the *demos*, and to replace their anger with mildness.

Appendices

I: IS *MENO* 77B–78B COMPATIBLE WITH *REPUBLIC* IV?

Irwin's view

On pages 46–53 I interpreted Socrates' conclusion in the argument of 77b–78b as being that all our self-interested desires are for good things and that no one ever desires anything they know to be bad for them. But in *Plato's Ethics*, Terence Irwin claims that the argument is susceptible of a very different interpretation, one that would make it compatible with the position of *Republic* IV.[1] He interprets the negative thesis – that no one knowingly desires bad things – as meaning that no one desires something *on the grounds that* it is bad, or *qua* bad. Then he interprets the positive thesis – that everyone desires good things – to mean only that some of our desires are for good things *qua* good, not that they all are. This leaves open the possibility of our having non-rational desires, focused on objects other than the good, e.g. pleasure or honour. The function of the argument is merely to insist that we never desire something *qua* bad, which is compatible with the moral psychology of the *Republic*.

Irwin's reading of the negative thesis seems to me implausible for the following reason. Meno would have to be intent on defending the view that some people desire certain things *qua* bad. It is difficult to see why he would do this. If the explanation is that he wants to insist that there are people with self-destructive urges, why at 78a5 does he cave in immediately to the claim that no one desires to be wretched (or that everyone desires not to be wretched)?[2] This would be the very thesis he is out to defend if Irwin's view were correct.

Irwin's reading of the positive thesis is also doubtful. For one thing, what did Meno's poet have in mind when he defined virtue as the desire for fine things and the ability to acquire them? Was he really saying that virtue

---

[1] Irwin 1995: 138–9.   [2] I would like to thank Theresa Robertson for this point.

involves having fine things as the objects of some desires? This would allow someone to be virtuous simply by having a small handful of desires for fine things, even though he also had an enormous number of extremely destructive irrational desires. This is highly implausible, and it is doubtful whether anyone would seriously have proposed it as a definition of virtue. If the proposal is to be plausible, it should mean, *pace* Irwin, that virtue requires desiring *only* fine things.

Another argument against Irwin's reading of the positive thesis is that, if correct, there would be no reason for Socrates to use any part of the argument apart from the attack on 3b. For all he needs to do is to eliminate the possibility of desiring something *qua* bad. Furthermore, if we ask why he also discusses 2a and 3a, the answer is surely that he intends to re-describe what Meno calls desiring the bad as desiring the good. But if, all along, Socrates believed also in the possibility of desiring something conceived as neither good nor bad, it is very strange that he does not mention it. When re-describing the people Meno thinks of as desiring the bad, the only possibility he canvasses is that they desire the good. It is very difficult to see why he should do this, if Irwin's view were correct.

The Croiset–Bodin view
Yet another interpretation that reads the possibility of non-rational desires into the *Meno* can be found in Croiset and Bodin (1923: III, 245–6) and Weiss (2001: 36). At 78a4, just as Socrates is drawing his conclusion against the existence of 3b, he changes the verb that he has been using for 'desire' from ἐπιθυμεῖν to βούλεσθαι. These commentators claim that this is highly significant. At *Charmides* 167e1–6, Socrates implies that there is a difference between these two verbs, the first picking out desires that have pleasure as their object, the second the good. This distinction seems to conform to the distinction made in the *Republic* between non-rational appetites and rational desires for the good. If the same distinction between ἐπιθυμεῖν and βούλεσθαι is at work in the *Meno*, we might be able to say that, by switching verbs at the crucial moment, Socrates is only insisting that no one can have a *rational* desire for bad things. This leaves open the possibility that they could have a non-rational appetite for them. (This interpretation is not the same as Irwin's, which does not require the two verbs to have different meanings.)

However, there are two problems with this view. First, immediately after Socrates has deployed his argument against 3b, he asks: 'weren't you saying just now that virtue is desiring (βούλεσθαι) fine things ...' (78b3–4). Since Meno immediately endorses the substitution of βούλεσθαι for ἐπιθυμεῖν, the two words ought to be acting as synonyms in this passage. Second, if Socrates is distinguishing the two words, what are we to make of the occasions when he says that people desire (ἐπιθυμεῖν) the good (77b6, b8–c2 and e3)? According to the *Charmides*, from which this interpretation takes its cue, this would be a misuse of the term. Again, it is much more plausible to suppose that Socrates is simply treating the two words as synonyms.

2. THE METHOD OF HYPOTHESIS: THE BI-CONDITIONAL INTERPRETATION

When discussing the hypothetical method on page 138 above, I said that there are broadly two interpretations of the way it is applied to answer the question of how virtue is acquired. According to the interpretation I adopted, the hypothesis Socrates uses is 'virtue is knowledge'; according to the other, it is the bi-conditional 'if virtue is knowledge it is teachable, and if it is not knowledge it is not teachable'. I now wish to say more about this second interpretation: the arguments for and against, and the broader implications of holding it.

One argument for adopting the bi-conditional interpretation can be made by looking back at the geometrical example. At 87a2–7, the geometer announces that he has 'the following hypothesis' to offer and proceeds to set it out. A very natural interpretation is that everything that follows the words 'the following hypothesis' (87a3) down to the end of the sentence (87a7) is the hypothesis. Thus, in the geometrical example, the hypothesis is: if the area is such and such (leaving the details on one side) it can be inscribed in the circle as a triangle, and if it is not, it cannot. So when Socrates moves on to the ethical argument, we should expect him to make the corresponding proposition the hypothesis of that argument. This he has done, according to the current interpretation, by 87c8–9: 'so we've made short work of that problem: *if it is of this sort it is teachable; if not, it is not teachable.*' True, he does not say explicitly that this is the hypothesis but, if we are prepared to apply the geometrical case strictly, he seems to imply as much. On this view, the hypothesis is the full bi-conditional. A closely related interpretation is that the hypothesis is actually only the positive half: 'if virtue is knowledge, it is teachable'. In what follows, however I shall group these interpretations together.[3]

---

[3] Weiss (2001: 131–2 n. 10) opts for the full bi-conditional as the hypothesis. In the first edition of *Plato's Earlier Dialectic*, Robinson (1941: 122–3) argued in favour of identifying the first half as the hypothesis. He then retracted this view in the light of Friedländer (1945) and Cherniss (1947), and

Though this argument has some weight, I do not find it compelling and even Robinson, who deployed it in 1941: 122–3, is lukewarm:

[The proposition that if virtue is knowledge it is teachable] seems to have the same form as the geometrical example; for, though Plato there also is not very explicit as to which of the geometer's words constitute the hypothesis, it seems probable on the whole that the geometer's hypothesis is of the form 'If A is B, then A is X.'[4]

There is another argument for the bi-conditional interpretation. If the alternative were right, once Socrates starts to apply the geometrical method to the case of virtue (87b2) the pattern of his argument ought to run as follows: he would simply posit the truth of 'virtue is knowledge' as something plausible to believe, just as he posits the existence of forms in the *Phaedo*. After doing this, he can then provide an argument for the hypothesis (just as in the *Phaedo* he anticipates searching for a 'higher' hypothesis to support the existence of forms). But there is no explicit stage in the argument of the *Meno* where virtue is just assumed to be knowledge (in the way that virtue is assumed to be good at 87d2–3). So if the proposition, 'virtue is knowledge', is not explicitly hypothesised, why assume that it is the hypothesis? The only thing that is just assumed at this stage is the bi-conditional, which provides another reason for taking it to be the hypothesis of this phase of the argument.[5]

Before considering the main objections to the bi-conditional interpretation, we should pause to ask what is at stake in accepting it. On the interpretation that I adopted above, I stressed that a hypothesis is something provisional. Not so on the current view: at 87c1–2 Socrates describes the proposition, 'knowledge alone is teachable', as 'plain to everyone'. Presumably he would therefore say the same of the proposition, 'if virtue is knowledge it is teachable', as nothing controversial is assumed in the course of inferring from the former to the latter. This means that, as a 'method', hypothesising has nothing *per se* to do with provisionality;

instead made the hypothesis 'virtue is knowledge'. See Robinson 1953: 116–20. For other proponents of the bi-conditional view, see Crombie 1963: II, 533, Sternfeld and Zyskind 1978: 54–5 and Bedu-Addo 1984: 9.

[4] On the closeness of fit between the geometrical example and its philosophical application, see Mueller 1992: 179–80.

[5] In the first edition of his book, Robinson also adduced another consideration in favour of the bi-conditional interpretation: at 89d4, in the course of reconsidering the whole argument of 87b–89a, Socrates says that he will not 'take back' the claim that if virtue is knowledge it is teachable. In Greek he says οὐκ ἀνατίθεμαι. Robinson (1941: 122) took this to suggest that the proposition was originally the result of ὑποτιθέναι. This, however, is not decisive: it certainly does not follow from the very meaning of the word ἀνατίθημι that whatever has been 'taken back' was once put forward as a hypothesis. This would be a very thin thread on which to hang so much.

rather, a hypothesis is 'something whose truth will not be questioned in the argument'.[6] How then does this 'method' differ from any other Socratic argument? The answer is: not at all. In every Socratic argument there are assertions, often considered obvious, that are simply laid down as premises. This means that the bi-conditional interpretation is entirely deflationary. Moreover, there is no sense in which the *Meno* anticipates the distinguishing mark of hypotheses in the *Phaedo* and the *Republic*, which are of their nature provisional and subject to revision.

Another point to bear in mind concerns the relation that this interpretation conceives to exist between the two levels of argument distinguished above (see p. 139). My interpretation yielded the beginnings of a deductive hierarchy: the 'higher' hypothesis that virtue is good supports the 'lower' one that it is knowledge. On the second interpretation, the two arguments are not related in this way. Rather, there are two main premises in the proof that virtue is teachable:

1 If virtue is knowledge it is teachable;
2 Virtue is knowledge.

The first is based (if we are being precise) on the 'obvious' hypothesis that only knowledge is teachable; the second is based on the hypothesis that virtue is good. These hypotheses are co-ordinate, not related as super- and subordinate, which suggests again that there is nothing new being introduced by all the talk of hypotheses: the proposition 'virtue is good' is, like the bi-conditional, merely an assumption necessary to make the argument work, and any Socratic argument has to rely on assumptions.

What are the arguments against the bi-conditional interpretation? For one thing, there are difficulties with the sentence at 89c2–4, which we translated on page 138 above as, 'it is clear, Socrates according to the hypothesis, if virtue is knowledge, that it is teachable'. There we took 'if virtue is knowledge' in apposition to 'the hypothesis'. But proponents of the bi-conditional view have claimed it to be susceptible of a different reading: 'it is clear, Socrates, according to the hypothesis, since virtue is knowledge, that it is teachable'. On this translation, Meno's statement breaks down as follows: (A) Given the initial hypothesis (viz. if virtue is knowledge, it is teachable), and (B) if (or 'since': εἴπερ) virtue is knowledge, then (C) it is clear that virtue is teachable. In (A) he states the major premise, in (B) the minor, and in (C) he draws the conclusion by *modus ponens*.[7] This, however, is unconvincing. Unless the clause 'if virtue is knowledge' explicates

---

[6] Weiss 2001: 131 n. 10. See also Robinson 1941: 122.
[7] For this reading see Sternfeld and Zyskind 1976: 133.

'the hypothesis', we are left with no signal at all as to which hypothesis Meno has in mind. Remember that only the proposition 'virtue is good' has explicitly been called a hypothesis; it has never been explicitly stated that the bi-conditional (or its first half) is the hypothesis. If the expression 'the hypothesis' is left with no gloss in 89c4, as the bi-conditional interpretation has to claim, the whole sentence becomes unacceptably opaque.[8]

But the real difficulty for the bi-conditional interpretation is that it cannot do any justice to the context in which the method of hypothesis is introduced at 86d3–e4. If, as I have repeatedly stressed, Socrates is trying to broker a deal with Meno, we must be able to explain just what this deal actually is. In allowing that they may investigate the attribute question without prior knowledge of the definition he is conceding the strict chronological priority of the definition. But he must be preserving *some* element of this principle otherwise he is not making a concession, but conceding outright defeat. This can only be so if Socrates is still insisting that they proceed from a hypothesis about the nature of virtue.

If this is right we ought to accept the first interpretation and reject the second. Since adopting a hypothesis is a response to renouncing the chronological priority of definition, a hypothesis must be something tentative.[9] Yet, as we have seen, Socrates must think it obvious that, if virtue is knowledge, it is teachable. Furthermore, for the reasons stated, the hypothesis had better concern the nature of virtue directly. On the bi-conditional, it does not do this.

At the level of textual detail, both interpretations have their difficulties, although I think the problem posed by 89c2–4 for the bi-conditional interpretation probably outweighs the two arguments in its favour mentioned above. In the end, however, I would take considerations about the context in which the method of hypothesis is introduced to be pivotal; and it is the fact that the bi-conditional interpretation cannot do justice to Socrates' very emphatic methodological remarks at 86d–e that rules it out of court.

---

[8] As noted above, proponents of this interpretation have also claimed that what suits the bi-conditional to be the basic hypothesis is that it is something whose truth is simply assumed in the argument: see Robinson 1941: 122 and Weiss 2001: 131 n. 10. It functions only as a premise, and is not treated as a demonstrandum, nor is it subject to testing. By contrast, the proposition, 'virtue is knowledge' is the subject of a demonstration in 87–9, and so cannot be treated as the hypothesis. However, this is a weak argument, as Friedländer (1945: 155) and Bluck (1961: 89) have shown: there is no reason why something that functions as a premise in one argument cannot be called a hypothesis, even if it is subsequently treated as a conclusion of a different argument.
[9] See above p. 138.

3. LLOYD ON MATHEMATICS AND THE MYSTERIES

In answer to the question of why the geometrical example is so opaque on page 137, I accepted the suggestion of Roslyn Weiss – that Socrates is deliberately (and somewhat mischievously) pandering to Meno's desire for the exotic and technical, just as he had done in giving the Empedoclean definition of colour.

Another scholar who argues that Socrates is being self-consciously opaque is Geoffrey Lloyd. For him, however, the underlying reason is quite different, stemming from a much more general view about how philosophical progress has to be made.[10] He argues that the point of the passage is to show that philosophy requires one to undergo a disorientating process of initiation (cf. 76e6–9). Central to his interpretation is a particular way of distinguishing between initiation and education:

In education the teacher does all he or she can to help the pupil, starting with elementary materials and proceeding gradually to more advanced ones, making sure at each stage that the pupil has grasped the simpler points before progressing to more complicated ones . . . In the *Meno* itself, the long exchange between Socrates and the slave-boy, 82b–85b, offers as fine an example as anyone could wish of careful and painstaking *education*.

But by initiation I mean rather the process whereby the initiates themselves come to see some subject in quite a different light. They may even discover that what they had been taught, or what they thought they had learnt, at an early stage in the process, later turns out to be quite false.[11]

Lloyd is not claiming that, on its own, the mathematical example initiates either Meno or the reader; but the example at least suggests that mathematics requires some form of initiation and patience. Indeed it suggests that mathematics is only for initiates. This, according to Lloyd, prepares Meno for the message that philosophy too is only for initiates.

But the distinction that Lloyd draws between initiation and education does not fit well with the dialogue. In the passage quoted, he talks of initiation as a process whereby 'the initiates themselves come to see some subject in quite a different light'. He contrasts this with education, of which he calls the slave-boy demonstration a good example. But one of the most important points that Socrates has to make about this demonstration is just that the boy learns for himself. Another feature that Lloyd affixes to the initiation side of his contrast also belongs to the Socratic concept of education: as one proceeds, one comes to see things in a quite different light, and may realise that what one decided at an earlier stage in the

---

[10] Lloyd 1992.   [11] Lloyd 1992: 178–9.

process was actually false. The slave-boy passage is again a good example; another will appear in the dialogue shortly, when they agree to retract one of the premises supporting the argument identifying virtue and knowledge (96d4–97a7). Education in the *Meno*, as so often in Plato, is revisionary.

This is not to deny the significance of initiation in the *Meno*.[12] But if we are to give it a high profile, we should not contrast it with education in the way Lloyd does, but see the two as complementary – different ways of describing the same process.

A better way of understanding their relation is to think of a process as one in which the learner-initiate is successively disorientated by the sheer difficulty of the subject and then encouraged by making progress.[13] Yet, if initiation and education are two sides of the same coin, a serious problem arises for Lloyd's approach to the geometrical passage. He is certainly right that, as a rule, education in the *Meno* requires the 'teacher' to make sure at each stage that the pupil has grasped the simpler points before progressing to the more complex. But if education cannot involve deliberate obfuscation (except as part of the occasional joke), nor should initiation. The geometrical example may be deliberately opaque, but we should not seek to explain this as falling out of the concept of initiation.

---

[12] On the philosophical significance of initiation, and its connection with education and recollection, see pp. 58, n. 13 and 107 above.
[13] See p. 213 above on the alternation of *euporia* and *aporia*.

References

Adkins, A. W. H. (1960) *Merit and Responsibility: a Study in Greek Values*. Oxford
Annas, J. (1981) *An Introduction to Plato's* Republic. Oxford
Anscombe, G. E. M. (1979) 'Understanding proofs: *Meno*, 85d9–86c2, continued', *Philosophy* 54: 149–58
Barnes, J. (1972) 'Mr. Locke's darling notion', *Philosophical Quarterly* 22: 193–214
    (1980) 'Socrates and the jury: paradoxes in Plato's distinction between knowledge and true belief', *Proceedings of the Aristotelian Society*, suppl. vol. 54, 193–206
Bedu-Addo, J. T. (1984) 'Recollection and the argument "from a hypothesis" in Plato's *Meno*', *Journal of Hellenic Studies* 104: 1–14
Benson, H. H. (1990) 'The priority of definition and the Socratic elenchus', *Oxford Studies in Ancient Philosophy* 8: 19–65
    (2000) *Socratic Wisdom*. Oxford
    (2002) 'The method of hypothesis in the *Meno*', *Boston Area Colloquium in Ancient Philosophy* 18: 95–126
Berti, E. (1981) ed. *Aristotle's* Posterior Analytics. Padua
Beversluis, J. (1987) 'Does Socrates commit the Socratic fallacy?', *American Philosophy Quarterly* 24: 211–23.
Blondell, R. (2002) *The Play of Character in Plato's Dialogues*. Cambridge
Bluck, R. S. (1961) *Plato's* Meno. Cambridge
Bostock, D. (1986) *Plato's* Phaedo. Oxford
Brague, R. (1978) *Le Restant: Supplément aux Commentaires du* Ménon *de Platon*. Paris
Brickhouse, T. C. and Smith, N. D. (1994) *Plato's Socrates*. Oxford
Brown, L. (1991) 'Connaissance et réminiscence dans le *Ménon*', *Revue Philosophique* 181: 603–19
Brown, M. S. (1967) 'Plato disapproves of the slave-boy's answer', *Review of Metaphysics* 20: 57–93
Brumbaugh, R. (1975) 'Plato's *Meno* as form and as content of secondary school courses in philosophy', *Teaching Philosophy* 1: 107–15
Brunschwig, J. (1991) 'Pouvoir enseigner la vertue?', *Revue Philosophique* 181: 591–602
Burnet, J. (1900–7) ed. *Platonis Opera*. 5 vols. Oxford
    (1908) *Early Greek Philosophy*. 2nd edn. London

Burnyeat, M. F. (1977) 'Examples in epistemology: Socrates, Theaetetus and G. E. Moore', *Philosophy* 52: 381–98
    (1980) 'Socrates and the jury: paradoxes in Plato's distinction between knowledge and true belief', *Proceedings of the Aristotelian Society*, suppl. vol. 54: 173–91
    (1981) 'Aristotle on understanding knowledge', in Berti (1981) ed. 97–139
    (1987) 'Wittgenstein and Augustine *De Magistro*', *Proceedings of the Aristotelian Society* suppl. vol. 61: 1–24
    (1997) 'First words: a valedictory lecture', *Proceedings of the Cambridge Philological Society*, 3rd series, 43: 1–20
    (2003) 'By the dog', Review of Blondell (2002), *London Review of Books*, vol. 25, no. 15: 23–24
Bury, R. G. (1932) *The Symposium of Plato*. 2nd edn. Cambridge
Calvert, B. (1974) 'Meno's paradox reconsidered', *Journal of the History of Philosophy* 12: 143–52
    (1984) 'The politicians of Athens in the *Gorgias* and *Meno*', *History of Political Thought* 5: 1–16
Canto, M. (1987) *Platon: Gorgias*. Paris
Canto-Sperber, M. (1991) *Platon: Ménon*. Paris
Carcopino, J. (1927) *La Basilique Pythagoricienne*. Paris
Cherniss, H. (1947) 'Some war-time publications concerning Plato', *American Journal of Philology* 68: 113–46
Cook Wilson, J. (1903) 'On the geometrical problem in Plato's *Meno*, 86E sqq.', *Journal of Philology* 28: 222–40
Cooper, J. M. (1997) ed. *Plato: Complete Works*. Indianapolis
Cottingham, J., Stoothof, R. and Murdoch, D. (1984–91) eds. *The Philosophical Writings of Descartes*. 3 vols. Cambridge
Cowie, F. (1999) *What's Within? Nativism Reconsidered*. Oxford
Croiset, A. and Bodin, L. (1923) *Platon: Gorgias et Ménon*. Paris
Crombie, I. M. (1963) *An Examination of Plato's Doctrines*. 2 vols. London
Day, J. M. (1994) ed. *Plato's* Meno *in Focus*. London
Desjardins, R. (1985) 'Knowledge and virtue: paradox in Plato's *Meno*', *Review of Metaphysics* 39: 261–81
Devereux, D. T. (1978) 'Nature and teaching in Plato's *Meno*', *Phronesis* 23: 118–26
Diels, H. and Kranz, W. (1985) eds. *Die Fragmente der Vorsokratiker*. 3 vols. 6th edn. Zürich and Hildesheim. (Cited as DK)
Dodds, E. R. (1959) *Plato's Gorgias*. Oxford
Dover, K. J. (1974) *Greek Popular Morality*. Oxford
Ebert, T. (1973) 'Plato's theory of recollection reconsidered: an interpretation of *Meno* 80a–86c', *Man and World* 6: 163–81
    (1974) *Meinung und Wissen in der Philosophie Platons*. Berlin
Everson, S. (1990) ed. *Epistemology (Companions to Ancient Thought I)*. Cambridge
Fine, G. (1990) 'Knowledge and belief in *Republic* V–VII', in Everson (1990) 85–115
    (1992) 'Inquiry in the *Meno*', in Kraut (1992) ed. 200–26
    (1999) ed. *Plato (Oxford Readings in Philosophy)* 2 vols. Oxford
    (2003) *Plato on Knowledge and Forms*. Oxford

(2004) 'Knowledge and true belief in the *Meno*', *Oxford Studies in Ancient Philosophy* 27: 41–81

Fowler, H. N. (1926) trans. *Plato:* Cratylus, Parmenides, Greater Hippias, Lesser Hippias. Loeb translation. Vol IV. Cambridge, Mass.

Franklin, L. (2001) 'The structure of dialectic in the *Meno*', *Phronesis* 46: 413–39

Friedländer, P. (1945) Review of Robinson (1941). *Classical Philology* 40: 253–9

(1958) *Plato I: An Introduction*. London

(1964) *Plato II: The Dialogues (First Period)*. London

Gaiser, K. (1963) Review of Bluck (1961). *Gymnasium* 70: 440–2

Geach, P. T. (1966) 'Plato's *Euthyphro*: an analysis and commentary', *Monist* 50: 369–82

Gedike, F. (1780) ed. *Platonis Dialogi IV:* Meno, Krito, Alcibiades uterque. Berlin

Gomperz, T. (1905) *A History of Greek Philosophy*. Vol. II. London

Gordon, J. (1999) *Turning Toward Philosophy*. Pennsylvania

Gulley, N. (1962) *Plato's Theory of Knowledge*. London

(1969) Review of Klein (1965). *Classical Review*, new series, 19 no. 2: 162–3

Guthrie, W. C. K. (1956) trans. *Plato:* Protagoras *and* Meno. Penguin Translation. Harmondsworth

(1971) *The Sophists*. Cambridge

Hackforth, R. (1952) *Plato's* Phaedrus. Cambridge

(1955) *Plato's* Phaedo. Cambridge

Hacking, I. (1975) *Why Does Language Matter to Philosophy?* Cambridge

Hall, R. W. (1981) *Plato*. London

Heath, T. E. (1921) *A History of Greek Mathematics*, vol. I. Oxford

Hobbs, A. (2000) *Plato and the Hero: Courage, Manliness and the Impersonal Good*. Cambridge

Hoerber, R. G. (1960) 'Plato's *Meno*', *Phronesis* 5: 78–102

Irwin, T. (1977) *Plato's Moral Theory*. Oxford

(1979) *Plato: Gorgias*. Oxford

(1995) *Plato's Ethics*. Oxford

Jolley, N. (1984) *Leibniz and Locke*. Oxford

Kerferd, G. B. (1981) *The Sophistic Movement*. Cambridge

Kirk, G. S., Raven, J. E. and Schofield, M. (1983) *The Presocratic Philosophers*. 2nd edn. Cambridge

Klein, J. (1965) *A Commentary on Plato's* Meno. Chicago

Knorr, W. R. (1986) *The Ancient Tradition of Geometric Problems*. Boston

Korsgaard, C. M. (1983) 'Two distinctions in goodness', *Philosophical Review* 92: 169–95

Kraut, R. (1984) *Socrates and the State*. Princeton

(1992) ed. *The Cambridge Companion to Plato*. Cambridge

Lamb, W. R. M. (1924) trans. *Plato:* Laches, Protagoras, Meno, Euthydemus. Loeb translation. Cambridge, Mass.

Lloyd, G. E. R. (1992) 'Plato and the mysteries of mathematics', *Phronesis* 37: 166–83

McCabe, M. M. (1994) *Plato's Individuals*. Princeton

Menn, S. (2002) 'Plato and the method of analysis', *Phronesis* 47: 193–223

Mill, J. S. (1979) *Essays on Philosophy and the Classics*, in *The Collected Works of John Stuart Mill*, vol. XI, J. M. Robson ed. Toronto

Moline, J. (1969) 'Meno's paradox?', *Phronesis* 14: 153–61

Moravcsik, J. (1978) 'Learning as recollection', in Vlastos (1978) ed. 53–69 [repr. in Day (1994) ed. 112–28]

Moser, P. K. (1987) *A Priori Knowledge (Oxford Readings in Philosophy)*. Oxford

Mueller, I. (1992) 'Mathematical method and philosophical truth', in Kraut (1992) ed. 170–99

Nakhnikian, G. (1973) 'The first Socratic paradox', *Journal of the History of Philosophy* 11: 1–17 [repr. in Day (1994) ed. 129–51]

Nehamas, A. (1985) 'Meno's paradox and Socrates as a teacher', *Oxford Studies in Ancient Philosophy* 3: 1–30 [repr. in Day (1994) ed. 221–48]
    (1987) 'Socratic intellectualism', *Proceedings of the Boston Area Colloquium in Ancient Philosophy* 2: 275–316

Newman, W. L. (1887) *The Politics of Aristotle*. 4 vols. Oxford

Nussbaum, M. (1980) 'Aristophanes and Socrates on learning practical wisdom', *Yale Classical Studies* 26: 43–97

O'Brien, M. J. (1967) *The Socratic Paradoxes and the Greek Mind*. Chapel Hill

Parkinson, G.H.R. (1973) ed. *Leibniz: Philosophical Writings*. London

Penner, T. (1973) 'The unity of virtue', *Philosophical Review* 82: 35–68

Phillips, B. (1948) 'The significance of Meno's paradox', *Classical Weekly* 42: 87–91

Popper, K. R. (1966) *The Open Society and its Enemies*. 5th edn. London

Prior, W. J. (1998) 'Plato and the Socratic fallacy', *Phronesis* 43: 97–113

Rackham, H. (1959) trans. *Aristotle: Politics*. Loeb translation. Cambridge, Mass.

Remnant, P. and Bennett, J. (1982) eds. *G. W. Leibniz: New Essays on Human Understanding*. Cambridge

Reuter, M. (2001) 'Is goodness really a gift from god? Another look at the conclusion of Plato's *Meno*', *Phoenix* 55: 77–97

Robinson, R. (1941) *Plato's Earlier Dialectic*. 1st edn. Ithaca
    (1953) *Plato's Earlier Dialectic*. 2nd edn. Oxford

Robinson, T. M. (1995) *Plato's Psychology*. 2nd edn. Toronto

Rose, L. (1970) 'Plato's *Meno* 86–9', *Journal of the History of Philosophy* 8: 1–8

Ryle, G. (1976) 'The *Meno*: many things are odd about our *Meno*', *Paideia (Special Plato Issue)* 5: 1–9

Santas, G. (1972) 'The Socratic fallacy', *Journal of the History of Philosophy* 10: 127–41
    (1979) *Socrates*. London
    (2001) *Goodness and Justice: Plato, Aristotle and the Moderns*. Blackwell

Saunders, T. J. (1995) *Aristotle: Politics, Books I and II*. Oxford

Savile, A. (1972) 'Leibniz's contribution to the theory of innate ideas', *Philosophy* 47: 113–24

Scolnicov, S. (1988) *Plato's Metaphysics of Education*. London and New York

Scott, D. (1988) 'Innatism and the Stoa', *Proceedings of the Cambridge Philological Society*, 3rd series, 33: 123–53

(1991) 'Socrate prend-il au sérieux le paradoxe de Ménon?', *Revue Philosophique* 181: 627–41
(1995) *Recollection and Experience*. Cambridge
(1999) 'Platonic pessimism and moral education', *Oxford Studies in Ancient Philosophy* 17: 15–36
Sedley, D. (1999) 'The ideal of godlikeness', in Fine (1999) ed., vol. II, 309–28
(2004) *Plato's Cratylus*. Cambridge
Seeskin, K. (1987) *Dialogue and Discovery: a Study in Socratic Method*. Albany, New York
Sharples, R. (1985) *Plato's Meno*. Warminster
Shorey, P. A. (1909) 'φύσις, μελέτη, ἐπιστήμη', *Transactions of the American Philological Association* 40: 184–201
(1930) *Plato: Republic*. Loeb translation. 2 vols. Cambridge, Mass.
Sternfeld, R. and Zyskind, H. (1976) 'Plato's Meno 89c: "Virtue is knowledge" – a hypothesis?', *Phronesis* 21: 130–4
(1978) *Plato's Meno: a Philosophy of Man as Acquisitive*. Carbondale and London
Stock, St. G. (1904) *The Meno of Plato*. 3rd edn. Oxford
Tarrant, H. (2003) Review of Gordon (1999). *Ancient Philosophy* 23: 435–9
Taylor, A. E. (1926) *Plato: The Man and His Work*. London
Thomas, J. E. (1980) *Musings on the Meno*. The Hague
Thompson, E. S. (1901) *The Meno of Plato*. London
Umphrey, S. (1990) *Zetetic Skepticism*. Wakefield, New Hampshire
Verdenius, M. J. (1957) 'Notes on Plato's *Meno*', *Mnemosyne*, 4th series, 10: 289–99
Vlastos, G. (1965) 'Anamnesis in the *Meno*', *Dialogue* 4: 143–67 [repr. in Vlastos (1995) vol. II: 147–65]
(1969) 'Socrates on *acrasia*', *Phoenix* 23: 71–88 [repr. in Vlastos (1995) vol. II: 43–59]
(1978) ed. *Plato I: Metaphysics and Epistemology*. Notre Dame
(1980) ed. *Socrates: a Collection of Critical Essays*. Notre Dame
(1991) *Socrates: Ironist and Moral Philosopher*. Cambridge
(1994) *Socratic Studies*. Cambridge
(1995) *Studies in Greek Philosophy*. 2 vols. Princeton
Weiss, R. (2001) *Virtue in the Cave: Moral Inquiry in Plato's Meno*. Oxford
West, M. L. (1983) *The Orphic Poems*. Oxford
White, N. P. (1974) 'Inquiry', *Review of Metaphysics* 28: 289–310 [repr. in Day (1994) ed. 152–71]
(1976) *Plato on Knowledge and Reality*. Indianapolis
Wilkes, K. V. (1979) 'Conclusions in the *Meno*', *Archiv für Geschichte der Philosophie* 61: 143–53 [repr. in Day (1994) ed. 208–20]
Wittgenstein, L. (1967) *Philosophical Investigations*. 3rd edn. Oxford
Woodruff, P. (1987) 'Expert knowledge in the *Apology* and *Laches*: what a general needs to know', *Proceedings of the Boston Area Colloquium in Ancient Philosophy* 3: 79–115

Index of ancient passages

Aristotle
History of Animals
620b19–25: 70
Metaphysics
981a30–b17: 181
1078b23–5: 21, 132
Nicomachean Ethics
1099b9–11: 17, 18
1144a29–b1: 152
1179b20–1: 18
Politics
1260a20–24: 28
1260a25–8: 24
Posterior Analytics, 21
71a1–2: 84
72b3–4: 180
75a18–19: 21
99b28–30: 84
100a6–9: 180
Rhetoric
1402a24–6: 15
Sense and Sensibilia
439a33–4: 42
Sophistical Refutations
183b36–184a8: 12–13,
71
Topics
141b22: 38

Isocrates
Antidosis 187–8: 16

Plato
Alcibiades I, 15
124c10: 41
Apology, 20, 74, 167
20d6–e3: 90
23a5–b4: 90
30e5: 69
38a5–6: 89

40c4–41c7: 113
Charmides
163d7: 89
166c4–6: 73
166d2–e2: 123
167b1: 89
167e1–6: 220–1
176b5–d5: 63
Cratylus
432b3–c5: 39, 40, 41
Crito, 20
53d4–7: 41
Euthydemus, 15, 70, 73,
164
277e7–278a5: 116
278e–282d: 149–50
288b8: 70
288d–292e: 155–7
Euthyphro, 86
5c8–d5: 28–30
11a6–b1: 20, 44
11b2: 89
11b6–d6: 180
15c11–12: 89, 90, 123
Gorgias, 20, 47, 189, 194–208
463c3–5: 20
474d1: 46
474d4: 41
474e7–475a3: 48
477a1–2: 48
483c8–491d3: 62
497c3–4: 58
483e4–484a2: 70
485d4: 123
Hippias Major, 164
Ion
534b: 193
Laches, 15
189e3–190c2: 20
190b7–c2: 141

190c9: 14
191d4: 89
191e12: 28–30
194a1–5: 123
194a1–c3: 89
198a1: 89
201a2–3: 90
Laws
654e3–655b5: 39
669a1: 40, 41
700b1: 39
737d6: 39
802e5: 39
Phaedo, 107, 113, 121, 204–5
65c11–e5: 104–5
69c3–d2: 58
74b4–75b8: 104–5
77c1–d5: 118
79a1–11: 104–5
81c8–82c8: 16, 96, 152
82a11–b8: 197
85c6: 123
89c11–90d7: 73
90c7–d7: 124
90e3: 123
91a7–b7: 122
96a5ff.: 148–9
96b3–8: 180
100a3–102a2: 139, 157, 222, 223
100b1–102a2: 109
100d1: 41
105e2–107a1: 118
Phaedrus
237d6–9: 159
245c5–246a2: 113
245d1–3: 113
246a–257a: 93–4, 109, 112
248c2–e3: 107
249c6–250c6: 58, 160
Philebus
51b4: 41
Politicus
291d6: 39
Protagoras, 15, 20, 47, 164
312c1–4: 20
318d9–e4: 15
318e5–319a2: 14
320b1–3: 166
322c1–323c2: 197
323c5–8: 158–9
323c5–324c5: 17
329c6: 14
333d3: 89
333d8–e1: 48

349a7: 89
349e–360e: 3
352d4–7: 50
360e6–361d6: 20
361c4–d5: 141–2
Republic, 15, 20, 46, 47, 107, 156–7, 164,
217
344a3–c6: 62
344e1–3: 140–1
348d5–6: 62
357b4–d2: 154
365b1–c6: 40
373b5–6: 40
379b11: 48
414b8–415d5: 122
415a2–c7: 158
430b6–c4: 152
435d1–5: 140–1
437a6: 140–1, 223
438a1–442c8: 52, 150, 219, 220–1
476b4–5: 41
476e–480a: 184
479a5–c5: 181
490e–495b: 167
500d4–8: 152
500d–501c: 192, 199
501c4–502a4: 218
504b1–4: 140–1
511d–e: 184
515c6–8: 129
517a4–6: 217
518b6–d1: 107
518d9–519a1: 16, 150, 152
521c2–3: 217
522c–531c: 34–5, 204
523a10–524b6: 129
533c8: 223
537d7–539d6: 73–4
540a4–9: 140–1
546b–d: 203
548c10: 39
587c–588a: 203
600e6–601a2: 40, 41
608d3–611b10: 113
Symposium, 46, 204
175c7–e2: 143, 144
208a7–b4: 113
209e5–210a2: 58
215a–222c: 167
216d1–7: 40
Theaetetus
147e6–148a4: 39
149a–151d: 143, 144
155e3–156a3: 58

Timaeus
33b1–3: 39
41c3–d3: 113
51e4: 180
55c3–4: 39
67c4–7: 44

[Plato]
On Virtue, 18

Xenophon
Anabasis
2.6.21–9: 65, 211
Memorabilia
3.9.14: 16
4.1.4: 16
4.2.11: 14
4.6.8: 48
4.6.9: 46

General index

acrasia, 51–2, 147, 152–3
Adkins, A. W. H., 64
Alcibiades, 74, 162, 167
Alcmaeon, 180
Anaxagoras, 148
Annas, J., 185
Anscombe, G. E. M., 101, 115
Anthemion, 168
Anytus, 5, 33, 37, 100, 108, 162–73, 188–9, 209, 212, 215–17
aporia, 33, 69–70, 72, 81, 130, 201, 212–13, 226
Aristides, 164, 188, 197, 208
aristocracy, 15
Augustine, 101, 105, 108

Barnes, J., 115, 185
Bedu-Addo, J. T., 3, 132, 212, 222
Benson, H. H., 22, 86, 90, 133, 141, 205
Beversluis, J., 22
Bluck, R. S., 17, 35, 43, 62, 65, 88, 96, 109, 134,
    136, 138, 139, 143, 147, 165, 166, 172, 174,
    177, 187, 189, 190–2, 193, 205, 224
Bostock, D., 103, 106
Brague, R., 170
Brennan, T., 88
Brickhouse, T. C. and Smith, N. D., 20
Brown, L., 96, 114
Brown, M. S., 212
Brumbaugh, R., 209
Brunschwig, J., 22, 162
Burnet, J., 17, 43
Burnyeat, M. F., 5, 12, 20, 22, 48, 129, 174, 179,
    183, 185
Bury, R. G., 40

Callicles, 62, 64, 123, 202, 204, 207, 210
Calvert, B., 75, 80, 103, 109, 189, 208
Canto-Sperber, M., 62, 78, 207
Carcopino, J., 207
Characterisation, 5–6
    see also Meno, character of; Anytus,

Charmides, 162–3
Cherniss, H., 138, 139, 221
Cimon, 196, 197
coercion, Meno's use of, 62–3, 81, 211
colour, 32, 35, 40–5, 48, 58, 81, 137, 225
Cook Wilson, J., 134, 136
courage, 14, 28, 31, 121–4, 145, 146, 151
Cowie, F., 115
craft (*techne*), 195–6, 198
Critias, 16
Croiset A. and Bodin, L., 52, 220–1
Crombie, I. M., 3, 222

daring (*tharros*), 146–53, 212
Day, J. M., 82, 103, 174, 204, 205
definition
    and circularity, 56–9
    priority of, 20–2, 56, 85–7, 89, 90, 109, 132,
        138, 193, 198, 215
    unity of, 20, 24–30, 32, 44, 72
democracy, 15, 162–3, 165
Democritus, 16
Descartes, R. , 105, 108
desire
    for bad, 49–52, 219–21
    for good, 48–9
    intended *vs* actual object of, 49
    self- *vs* other-regarding, 47, 53
    self-destructive, 50, 219
Desjardins, R., 35, 75, 143
developmentalism, 6–7
Devereux, D. T., 143
dialectical requirement, 35–7, 44, 45, 56–9, 81,
    85
discovery, problems of, 77, 82, 83–7, 88, 117, 118,
    123, 129, 133
Dissoi Logoi, 16
divine dispensation, 16, 17, 115, 160, 176, 177,
    184, 192–3, 199, 215
Dodds, E. R., 189, 207
Dover, K. J., 14, 16

Ebert, T., 78
elenchus, 69–74, 75, 170, 201–2, 205–7
Empedocles, 41–3, 45, 94
encrateia, 51–2
Epicharmus, 16
Epicurus, 42
epiphaneia (surface), 39, 41–2
eristic, 15, 35–6, 70, 73, 76, 80–1, 88, 122–3,
    211
essence, 20–1
Euclid, 37–9, 41, 43, 109
eudaimonism, psychological, 51–2
Euripides, 16, 217
explanation, 19–21, 87, 133, 176, 179–80,
    181–5
external goods, 53–6, 62, 124, 145, 148, 150–1

fine (*kalon*), 46
Fine, G., 75, 80, 82, 110–12, 185, 202
foreknowledge principle, 84–6, 89–90, 106, 117,
    132
forms, transcendent, 94, 104
Franklin, L., 36, 58
Friedländer, P., 42, 138, 207, 221, 224

Gaiser, K., 78
Geach, P. T., 22
Gedike, F., 35
genus/species distinction, 31, 32, 38, 56, 87
geometry, 34–5, 42, 103, 107, 113, 133–7, 196, 202,
    221–2, 225–6
Golding, W., 103
Gomperz, T., 189
good (*agathon*)
    how related to fine (*kalon*), 46
    instrumental *vs* final, 153–7, 176
    intrinsic *vs* extrinsic, 155
Gordon, J., 209, 211
Gorgias, 12–13, 23–5, 27–8, 30, 43–4, 48, 60–2,
    70–1, 78, 143, 174, 180
Grube, G. M A., 106, 174, 175
Gulley, N., 5, 113, 117
Guthrie, W. C. K., 14, 15, 24, 47, 106, 174, 209

Hackforth, R., 189
Hacking, I., 115
Hall, R. W., 189
happiness, 18, 51, 94, 154–6
Heath, T. E., 134, 136
Hippias, 15, 163
Hobbs, A., 46
Hoerber, R. G., 43, 78
Homer, 14, 186–8, 217
hypothesis, method of, 131–42, 156–7, 202,
    204–5, 221–4

immortality, 92–3, 97, 100, 112–20, 122
initiation, 58–9, 107, 225–6
innatism
    dispositional, 108–9
    and recollection, 158–9
inquiry, 13, 61, 71, 129–30, 171–3
    duty to engage in, 89, 91, 122–5
    problem of, 76–7, 79–80, 201
intellectualism, Socratic, 51, 151–2, 211
irony, 185
Irwin, T., 20, 26, 36, 51, 52, 74, 83, 91, 147, 181,
    187, 189, 202, 219

Jolley, N., 115
justice, 14, 19, 26–7, 31, 40, 54–6, 62, 64–5, 145,
    153, 203
justification, 184–5

Kant, I., 155
Kerferd, G. B., 15
Klein, J., 12, 36, 42, 78, 158, 170, 189
knack (*empeiria*), 195, 208
Knorr, W. R., 134, 136
knowledge
    a priori, 103–5
    and the dialectical requirement, 36–7, 57–9
    latent *vs* explicit, 79, 80, 85, 100, 106, 108–12,
        114, 116, 118–20, 129, 144
    stability of, 175, 178–81
    vs true belief, 6, 19–20, 79–80, 83–4, 100, 107,
        144, 153, 176–92, 208, 213
Korsgaard, C. M., 155
Kraut, R., 187, 189, 193, 203, 204

Lamb, W. R. M., 47, 174
laziness, intellectual, 60–2, 70–1, 88, 121–3
Leibniz, G., 104, 114, 116
Lloyd, G. E. R., 4, 38–9, 134, 136, 137, 225–6

mathematics, 202–5
    see also geometry
magnificence, 31, 145
McCabe, M. M., 75
Menn, S., 134
Meno, character of, 5, 12, 60–5, 74, 80–1,
    99–100, 140–2, 170–3, 204, 209–13, 215–17
'Meno's paradox'
    Meno's challenge, 76–9
    eristic dilemma, 77–9, 82, 88
    see also inquiry, problem of; discovery,
        problems of
mildness, 37, 153, 172, 209, 212, 216–17, 218
Mill, J. S., 3
Miltiades, 196, 197
misology, 73, 125

Moline, J., 75
moral education, 5, 60, 214–17
    see also teaching; virtue, acquisition of
Moravscik, J., 103
Moser, P. K., 104
Mueller, I., 222

Nakhnikian, G., 48, 50
nature, 15–17, 157–60, 166–7
necessity, logical, 101, 104
Nehamas, A., 22, 75, 77, 101, 182, 183, 185
Newman, W. L., 28
Nussbaum, M., 74

O'Brien, M. J., 16, 17
Orphics, 94

Parmenides, 84, 180
Pascal, B., 124
Penner, T., 198
Pericles, 17, 154, 164, 176, 177, 186, 188, 192, 196, 197, 200
Persephone, 92–3
Phillips, B., 75, 88
piety, 19, 54–6, 62, 86, 92–4, 122
Pindar, 16, 43, 94–5
poets, 95, 192, 215
Polus, 64, 202, 204, 210
Popper, K. R., 108
Posidonius, 37–8
power, 31, 61, 81
practice, 16–18, 35
Prior, W. J., 21, 22
Proclus, 38
Prodicus, 36, 213
Protagoras, 14–16, 163, 165
Pythagoras, 96
Pythagoreans, 42, 94, 97, 205, 207

recollection, 6, 12, 13, 23, 71, 82, 129–30, 140,
    158–60, 179–80, 201–2, 205–7, 211–13,
    214–15, 216–17
    argument for, 98–112, 171
    metaphorical interpretation of, 121–2
    and religion, 92–7, 112, 122, 124
    sequential, 97, 101, 102
    see also synoptic reasoning
    as solution to the eristic dilemma, 79–83
redemption, 93–4, 122, 124
reincarnation, 92–4, 121–2, 207
Reuter, M., 19
rhetoric, 13, 15, 194–9
Robertson, T., 219
Robinson, R., 27, 86, 132, 138, 139, 221, 222, 223, 224

Robinson, T. M., 112
Rose, L., 138
Ryle, G., 75

Santas, G., 22, 49, 50, 86, 146
Saunders, T. J., 28
Savile, A., 115
schema
    definition of, 32–4, 35
    as shape/figure, 37–9, 44
    as surface, 39–42, 44, 57, 202
Scolnicov, S., 12
Scott, D., 75, 88, 109, 114, 115, 159, 193, 198, 210,
    217
Sedley, D., 45, 150, 216
Seeskin, K., 12, 209
self-discipline, 150, 153, 212
sense perception, 96, 103–5
shame, 34, 81, 171
Sharples, R., 35, 41, 109, 117, 138, 147, 165, 189
Shorey, P. A., 16
Simonides, 46
Socrates (historical), and
    the disavowal of knowledge, 20
    discovery, 89–90
    the duty to inquire, 89, 91
    the elenchus, 72–4
    the foreknowledge principle, 90
    the priority of definition, 89–90, 141–2
    the unity of definition, 27–8, 30
soothsayers, 95, 176, 193, 215
sophists, 15, 163–4, 165
Sophocles, 217
Sternfeld, R. and Zyskind, H., 222, 223
Stock, St. G., 114
Stoics, 109
synoptic reasoning, 61–2, 97, 107, 171, 183–4,
    210–12
    see also recollection, sequential

Tarrant, H., 211
Taylor, A. E., 11, 169, 198
teaching, 12–13, 15–18, 101, 142–4, 158–60, 177–8,
    225–6
    see also moral education; virtue, acquisition of
Teiresias, 186–7, 217
temperance, 14, 19, 26–7, 31, 54–6, 62, 65, 145,
    146, 151
testimony, 101–5, 115, 143–4, 171–2
Themistocles, 17, 164, 177, 188–90, 196, 197, 200
Theognis, 174
Theophrastus, 43
Thomas, J. E., 38, 41
Thompson, E. S., 3, 35, 46, 92, 112, 147, 174,
    209

Thrasymachus, 62, 64, 210
Thucydides (historian), 16
Thucydides (politician), 164, 186–8, 197
true belief
  and Athenian politicians, 187–92
  vs knowledge, *see* knowledge
  instability of, 130, 133
tyranny, 63–4

Umphrey, S., 81

Verdenius, M. J., 36, 43
virtue
  acquisition of, 15–18, 37, 130–1, 140–2, 157–60,
    161–75, 211–13, 214
  see also divine dispensation; moral
    education; nature; teaching
  demotic, 16
  Gorgias' conception of, 24–5
  immoralist conception of, 62, 64–5
  as knowledge, 15, 19, 53, 124, 138–9, 145–57,
    176–7, 214, 222–4

nature of, 14, 214, 224
parts of, 53–7
political, 197–200
real *vs* shadow, 186–7, 198–9
as true belief, 124, 176–93
as unitary, 19, 25–30, 32, 61, 74, 187
Vlastos, G., 7, 19, 20, 21, 22, 28, 34, 41, 42, 44,
  51, 75, 86, 88, 90, 101, 102, 103, 110, 129,
  134, 138, 142, 145, 154, 183, 189, 192–3,
  201–7

Weiss, R., 3, 4, 52, 75, 81, 88, 90, 95, 109, 137, 158,
  189, 209, 211, 220–1, 223, 224, 225
West, M. L., 93
White, N. P., 29, 75, 103
Wilkes, K. V., 4, 103, 212
wisdom, as a part of virtue, 14, 31
  see also knowledge
Wittgenstein, L., 25
Woodruff, P., 20

Xenophanes, 84

Printed in the United States
139933LV00008B/60/P